Anonymous

The Satires of Horace in Rhythmic Prose

Anonymous

The Satires of Horace in Rhythmic Prose

ISBN/EAN: 9783337372057

Printed in Europe, USA, Canada, Australia, Japan

Cover: Foto ©Thomas Meinert / pixelio.de

More available books at **www.hansebooks.com**

THE

SATIRES OF HORACE

In Rhythmic Prose

FOR THE STUDENT.

WITH ILLUSTRATED ARTICLES BASED ON THOSE IN
RICH'S "ANTIQUITIES"

ON THE

ROMAN HOUSE, AMPHITHEATRE, THE PRINCIPAL ARTICLES OF
DRESS, THE FORUM, THE BATHS, AND THE LOOM.

AND

NOTES TRANSLATED FROM THOSE IN ORELLI'S EDITION.

By R. M. MILLINGTON, M.A.

LONDON:

LONGMANS, GREEN, READER, & DYER,

PATERNOSTER ROW.

1870.

INTRODUCTION.

THE special object of this translation is to offer to the student an accurate and readable version of this portion of the works of Horace.

The iambic rhythm has been adopted with the idea that prose with a rhythm is smoother and more harmonious than prose without it, and consequently is, to a certain extent, nearer the original.

It is believed that the illustrated articles will be found very useful to the student.

Orelli's text and notes have been consulted throughout.

It may be as well to say a few words on the distinctive features of the satire and philosophy of Horace, as it is very possible that some may conclude that the one is merely a denunciation against men's vices and defects, and that the other is either vague and dreamy, or Utopian and impossible.

The chief characteristic of Horatian satire is, that instead of lashing vice and human weakness with the uncompromising severity and indignant sarcasm of a Juvenal, it rather, with a pleasant vein of irony and playful personality, gently reproves and remonstrates than summarily condemns. And while entirely allowing that it was quite desirable that there should arise a Juvenal to brand with infamy such reigns of terror and excess as that of Domitian, the author unhesitatingly claims for Horace immunity from the charge of sympathizing with vice. If the real end and purpose of satire be to check, not merely to inveigh against vice, Horace's method of handling the subject seems the best calculated to attain that end. And that he deliberately chose that method, not from a secret leaning to the vices and follies he satirized, but with the true instinct of a master of his art, and from the teaching of his own philosophy, those who attentively read this portion of his works can have no reasonable doubt. Men are not so likely to listen to or profit by the fierce strictures of a satirist who in his writings apparently exhibits not only the utmost disdain and abhorrence of vice, but seems to arrogate to himself exemption from most of the weaknesses poor humanity has ever been subject to. The feeling created in the minds of the satirized is much more likely to be one of antagonism, or even more likely of indifference, on the ground that such a satirist really cannot fully understand human nature.

Horace, on the contrary, knew human nature thoroughly; and the consummate address with which, while holding vice up to ridicule, he carefully avoids giving any impression that he is himself exempt from it, combined with the genial kindliness of a nature that satire cannot conceal, must have at once given him the advantage of being fully intelligible to his readers as a satirist, and, from his relations with Mæcenas his patron, and through him with the Emperor Augustus, must have secured for his writings the attention of most of the influential men of his day. No one had more real friends than Horace, no poet was more really liked by the powerful, although the aristocracy of Rome were as exclusive and haughty as the old Bourbons themselves. The bearing, at once liberal and independent, and yet modest and unassuming, that he ever preserved, in spite of the suddenness of his rise and the consequent difficulty of the *rôle* he had to play in a city where adroit flattery was far more acceptable than real and unpretending merit, deserves the warmest commendation. Shall we assign as reasons for this popularity (as a satirist) that he tacitly approved of, at all events, the milder vices, and that, with the spirit of a courtier, he merely modified his tone to suit the times, or that he recognised the absurdity of attempting to preach to an audience in a language which, if they heard, they would not understand; and which, if they understood, they would probably pretend not to hear? Let those who read him judge. The author is quite content to believe as much good as possible of a writer who, beyond dispute, was not only a great satirist, but who was a genial companion, a thorough gentleman, a firm friend, and singularly free from prejudice.

With regard to his philosophy it is enough to say that, while carefully and critically culling the good from the various systems that then engrossed men's minds and attention, he never absolutely adhered to the tenets of any one, but seems to have had firmer faith in the wisdom to be derived from that maxim, "the golden mean," which more or less tinctures his writing.

LIFE OF HORACE.

In December of the year 65 B.C., in the consulship of Lucius Aurelius Cotta and Lucius Manlius Torquatus, was born the great Roman poet and satirist of the Augustan age, Quintus Horatius Flaccus. His birthplace was a small town then called Venusia or Venusium, and now Venosa, situated in Apulia, and only separated from Lucania by a chain of mountains about one mile to the south of the town, which formed the natural boundary between the two countries. His father, whose condition was that of a freedman, while exercising the humble calling of collector of the salt fish revenues, had acquired means enough to purchase a small farm near Venusia, on the banks of the river Aufidus, now called the Ofanto. The first ten or eleven years of the poet's life were passed in this small town, when the father, dissatisfied with the advantages afforded by the tenth-rate academy of Flavius at Venusia, and probably even then perceiving some indications of the genius his son afterwards manifested, removed to Rome, and placed him under the care of a celebrated schoolmaster named Orbilius Pupillus of Beneventum, now Benevento; under whose tuition he became acquainted with the more ancient poets of Rome, such as Livius, Ennius, and Lucilius, whose satiric writing Horace has himself told us that he imitated. He next learned the Greek language, and read some of the literature of Greece; and so, while the father was plying his humble calling of broker's clerk, or tax-gatherer, the son was

receiving instruction and advantages suited even to the sons of
the oldest aristocracy of Rome.   The poet himself pays a graceful tribute of acknowledgment to this self-denial on the part of
the father, and to his careful training, in the Sixth Satire of the
First Book, where, alluding to the former, he says,—

"But if my character be sullied by more venial defects, and
those but few, and be good in the main; if none shall fairly
charge me with the fault of avarice, or meanness, or bad company; if I be pure and guiltless; if, to praise myself, I live
dear to my friends,—my father was the cause of this; for he,
though poor, sent me to Rome to learn accomplishments
which any gentleman of property, or any member of the House,
might get his children taught."

And to the latter,—

"In fine, he kept me chastely free from all immoral deeds;
nor that alone, but e'en from slander's slur, and purity like this
is youthful virtue's brightest crown."

When about twenty or one-and-twenty years of age, Horace
went to Athens to complete his education; and here, while
"learning philosophic truth 'mid Academus' groves," he found
for his fellow-students, the son of Cicero, Varus, and Messalla.
Meantime the crash of civil war had burst in Rome: the Dictator Cæsar had fallen by the assassin's dagger:—Antony was
bending all his energies to raise from the embers of his power
a tyranny more to be dreaded, while Brutus and Cassius were
at Athens endeavouring to enrol under their banner the young
Romans who were there quietly pursuing their studies, as yet
uninfluenced by the tide of anarchy and the fierce rivalry of
faction.   Horace joined the republican army, and finished an
uneventful campaign of nearly two years in Macedonia by
serving as a general officer at the battle of Philippi, now
Filibah, against Mark Antony and Octavianus, as Augustus
then was called, in which Brutus and Cassius were totally

defeated : and the poet fled from the battle-field, and repaired
to Rome, after saving his life (but not his small property at
Venusia, which was confiscated), intending to maintain himself
by his pen. His father was now dead, and it was no bright
opening for the young Venusian to appear as a political rene-
gade, without fame and without patronage, in a town like Rome,
where the courtier and the informer too often found the way
to honour and distinction more easily than the man of genius
or merit. However, as he says himself, " my poverty compelled
me to write verses," and although it was satire that he wrote
(for from his satires alone he gained his early and most lasting
fame), we find him soon attracting the notice of Virgil and
Varius, and, through their recommendation, securing the
patronage of Caius Cilnius Mæcenas, the intimate friend and
chief counsellor, together with Agrippa, of the Emperor Augustus. He was now twenty-seven years of age ; had won for
himself a name among the most celebrated literary men of the
day, such as Virgil, Ovid, and Tibullus ; enjoying the friendship of the Emperor, of Mæcenas, and of such men as Marcus
Vipsanius Agrippa, Caius Asinius Pollio, and Quintus Ælius
Lamia.

He was now secured from want, and received, as marks of
his patron's favour and esteem, a romantic villa at Tibur, now
Tivoli, on the banks of the Anio, now the Teverone, and a
retired farm in the eastern extremity of the country of the
Sabines, in one or other of which he spent a great part of his
time, and ever preferred the simple country life to the pomp
and bustle of Rome. And there is no need to suppose that
this love of retirement was due to anything but the teaching of
his own philosophy, for he had offers of positions of emolu-
ment ; and, indeed, the Emperor Augustus, when the weight of
supreme rule began to be felt and his health to suffer, desired
that Horace would accept the office of private secretary, and

this Augustus more especially wished so that the poet might
conduct the correspondence between himself and his private
friends,—an office for which Horace must have been singularly qualified.   The poet, however, declined the offer; and
still enjoyed the imperial friendship.   Mæcenas gave a signal
proof of the affection with which he regarded him, for in
his last communication to the Emperor he said, " Remember
Horatius Flaccus even as you remember me."   We learn
from his own writings that Horace was fond of warmth and
sunny weather; that his hair was grey early in life; that he
was short and corpulent, and suffered from weak digestion
and sore eyes,—a bodily defect very common among the
Romans.   His manner of living was abstemious, and he was
moderate and temperate in his pleasures; and his convivial
hours were ever marked by social wit and philosophical wisdom.
He died in November of the year 8 B.C., or the early part of
December, in the fifty-eighth year of his age, having survived
his patron by a few weeks only, was buried near him on the
Esquiline hill, and left his property to the Emperor.

The dates and order of his publications are as follow :—

     I. The First Book of the Satires, B.C. 35.
    II. The Second Book of the Satires, between 35 and
        30 B.C.
   III. The Epodes, B.C. 29 or 30.
   IV. The First Three Books of the Odes, between 30 and
       24 B.C.
    V. The First Book of the Epistles, between 24 and 20 B.C.
   VI. The Carmen Seculare, 17 B.C.
  VII. The Fourth Book of the Odes, between 17 and 13 B.C.
VIII. The Second Book of the Epistles, after the Carmen
      Seculare, but the year is uncertain.
   IX. Art of Poetry,—quite uncertain.

The reader will find his philosophy alluded to in the following parts of the Satires and Epistles :—

Satires.	Bk. I., Satire	1.	
,,	Bk. II., Satire	2.	First paragraph.
,,	,, Satire	4.	Apology for Epicurus.
,,	,, Satire	6.	
,,	,, Satire	7.	By the mouth of Davus, in the last long paragraph.
Epistles.	Bk. I., Epistle	1.	In the first part.
,,	,, Epistle	4.	In the latter part.
,,	,, Epistle	6.	In the first part.
,,	,, Epistle	18.	In the latter part.
,,	,, Epistle	20.	In the latter part.
,,	Bk. II., Epistle	2.	In the latter part.

By the same Author.

THE BUCOLICS, OR ECLOGUES OF VIRGIL, with Notes based on those in Conington's Edition, a Life of Virgil, more than 100 Woodcuts from Rich's "Antiquities," and an Illustrated Article on the Ancient Musical Instruments, translated into English Heroic Verse. Fcap. 8vo., cloth boards, illuminated, gilt edges, 5s.

THE BUCOLICS, translated into Rhythmic Prose, with Notes for the Student. Fcap. 8vo., cloth boards, 2s. 6d.

LONGMANS & CO.

D O M U S,

The Roman houses were generally built upon the same plan, differing from one another only in the size, number, and arrangement of the apartments they contained, or the extent and character of the ground on which they stood. They were divided into two principal members, as shown by the ground plan annexed. The several apartments mentioned made the nucleus of the house on its ground plan, and are always found

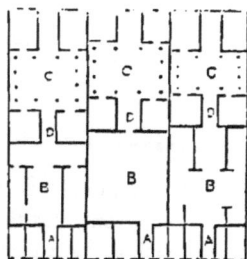

Ground plan of private house.

in every Roman house of any size. The relative situations were always fixed, and they were constructed according to a received model, as shown in the above plan. A A A represents the *prothyium* * or entrance passage from the street (for which see illustration on next page representing the *prothyrum*), and at its further end the *ostium*, a door half closed, which was used

to shut off the *atrium* (see woodcuts to *Atrium* on page xiv)
from the entrance passage. The pavement was generally mosaic,
and the usual word of salutation (*salve*) was inlaid in coloured
stone at the entrance (see illustrations to *Pavimentum* on pages
xix and xx). *Janua* † was the street door, as distinguished from
the *ostium*, as shown by the annexed illustration.

B B B, in the ground plan, refer to the *atrium*, or principal
apartment in a Roman house, with its appropriate dependences

* *Prothyrum*, or entrance passage   † *Janua*, front or street door.
from the street. '

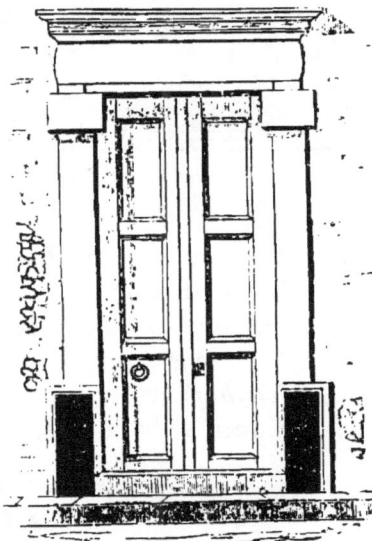

all round it, as shown by the illustrations on page xiv, and also
by the one termed *cavædium* (*cavum ædium*), which shows the
atrium from the outside.

c c c, in the ground plan, refers to the *peristylium*, with its
appurtenances beyond. The parts of the house belonging to
the *peristylium* were connected by an intermediate room called

the *tablinum*, or one or two corridors termed *fauces*, and occasionally by both.

The letters D D D, in the ground plan, refer to the *tablinum*,* as shown by the illustration on page xv. The part immediately in front of the drawing is the floor of the *atrium*, with a portion

Atrium Tuscanicum, or principal apartment, in the Tuscan style.

Atrium Tetrastylum, or principal apartment, supported by four columns.

of its * *impluvium;* the dark open recess occupying the left half of the middle ground is the *tablinum*, with the colonnade of the *peristylium* † showing through, and the small door at the right of it is the *faux*, or corridor, which also opens upon the *peristylium* at its further extremity. The apartment is entirely open at both ends, so as to permit a continuous view

Cavædium (*cavum ædium*), or outside view of the *atrium*.

through both divisions of the house; but those ends were closed when desired by moveable screens or partitions of wood called *tabulæ*, which is evident, from there being a separate passage at the side to afford communication between the *atrium*

and *peristylium*, which would not be required if the *tablinum* *
permitted a thoroughfare always through it. The name
tablinum is probably derived from these *tabulæ*, or screens.

† *Peristylium*, or second and inner division of a Roman house, generally
the domestic apartments occupied
by the proprietor and family.

* *Tablinum*, one of the principal private apartments in a Roman house,
adjoining the *atrium* and *fauces*,
or corridors, and showing the *ara.*

Compluvium, a large square opening in the centre of the
roof which covered the four sides of the *atrium*, and towards

Latrina, showing the washing-places, w.c., &c., and offices near
kitchen, in a private house.

which three sides converged for the purpose of carrying down the rain into a reservoir (*impluvium*).   See woodcut to *Atrium Tuscanicum* on page xiv.

Latrina (*lavatrina*), (see cut on page xv,) the wash-places and offices contiguous to the kitchens. The two small arches on the right form the kitchen stove.   Four steps lead down to the room, and have a hand rail by their side to aid the ascent or descent, the mark of which is shown on the wall. The recess to the left is the *latrina*, originally closed by a wooden door, which has left the marks of its hinges and bolt on the edge of the door-frame ; and the mouth of the pipe through which the place was supplied with water is observable in the right-hand corner.

Ara, or altar, placed close by the *impluvium* of a private house, on which the family sacrifice was made.   The *ara* is on the margin of the reservoir, or *impluvium*, in the right-hand woodcut on page xv, which shows both.

Alæ were large recesses in, Roman houses of any pretensions to magnificence, generally one on each side of the *atrium*, furnished with seats, and closed in front with curtains, intended

* *Cellæ*, or dormitories for slaves of the house.

for the master of the house to receive his visitors in and to enjoy the conversation of his acquaintance.   The entrance to the *alæ* is formed by the two large doorways with the curtains drawn aside at the further angle of the chamber on the right and left. (See illustration to *Atrium Tuscanicum* on p. xiv).

* *Cellæ* were dormitories for household slaves, as the annexed

illustration represents. They were often found in Roman villas, and the fronts were originally bricked in with only an entrance door.

Chalcidicum.—This was a large, low, deep porch, covered with its own roof, supported on pilasters, and appended to the entrance front of a building, and forming a grand entrance to the whole edifice. It was added to private as well as public buildings, not merely as an ornament, but also to give shelter to persons waiting outside to be admitted, or to transact public business in.

Chalcidicum, or large entrance porch to a private or public building.

Fenestra.—The illustration on p. xviii represents three ancient windows of different designs : the one on the left hand being from a Greek bas-relief in the British Museum ; that on the right from the Vatican Virgil, and the centre one from a marble sarcophagus of a later period found in the Vatican cemetery.

In later times the walls of dwelling-houses and rooms were sometimes decorated with imaginary views of country scenery,

ports, and temples, termed *topia*, as shown by the annexed
illustration.

Pavimentum.—A flooring composed of small pieces of brick,
tile, stone, and shells, set in a bed of cement, and consolidated
by beating with a rammer (*pavicula*), which gave rise to the
name : afterwards applied to any kind of artificial flooring, even
of the most elaborate workmanship, like those shown by the
illustrations on next page.

Fenestræ, or windows

Topia, or landscape paintings.

Pavimentum sectile.—This was a flooring composed of pieces
of different coloured marbles, cut (*secta*) into sets of regular
form or size, so that when joined together the whole constituted
an ornamental design or pattern, as exhibited by the annexed
specimen.   The objects at the top show the different forms of
the pieces with which it is composed : the triangular ones, A
and B, consist of *serpentine* and *palombino* respectively ; the hex-
agonal, C, of *pavonazzetto ;* and the square, D, of red porphyry.

Pavimentum tesselatum, or *tesseris structum*. — This is a
flooring belonging to the class of *sectilia*, and also of an ornamental character, composed of coloured marbles.   The pieces
composing it were cut into regular dies without the admixture
of other forms, as in the annexed example, showing part of a
pavement in the Thermæ of Caracalla at Rome.   Square dies
(*tessellæ, tesseræ*) were likewise employed in making other kinds

of mosaic pavements, as in the following specimen; but in that case they were of smaller dimensions and less precise in their angles.

Pavimentum vermiculatum.—A mosaic flooring or pavement representing natural objects, both animate and inanimate, in

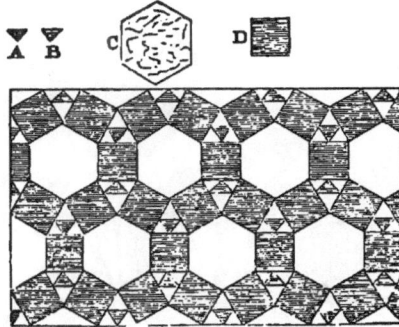

Pavimentum sectile, or flooring composed of pieces of different coloured marble.

their real forms and colours, as in a picture. It was composed with small pieces of different coloured marbles, inlaid in a bed of very strong cement, the colours and arrangement of the

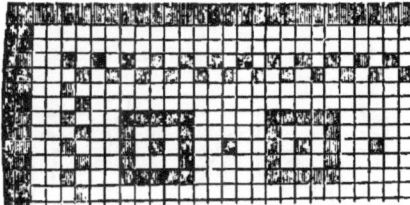

Pavimentum tesselatum, flooring with pieces of marble cut in regular dies.

pieces being selected and disposed so as to imitate the object designed with a good deal of pictorial effect. The dies were not exactly square, nor laid in parallel lines; but they followed the sweep and undulations in the contours and colours of the objects reproduced, which, when viewed at a little dis-

tance, presented a resemblance to the wreathing and twisting
of a cluster of worms (*vermes*), and thus suggested the name.

Pavimentum scalpturatum.—An ornamental flooring or pavement on which the design is produced by engraving (*scalptura*),
and perhaps inlaying, but, as the name implies, by a different
process or in a different manner from the kinds already de-

Pavimentum vermiculatum, a mosaic
flooring representing natural objects, animate or inanimate.

Pavimentum scalpturatum, ornamental flooring on which the
design is engraved or inlaid,
but by a different process from
any of the others.

scribed. Though this kind of pavement was simple at first, this
style of decorative art was sometimes carried to great perfec-

Alexandrinum opus, mosaic flooring for rooms.

tion, and in such a way that the effect of a finished cartoon was
produced on the pavement by inserting pieces of grey marble

for the half-tints into white ; then hatching across both with
the chisel, and filling in the incisions with black mastic for the
shade, so that the whole looks like a finished chalk drawing.
The illustration is a fac-simile of one of the groups designed by
the artist Beccafiume.

Alexandrinum opus. — A particular kind of mosaic work,
especially used for the flooring of rooms, and belonging to the
class of pavements termed *sectilia;* the distinctive character of
which consisted in this, that the frets or patterns forming the
designs were composed of the conjunction of *only* two colours
—red and black, for instance—on a white ground, as in the
example, which represents a portion of a pavement in a house
at Pompeii.

AMPHITHEATRUM.

1. AMPHITHEATRUM, a building constructed for the exhibition of gladiatorial combats, and sometimes used for other spectacles. The illustration shows the exterior view.

Exterior view of *amphitheatrum* still standing at Pola in Istria, showing the oval wall divided into stories of arcades, decorated with columns and pilasters.

2. The next illustration shows the interior view of the amphitheatre at Pompeii; but as the drawing is on a very reduced scale, and indistinct through the dilapidations of the building, it should be compared with the woodcut, No. 3, that follows this, in which full particulars are given.

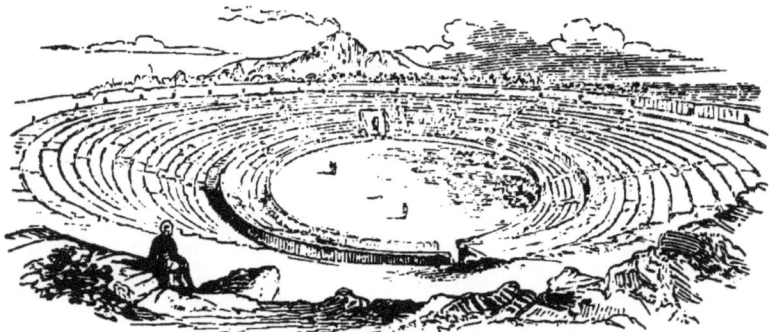

Interior view of amphitheatre, forming an elliptical cup (*cavea*), set round with seats, containing *arena*, and other parts enumerated in the next woodcut.

3. This woodcut shows a restored section and elevation of a portion of the amphitheatre at Pola. The company entered through the arches on the ground-floor at the left-hand side of the engraving. A is the *podium*, which is approached by a short staircase springing from the third or inner corridor in the centre of the woodcut. It is raised above the *arena* by a blank wall, surmounted by a balustrade, under which is seen one of the doorways through which the

Restored section and elevation of amphitheatre at Pola, with detailed account of the parts.

wild beasts or combatants emerged upon the *arena*. The staircase, which commences immediately from the ground entrance, leads directly to the first *mænianum* (1), or flight, into several of which flights the *gradus* or circles of seats occupied by the public were divided, when the building was lofty, by broad landing-places (*præcinctiones*) and raised walls (*baltei*), and vertically into compartments in the form of an inverted triangle (*cunei*) by a number of staircases (*scalæ*) which communicated with the avenues of ingress and egress (*vomitoria*) within the shell of the building. The spectator entered the *mænianum* 1, referred to above, through the doorways (*vomi-toria*) B, and descended the flights of stairs which divide the rows of seats between them into a wedge-shaped compartment (*cuneus*), until he came to the particular row where his seat was reserved. The high blank wall into which the entrance (B) opens is the *balteus*, and its object was to separate the various *mæniana* and prevent the classes who were only entitled to a seat in the upper *mæniana* from descending into the lower ones. A branch staircase diverging to the left leads up to the corridor formed by the arcades of the outer wall, from whence it turns to the right and conducts to the second *mænianum* (2), which is entered and distributed in the same way as the lower one, and separated from the one above by another *balteus* (c). Other staircases, though they cannot be shown on one section, conduct in like manner to the third *mænianum* (3), and to the covered gallery for the women above (D). The three solid arches in the centre of the engraving, constructed in the main brickwork of the building, form a succession of corridors encircling the whole edifice, from which the different staircases spring, while at the same time they support the seats of the *cavea* and the flights of stairs by which the company entered or left the amphitheatre.

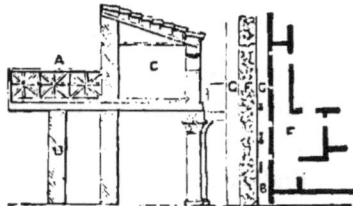

Mænianum, showing ranges of seats with compartments (*cunei*), from the theatre at Pompeii.

4. This illustration gives a separate view of *mæniana*, or entire ranges of seats rising in concentric circles between one

landing-place (*præcinctio*) and another, but divided perpendicularly into a number of compartments (*cunei*) by the flights of steps (*scalæ*) which the spectators descended or ascended to and from their places. The engraving shows a portion of two *mæniana* containing three *cunci*. Each *mænianum* comprised an entire circuit.

THEATRUM.

(*Orchestra, Pulpitum, Proscenium.*)

THE Roman theatre was originally a temporary wooden scaffolding, erected for the occasion, and when no longer needed, pulled down. It was afterwards constructed of brick or stone, with considerable architectural beauty and magnificence of decoration. It was usually built upon a level space within the town, and consisted externally of a semicircular elevation at one end, comprising one or more stories of arcades, through which the spectators entered and

Circular end of the theatre of Marcellus.

passed by staircases constructed within them to a number of semicircular tiers of seats in the interior of the building, which were enclosed by the external wall described, and exhibited by the illustration showing the circular end of

the theatre of Marcellus as it now exists in partial ruins at
Rome. Two stories only remain—the lower one, of the Doric
order, partly embedded in the soil : over this the Ionic is more
perfect. But there was originally a third story, of the Corinthian
order, which has entirely disappeared. The circular line of
the plan is distinctly apparent in the drawing, as well as the
columns which decorated each story and the stonework of the
arches between them, which formed so many open arcades,
now filled up by the wall and windows of modern houses, into

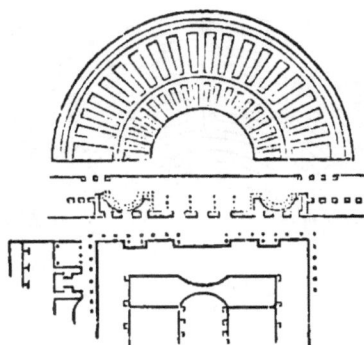

Ground plan of Pompey's theatre at Rome.

which the edifice has been transformed. The opposite extremity of the building, which contained the stage, apartments
for the use of the actors, and conveniences for storing property,
was flat, forming as it were a chord or base to the semicircle,
and was decorated externally by a portico (*porticus*), (see article
on *Amphitheatrum*, the exterior view,) sometimes of considerable extent, containing numerous colonnades, open or covered
walks, and corridors, and forming a favourite resort for the
idle and fashionable loungers of the city. A portion of these
appurtenances, sufficient to give an accurate notion of the
entire structure, is exhibited by the lowest part of the annexed
illustration, which represents the ground plan of Pompey's

theatre at Rome, showing the portico at the bottom marked in
black lines, then the walls of the scene and stage, and beyond
them the circular seats for the spectators, which were enclosed
externally by a wall similar to that exhibited in the first illustration.   The interior was open to the sky, having no roof, and
consisted of the following essential parts, distributed in the
manner shown by the annexed engraving representing the

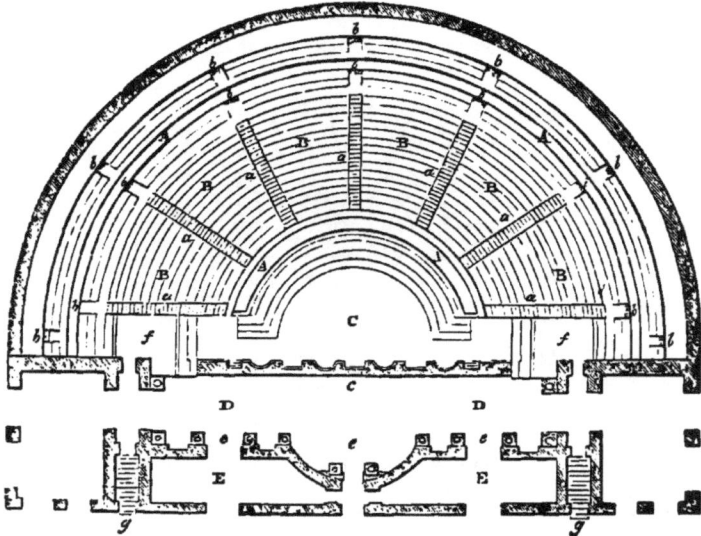

Ground plan of theatre at Herculaneum.

ground plan of the theatre at Herculaneum, which is constructed upon the Roman model.   The body of the house
(*cavea*), where the spectators sat, consists of a number of semicircular rows of seats formed by deep steps (*gradus*) rising
in concentric lines one above the other, which were sub-
divided horizontally into tiers (*maniana*), (see *Amphitheatrum* for the terms,) comprising several rows each by broad

landing-places (*præcinctiones*, A A, A A), and vertically into cuneiform compartments (*cunei*, B B B B B) by a number of staircases (*scalæ*, *a a a a a*), down which the spectators descended to the row where their respective places were situated, upon entering the house through the open doorways (*vomitoria*,

Orchestra of Greek or Roman theatre.

b b b b b) at the head of each staircase, which were reached by means of passages and covered lobbies constructed in the shell of the building, precisely in the same manner as explained and illustrated by the text and woodcut to restored section of *amphitheatrum*. At the bottom of the *cavea* was the *orchestra* (c), an exact half-circle, and answering in use and locality to

Proscenium, stage of theatre, bounded by the permanent wall of *scena* at the back and *orchestra* in front.

our *pit*, for it contained the seats appropriated to the magistrates and persons of distinction, and was not used like the Greek orchestra. for a chorus and musicians. A little in advance of this was a low wall (*pulpitum* or *proscenii pulpitum*, c), forming the front of the stage (*proscenium*, D D) towards the spectators, and separating it from the orchestra. At the back of the stage there was a lofty wall of brick or masonry (*scena*, *e e e*), which formed the permanent scene of the theatre, with three grand entrances for the chief actors ; and behind this the apartments for the actors and property (*postscenium*, E E), or what we call the part " behind the scenes." (See illustration to *proscenium* for *postscenium*, boundary wall of which is shown in a half-tint at the back.) The two divisions in advance of the stage on each side of it, like our stage boxes (*f f*), are supposed to have been reserved as places of honour for the chief magistrates of Herculaneum, for they have each a private entrance from the portico at the back of the house by a separate staircase (*g g*), but they do not appear to have been usual in every theatre.

CIRCUS.

THE annexed illustration shows a ground plan of a Roman racecourse called *Circus*. It was laid out in an oblong form, terminating in a semicircle at one extremity, and enclosed at the opposite end by a pile of buildings called the *town (oppidum)*, under which the stalls (*carceres*) for the horses and chariots were distributed, marked A A in the engraving. B represents a long low wall called *spina*, built lengthwise down the course, so as to divide it like a barrier into two distinct parts, and at each of its ends was placed a goal (*meta*), round which the chariots turned ; the one nearest to the stables (c) being termed *meta prima*, the farther one (D) *meta secunda*. D represents the goal at the bottom. The stalls (A A) are arranged in the segment of a circle, of which the centre falls

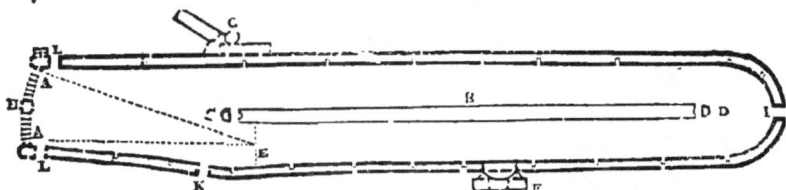

Ground plan of *circus* or Roman racecourse.

exactly in the middle point (E) between the first *meta* and the side of the building at which the race commenced. E represents a chalked rope (*alba linea*) fastened across from two small marble pillars (*hermulæ*), and loosened away from one side as soon as all the horses were brought up fairly abreast of it, and the signal for the start had been given. The out-building F is the Emperor's box (*pulvinar*), and the one on the opposite side (G) is supposed to have been intended for the magistrate called *editor spectaculorum*, at whose charge the games were exhibited. In the centre of the end occupied by the stalls was a grand entrance (H), called *porta pompæ*, through which the Circensian procession entered the ground before the races commenced. Another one was constructed at the circular extremity (I), called *porta triumphalis*, through which the victors left the ground in a sort of triumph. A third is situated on the right side (K), called *porta libitinensis*, through which

Ancient racecourse at Constantinople.

the killed or wounded drivers were conveyed away; and two others (L L) were left close by the *carceres* through which the chariots were driven into the ground.

The external and internal elevation of a circus was much like that of an amphitheatre (see *Amphitheatrum*), though the annexed engraving will afford a fair idea, as, though a ruin, it shows distinctly the arcades and outer shell of the building; some fragments of the rows of seats for the spectators; the *spina*, with its obelisks and columns nearly perfect; the *meta prima* on the right hand of it; the *oppidum* and *carceres* arranged on a curved line, as in the first example; and one of the gates through which the chariots entered the ground, like those marked L L on the ground-plan.

FORUM.

1. THE original meaning of the word *forum* was the un-
covered space of ground left in front of a tomb, in which
the same right of property existed as in the sepulchre itself.

2. A *market-place*, consisting of a large open area in the
centre, where the country people exhibited their produce for
sale, surrounded by outbuildings and colonnades, under which
the different trades erected stalls and displayed their wares
or merchandise. In small towns a single forum would suffice
for different markets; but in large cities, like Rome, almost

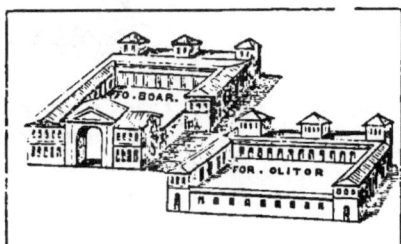

The cattle and vegetable markets at Rome.

every class of provision dealers had a market of their own
distinguished by the name of the produce sold in it—as *forum
boarium*, the cattle-market; *forum olitorium*, the cabbage or
vegetable market; both of which are represented in the
annexed illustration, which also distinctly shows the manner
in which an ancient market-place was laid out and enclosed.

3. The *Forum, i. e.*, a large open area of a nature somewhat
similar to the last one described, but laid out upon a much more
magnificent scale (see woodcut on page xxxvi), and intended as

c

a place for holding public meetings in the open air, and for the transaction of judicial and commercial business, rather than a

Arcus or *fornix*, triumphal arch.

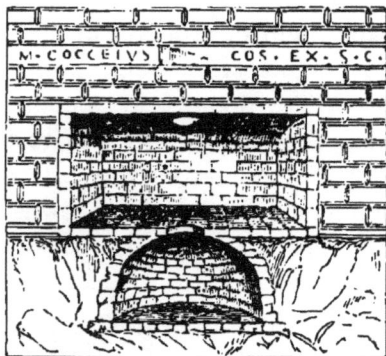

Carcer, or gaol, showing the *carcer inferior*, or dark underground dungeon, having access to the *carcer interior*, or middle gaol, by an aperture in the roof, which also opened into the place for *custodia communis*, or lighter imprisonment, through an aperture in the roof.

mere provision-market. It was surrounded by the principal public buildings and offices of state, courts of justice, *basilicæ*,*

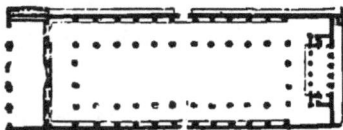

* Ground plan of a *basilica*, consisting of central nave and two side aisles divided from it by a row of columns on either side. At the further extremity of the principal nave a portion was railed off, as shown at the right hand of the cut, like the chancel of a church, to form a more private recess from the noise and activity of traffickers, in which the judges sat and the counsel pleaded.

places of worship, and spacious colonnades of one or more stories, in which the merchants, bankers, and money-dealers

had their counting-houses and transacted their business. The
famous Roman Forum is nothing but a mass of ruins. The
illustration on page xxxvi gives a plan of the Forum afforded by
the excavations at Pompeii. The central area is paved with
large square flags, on which the bases for many statues still
remain, and surrounded by a Doric colonnade of two stories,
backed by a range of spacious and lofty buildings all round.
The principal entrance is through an archway (*fornix*, A, see
page xxxiv), towards the left-hand corner of the plan, and by the
side of a temple of the Corinthian order (B), supposed to have
been dedicated to Jupiter. On the opposite flank of this temple
is another entrance into the Forum, and by its side the public

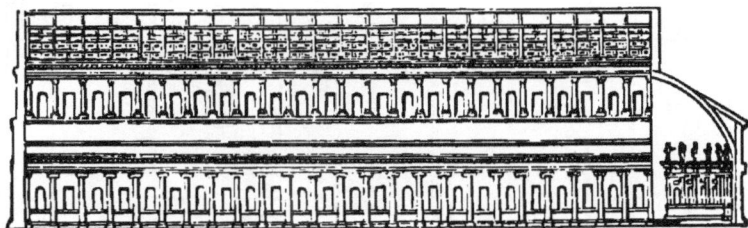

* The whole of the interior of a *basilica* was surrounded by an upper
gallery raised upon the columns which divided the aisles below, as
in this engraving, which shows a longitudinal section and elevation
down the centre of the ancient Basilica at Verona. These upper
galleries were intended for spectators and loungers. At the end is
shown a *tribune*, thrown out instead of the *chancel* in the woodcut on
page xxxiv to answer the same purpose as the recess there spoken of.

prison (*carcer*, C—see the illustration to *Carcer* on page xxxiv),
in which the bones of two men with fetters on their legs were
found. Adjacent to this is a long, shallow building (D), with
several entrances from the colonnade, which was probably a
public granary (*horreum*). The next building is another temple
of the Corinthian order (E) dedicated to Venus. It stands in
an area enclosed by a flank wall and peristyle, to which the

principal entrance is in a side street, abutting on the Forum,
and flanking the *basilica* (F—see illustration to *Basilica* on
page xxxv), beyond which there are three private houses out of
the precincts of the Forum.

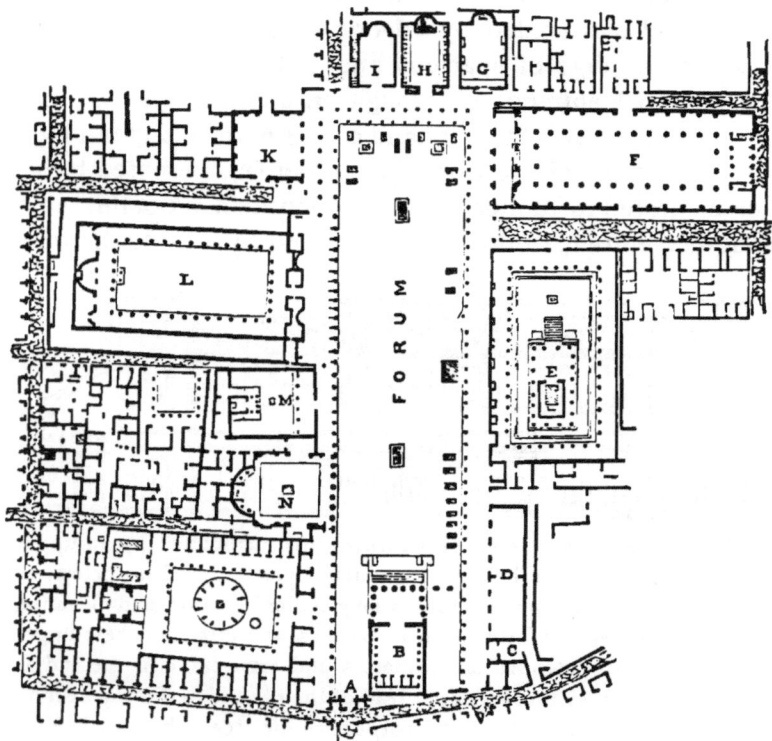

Plan of the Forum excavated at Pompeii, and answering in its
arrangements to the one at Rome.

The further or southern side of the square is occupied by
three public edifices (G. H, I), nearly similar to one another in
their plans and dimensions. All these have been decorated
with columns and statues, fragments of which still remain on

the floor ; but there are no sufficient grounds for deciding the uses for which they were destined. The first is merely conjectured to have been a council-chamber (*curia*) ; the second, the treasury (*ærarium*) ; and the last, another *curia*. Beyond this is another street opening on the Forum, and turning the angle are the remains of a square building (K) for which no satisfactory use can be suggested. The space behind is occupied by the sites of three private houses. The next object is

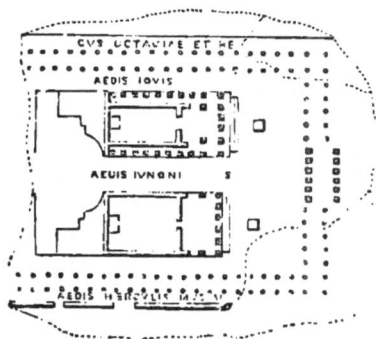

Porticus, ground plan of portico of Octavia, with the temples of Jupiter and Juno within its precincts. The double row of six columns on the right marks the principal entrance.

Chalcidicum, or large, low, and deep porch, covered with its own roof, supported on pilasters, and appended to the entrance front of many public buildings.

a large plot of ground (L) surrounded by a colonnade (*porticus*) and a cloister (*crypta*), and decorated in front where it faces the Forum by a spacious entrance-porch or vestibule (*chalcidicum*), all of which were constructed at the expense of a female named Eumachia. (See the illustrations above to *porticus* and *chalcidicum*, and to *chalcidicum* * on page xxxviii.)

Beyond this is a small temple (M), upon a raised basement, attributed by some to Mercury, by others to Quirinus, and adjoining to it an edifice (N) with a large semicircular tribune or absis at its further extremity, supposed to have been a

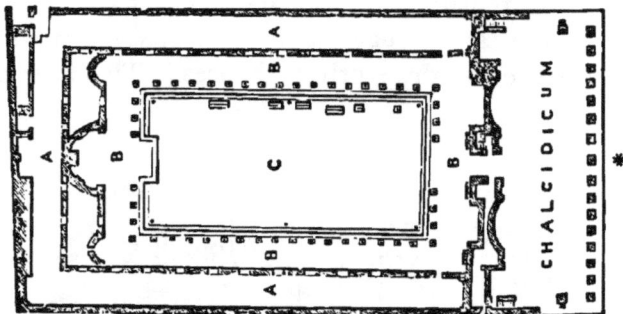

Ground plan of public edifice, consisting of A A A, three corridors or *crypta*, surrounded on three sides by a blank wall decorated with fresco paintings. On the inside are windows opening on a colonnade (*porticus*), marked B B B B, which surrounds a large central area (C).

meeting-hall for the Augustals or a town-hall (*senaculum*) for the Pompeian senate. The rear of both these structures is covered by the premises belonging to a fuller's establishment (*fullonica* *—see the illustration on page xxxix).

The last structure (O) is a magnificent building commonly called the Pantheon, with various appurtenances behind it, so called from twelve pedestals placed in a circle round an altar in their centre, supposed to have supported the statues of the Dii Magni, or twelve principal divinities, but the style of the decorations and the subject of the numerous paintings which ornamented its walls make it probable that it was a banqueting-hall for the Augustals.

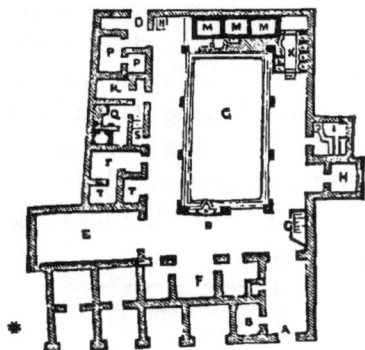

Fuller in his tub.

Ground plan of fuller's washhouse and premises at Pompeii. A, the principal entrance from the main street. B, the porter's lodge. C, the *impluvium*. D, a fountain with jet of water. E, a spacious apartment opening on the courtyard for drying clothes. F, a *tablinum*, with a room on each side where customers were received. G, closet for clothes already scoured. H, adjoining rooms where active trade operations were carried on. I, wash-house with tank for simple washing and rinsing. K, the place where dirt and grease were got out by rubbing and treading with the feet. L L L L L L, six niches on the sides of the room, separated from one another by low walls about the height of a man's armpits, in each of which was placed a tub where the fuller stood and trod out the impurities of the clothes with bare feet, raising himself on his arms to do so, which rested, as shown by the engraving, on the side walls. M M M, three smaller tanks for soaking clothes before washing. N, fountain or well for workmen. O, back gate opening on a small street contiguous to that portion of the premises in which the active part of the trade was performed. Γ P, spare rooms. Q, the furnace. R, apartment contiguous. S, stairs ascending to an upper story. T T T, apartments opening on the courtyard, painted in fresco, appropriated for the use of the master and mistress of the establishment. The rooms at the bottom of the plan without references are shops facing the street, and belonging to other tradesmen.

TELA.

TELA, a weaver's loom. The earliest looms, and those common among the Romans, were upright ones, such as are still used at the Gobelin's manufactory in India, for making tapestry, and in Iceland. The illustration,* though taken from an Egyptian model and slightly restored on one of its sides, exhibits distinctly all the different parts enumerated by the Latin writers, viz., the cross-piece or yoke (*jugum*), connecting

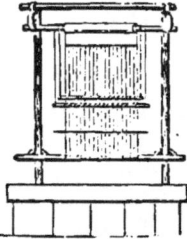

* *Tela*, a weaver's loom.

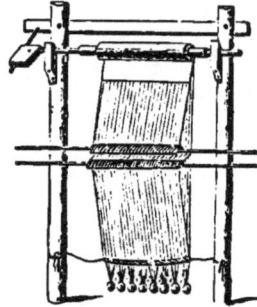

† *Liciatorium*, leash-rods shown upon a primitive Icelandic loom.

the two uprights at the top ; the cloth beam (*insubulum*) imme-diately under it, round which the cloth was rolled as the work progressed ; the pair of treadles or leash-rods (*liciatoria*), which are also shown by the engraving annexed (*Liciatorium*),† and are used to decussate the threads of the warp so as to open a shed for the passage of the shuttle (*alveolus*), ‡ or for

‡ *Alveolus*, weaver's shuttle.

the needle (*radius*), which conveys the weft across it. Below these is the reed (*arundo*), which is passed alternately over

and under every thread of the warp, in order to separate the
whole of them into two parcels for receiving the leashes (*licia*),
and finally the yarn-beam (*scapus*), to which the threads or
yarns forming the length of the cloth are fastened. In this
loom the web is driven from below upwards ; in the next
specimen (*tela jugalis*) it is driven downwards from above ;
but in both of them the weaver stood at his work instead of
sitting.

2. *Tela jugalis.** This is the commonest and simplest kind

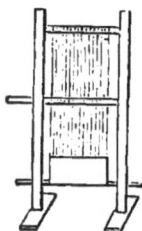

* *Tela jugalis*, weaver's loom with no cloth beam (*insubulum*).

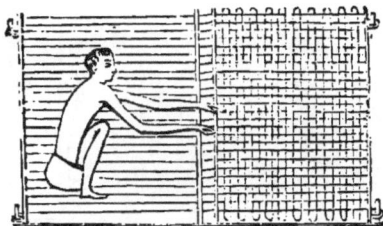

Subtemen, the weft or woof, *i.e.*, the cross thread passed alternately
under and over the warp (*stamen*). (See engraving to *stamen*.)

of loom that was used by the Romans, as shown by the
annexed illustration, and so called because it had no cloth
beam (*insubulum*), the yarns being merely attached to a yoke
(*jugum*) on its top. The word *tela* is also used for the warp
(as in Virgil's Georgics, 1., 285), *i.e.*, the series of strongly

twisted threads or yarns extended on a loom, into which the
finer ones of the weft (*subtemen*—see engraving for *subtemen*
on page xli) are woven to make a piece of cloth.   In this
sense the word is commonly accompanied by such epithets
as *stans, recta, pendula*—all of which imply that the warp was
fixed in a vertical position, and consequently upon an upright
loom, such as is exhibited by both the illustrations, viz., *tela*
and *tela jugalis.*

The annexed illustrations show the *stamen* or spun thread,
consisting of several fibres drawn down from the top of the
distaff (*colus*) and twisted together by the thumb, and the
rotary motion of the spindle (*fusus*) as it hung in a perpen-
dicular line from the distaff, the upright portion suggesting the
name.   All these particulars are shown by the left-hand woodcut representing a female spinning, while the other woodcuts
show two spindles with thread round them and one empty.

Neo, to *spin* or twist a number of separate fibres of wool
or flax into a single thread.   The annexed illustration, representing Hercules with the distaff and spindle of Omphale, will
elucidate the manner in which the process of spinning is
conducted and explain the terms employed to describe the
different steps in the operation.   The loaded distaff (*colus
compta* or *lana amicta*) was fixed to the left side of the
spinner by running the end of the stick through the girdle

(*cingulum*), instead of which the modern women use their apron strings. A number of fibres (*stamina*) are then drawn down from the top with the left hand (*ducere lanam*) and fastened to the spindle (*fusus*), which is then set twirling with the thumb and finger, as boys spin a teetotum (*stamina nere*), (*pollice versare*), (*versare pollice fusum*). The rotary motion of

Hercules, with the distaff and spindle of Omphale.

Colus, or *distaff*, as shown by the right-hand figure, made of a cane stick about a yard long, slit at the top so as to form a sort of basket to contain the wool or flax for spinning. The ring is a sort of cap to keep the mass together. The figure on the left shows a woman with a distaff filled (*colus plena* or *lana amicta*) in her left hand, the drawn thread (*stamen*) depending from it, and twisting the spindle (*fusus*) with the fingers of her right hand.

the spindle as it hangs suspended (see the left-hand woodcut above) twists these fibres into a thread (*filum*), which is constantly fed from above by drawing out more fibres from the distaff as the twist tightens (*ducere stamina versato fuso*). When the length of thread has grown so long that the spindle nearly touches the ground, the portion made is taken up and wound round the spindle, and the same process is again resumed, until other lengths are twisted and the spindle is entirely covered with thread so that it can contain no more, when the thread is broken from the distaff (*rumpere supremas colos*), and the whole rolled up into a ball (*glomus*) ready for use.

BALNEÆ.

THE illustration below on the left shows a plan of a complete set of public baths, including conveniences for warm and cold bathing, as well as sudorific or vapour baths, and provided with a double set of apartments for the male and female sexes.

These baths had six distinct entrances (1, 2, 3, 4, 5, 6) from the street, of which the first three were for visitors, 4 and 5 for the slaves and purposes connected with the business of the establishment, and the last gave access to the women's baths, which had no communication with the larger set.

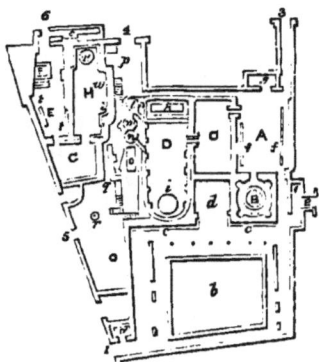

Balinea or *balnea*, ground plan of the double set of baths at Pompeii.

Commencing the circuit of the plan by the first door (1). at the bottom of the plan on the left hand, we have:—*a*, or a *latrina*, w.c. *b*, an open court, surrounded by a colonnade on three of its sides, which formed a sort of *atrium* to the rest of the edifice, something like the *atrium* of a private house (see page xiv). *c c*, stone seats along one side of the court for the slaves who were awaiting the return of their masters from the interior, or for the accommodation of the citizens, in like manner expecting the return of their friends. *d*, a recessed chamber, either intended as a waiting-room for visitors, or probably appropriated to the use of the superintendent of the

* *Apodyterium* or undressing-room, where every one was compelled by law to undress and leave his clothes as a check to robbery. It has three doors. The one on the left hand is the general entrance from the outside ; that on the right of it opens into the cold bath ; the nearest one on the right gives access to the warm bath. Seats for dressing and undressing upon run along three sides of the room, and holes are seen in the walls in which wooden pegs were fixed for hanging up the clothes. The small dark niche under the window served to hold a lamp.

baths. *e*, another *latrina*, near the second principal entrance (2), from which a corridor turning sharp to the right leads into A, the * *apodyterium* (as shown by the above engraving) or un-dressing-room, which has a communication with each of the principal entrances and with each of the apartments destined for the various purposes of hot and cold bathing. *f f*, seats of masonry on each side of the room for the bathers to dress and undress upon. B, the *frigidarium*, or chamber containing the cold -water bath (*baptisterium*—see the left-hand engraving below). *g*, a room for the use of the *garde-robe*, who took charge of the wearing apparel, kept for its owners while bathing.

Baptisterium, or cold plunging bath, constructed in the *cella frigidaria.*

* *Tepidarium*, containing three bronze benches (*subsellia*) and a brazier (*focus*). The walls all round are divided into recesses under the cornice by a number of male figures (*telamones*), which thus constitute a series of small closets, where the unguents and other necessaries used by the bathers were deposited. It is believed that the chamber also served for the oiling-room (*elæothesium*), to which bathers retired to be scraped with the strigil after the sweating bath.

Aliptes or *unctor*, a slave whose business was to rub the bather dry, scrape off the perspiration with a *strigil*, and then anoint the body with unguents.

c, the * *tepidarium* (see the engraving above), or tepid chamber, the atmosphere of which was kept at an agreeable warmth by means of a brazier formed in it : it was intended to break the sudden change of temperature from heat to cold, as the bather returned from the thermal chamber to the open air. This apartment also served sometimes as a place for being scraped with the strigil and anointed after the sweating bath (see the engraving—*aliptes*, on page xlvi). A door from this department conducted the bather into D, the *caldarium* * or thermal chamber, which contains (*h*) a hot water bath (*alveus*) at one extremity, and the *laconicum*, with its basin or *labrum*,

* *Caldarium* or thermal chamber, containing three parts :—1. *Laconicum*, a semicircular alcove at the right hand of the engraving, with a *labrum* upon a raised stem in the centre of it. 2. A vacant space in the centre of the room (*sudatorium*) and a warm water bath (*alveus*) at the other extremity. In the central portion the bather exercised himself by lifting weights and performing gymnastics for the purpose of exciting perspiration ; he then sat down in the *laconicum*, and underwent a profuse perspiration, induced by the hot air from the flues seen under the flooring, or, if preferred, he entered the *alveus* or warm bath.

at the other (see the engraving to *laconicum* on p. xlviii). *l*, the furnace, which, besides the use above mentioned, also heated the coppers containing the water for the baths, viz., *m*, the *caldarium*, or copper for hot water ; *n*, the *tepidarium*, or copper for tepid water. *o*, the cold water cistern. *p*, a room for the slaves who had charge of the furnace and its appen-

dages, furnished with a separate entrance from the street (4),
and two staircases, one of which led up to the roof, and the
other down to the furnace.   *q*, a small passage connecting the
last-named apartment with *r*, the yard, where all the things
necessary for the service of this part of the establishment, such
as wood, charcoal, &c., were kept : it has also its own separate
entrance from the street (5), and the remains of two pillars
which originally supported a roof or a shed are still visible.

Laconicum, so called because it originated with the Lacedæmonians.
One end contained the *alveus*, the other the *laconicum*, a semicircular alcove heated by a furnace and flues (*hypocausis*) under its
floor.   In the centre was placed a flat vase (*labrum*) containing
water for the bather to sprinkle himself with as he scraped the perspiration off. and immediately over it was a circular opening (*lumen*)
which could be closed or opened by means of a metal disc (*clipeus*)
to raise or lower the temperature.

The remaining portion of the plan is occupied by another
set of baths for females, more confined in space, but arranged
on a similar principle. They have but one entrance (6), which
gives access to a small waiting-room (*s*), with seats for the same

use and purposes as those marked *c c* in the larger set. E, the *apodyterium*, with seats on two of its sides (*t t*), and which, like the one first described, communicates with the *frigidarium* or cold water bath (F), and with the *tepidarium* or tepid chamber (G), through which the bather passes on, as he did in the preceding case, to the thermal chamber (H), provided in the same manner with its *laconicum* and *labrum* (*v*) at one end, and its *alveus* or hot water bath (*w*) on the side contiguous to the furnace and boilers, which are thus conveniently situated so as

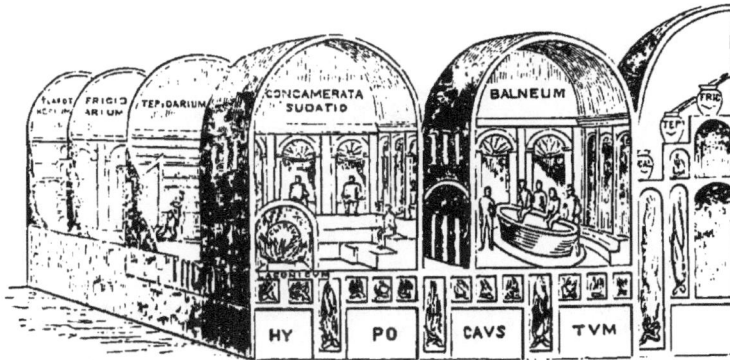

Sudatorium or sweating-room, heated by flues arranged under the flooring (*suspensura*), sometimes constructed in the walls of a chamber, when it was called *sudatio concamerata*. as in the woodcut here given, showing a set of baths from a painting of the *thermæ* of Titus, in which the *caldarium* is divided into two parts—the *balneum* (warm water bath) and sudatory.

to supply both sets of baths with hot air and warm water by a single apparatus. In these baths for the women the *tepidarium* has a suspended floor and walls fitted with flues, which is not the case in the corresponding apartment of the larger set.

The plan on next page represents a private bath (*balneum*) as contradistinguished from the plural *balneæ*, or public baths. The distribution and arrangement is on a similar principle to that in the other plan. The baths and appurtenances occupied

d

an angle at one extremity of the whole pile of building, and
were entered from the *atrium* through a door at *a*. Immediately
on the right of the entrance is a small room (*b*), perhaps used
as a waiting-room or intended for the slaves attached to this
department of the household.   Beyond this is the *apodyterium*
or undressing-room (A), situated between the cold and hot
baths, and having a separate entrance into both of them.   B is
a small triangular court partially covered by a colonnade on

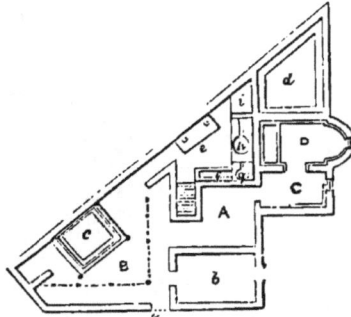

Ground plan of *balneum* or bath belonging to the suburban
villa of Arrius Diomedes, at Pompeii.

two of its sides, in the centre of which, and in the open air
(excepting that it had a roof overhead supported by two
columns at opposite angles), was the cold water bath (*c*) *piscina
in area*.   c is the *tepidarium ;* D, the *caldarium* (see the illustrations to the other plan) ;   *d*, the reservoir; *e*, a room for
furnace-slaves, which had a stone table in it (*e*) and a staircase
leading to an upper story on the roof; *f*, the cistern for cold
water ; *g*, the boiler for tepid water ; *h*, the boiler for hot water ;
i, the furnace—all arranged as in the public baths.

THERMÆ.

1. THERMÆ—literally, *hot springs;* thence a bath of hot water, whether warmed by natural or artificial heat. From this the name was subsequently transferred to the buildings which contained a set of baths, including cold as well as hot, and vapour as well as water baths; such, for instance, as those bequeathed by Agrippa to the Roman people, of which the noble edifice now called the Pantheon at Rome formed one of the apartments. In this general sense the name is nothing more than a new term for *balineæ.*

2. But after the age of Augustus, when the Romans cultivated the arts of peace, and expended a portion of the tributary wealth acquired from their extensive dominions in the embellishment of their Capitol, the name *thermæ* was applied particularly to those magnificent establishments modelled after the plan of a Greek gymnasium, but constructed on a still more sumptuous and extensive scale, which, in addition to conveniences for all kinds of bathing, contained rooms for intellectual conversation and philosophical discussion, libraries, picture galleries, apartments for games and exercises, open and shaded walks; covered corridors and porticos for running, leaping, racing, and other gymnastics; as well as every appurtenance which could conduce to the intellectual or physical enjoyment of a wealthy and luxurious population. Very extensive remains of *thermæ* are still to be seen at Rome.

The illustration on page lii shows the ground plan of the *thermæ* of Caracalla. The dark parts exhibit the actual remains, the light ones are restorations. The names and uses of the several apartments are to a certain extent conjectural, excepting where the ruins point to the original intention.

A A, a colonnade fronting the street annexed to the original building by Heliogabalus in part, and completed by Alexander Severus. The range of small apartments behind this colonnade are supposed to have been separate bathing-rooms, with an

Thermæ, ground plan of hot and cold baths, colonnades, exercising grounds, libraries, discussion-rooms, and picture galleries; theatre-like space for races, corresponding very much to the Greek γυμνάσια.

undressing-room (*apodyterium*—see page xlv) attached to each for the use of persons who did not wish to bathe in public. B, the entrance. C C C, three single corridors round the central pile of buildings, with a double one (D D) on the south-west. E E, *exedræ* for philosophers and literary men to sit and converse in, constructed with a semicircular *absis* or *alcove*, remaining on the left side, round which the seats were ranged. F F, corridors like the Greek *xysti* in front of the exercising ground, and having a separate apartment at each end, which probably served for some of the games or exercises adopted from the Greeks. G G G G, open walks (*hypæthræ ambula-tiones*), planted with trees and shrubs, and laid out with vacant spots between for active exercises. H, the *stadium* (see the annexed illustration), with seats round for spectators to view the racing and other exercises performed in it; hence also termed *theatridium*. In the general plan the *stadium was very like the Roman circus, with the barrier (*spina*) and stalls (*carceres*) forming a narrow oblong area, terminated in a semi-circle at one end and by a straight line at the other. A is the starting-place, B the other end of the *stadium*.

* *Stadium*, racecourse for foot-racing, 606¾ English feet long.

The works at the back of the *stadium* in the plan to *thermæ* contain the water tanks, and furnaces below them, which heated the water for the baths to a certain temperature before it was conveyed by pipes into the coppers immediately ad-joining the bath-rooms, with I, the general reservoir (*castellum*), and J, a portion of the aqueduct which supplied it. The other apartments at this extremity of the structure were probably intended for games or exercise of some sort. The central pile of buildings contained the bathing apartments, of some of which sufficient traces remain to indicate their uses. N, *natatio*, a large swimming bath, flanked by a suite of rooms on each side, which served as undressing-rooms (*apodyteria*, see page xlv), and chambers for the slaves (*capsarii*) who took charge of the clothes while their owners were bathing. O, the *caldarium* (see illustration to *caldarium* on page xlvii), with four baths (1, 2, 3, 4) for warm water (*alvei*) in each of its angles, and a *labrum* (5, 6) on each flank. The steps still remain which conducted into the baths, and part of a pipe through which the water was introduced into one of them. The roof over the central part, as well as that of the preceding one (N), was supported upon eight immense columns. The apartments beyond contained the *laconicum* (see page xlviii) or vapour bath, for which the circular room (P) served. Q Q were cisterns for water near the bath-rooms, and filled from the tanks at the further end of the edifice. The two spacious apartments (R R) within the lateral corridors on each flank were covered rooms for exercise in bad weather. The remaining ones on the further side, under the double portico (S S), were two cold plunging baths (*baptisteria*—see page xlvi), with an oiling room (*elæothesium*, T T) and a cold chamber (*frigidarium*, U U) on each side. The whole exterior occupied one mile in circuit; and the central pile had an upper story, traces of which remain, where the libraries and picture galleries were probably situated.

TOGA, STOLA, TUNICA, AND PALLA.

TOGA.—The distinctive national dress and principal outer garment of the Roman people was of white wool, except in cases of private mourning, or amongst the poorest classes, who could not afford to have it frequently cleaned, in both which cases dark wool of the natural colour was employed. The size and manner of adjusting the garment was modified according to the age in which it was used.

The woodcut below shows a figure adjusting a *toga* used in early times. This sort of toga was made of a lunated or semicircular piece of cloth, of moderate dimensions, so as not to form any bend or *sinus* across the chest. The numerous

Toga used in early times.

parallel folds at the extremities were produced by drawing the hollow edge of the garment into a straight line, or tight across the back, which constitutes the first process in adjusting the drapery to the person, as exhibited by the figure. After the centre of the smallest or upper curve had been raised against

the back of the neck, both ends were drawn over the shoulders
so as to hang down perpendicularly in front, but with no
brooch under the chin ; the right one was then taken up and
drawn tight under the chin, and then cast over the left shoulder,
so that the extremity fell like a lappet down the back, in
which case both the arms would be covered by the drapery.

But if the wearer wished to leave his right arm free for action,
as shown by the engraving below on the left, instead of drawing
the right side over the top of the shoulder he passed it *under* the
armpit (see the figure on page lv), and then threw it over the

Figure with *toga* of early times adjusted so as to leave the arm free
for action.

Toga of increased but moderate size, such as the one
called *neque restricta neque
fusa*, worn in the time of the
republic.

opposite shoulder.   All togas of the kind shown by the left-
hand engraving were termed *togæ restrictæ*, *i. e.*, togas of less
dimensions than those afterwards used.   The engraving on the
right hand shows a *toga* of the same character in outline, but of
larger dimensions, which made it necessary to adopt some altera-
tion in the manner of adjusting it, and led to the formation of a
very short fold (*sinus perquam brevis*).   The object of this *sinus*
was to carry off the additional length given to the drapery by

depressing a certain portion of it in front of the person, in order
that the end cast over the shoulder might not hang too low
behind. It will be perceived from the illustration that the
right side crossing the chest is depressed a little in front, instead of being drawn close under the chin, or tight under the
armpit, so as to form the *sinus*, and thus to create a bed for
the arm to rest in, leaving only the hand and a small part of
the chest exposed.

This is the attitude intended by the expression " *brachium
veste con.inebatur*," and was the one commonly adopted by the
orators of the republic.

The next woodcuts show the ample toga (*toga fusa* *), or last
style, which prevailed in the age of Augustus and the succeeding
emperors, and its different appearance is caused merely by its
increased size. It was enlarged until its outer circumference

* *Toga fusa*, or ample toga worn in the Augustan age and afterwards.

formed a complete circle (*rotunda*), when spread out upon the
ground in the manner of an Italian or Spanish cloak, the inner
edge being likewise hollowed out as in the preceding instances,
but in such a manner as would produce a greater breadth of
fold when wound round the person, as indicated by the expression *apte cæsa*. It was first put on the left shoulder in such a

manner that about a third of its entire length covered the left side, and fell down in front of the wearer to the ground between the feet, as shown by the parts marked 1 in both the front and back views in the illustrations on page lvii. The rest was passed behind the back, and *under* the right arm, then turned down or doubled together at about the middle of its breadth, carried across the front of the body, and thrown over the left shoulder, so that it hung down to the heels, as shown by the back view in the right-hand woodcut on page lvii. The portion thus folded down produced a double *sinus*, one formed by the outer edge of the drapery folded over, which in example referred to falls to the level of the knees (2), and in other statues reaches still lower, so as to set a little above the under edge of the drapery, *ima toga*, which was considered most becoming (*decentissimus*); the other was produced by the double part of the fold (4), and proceeding, as above mentioned, from under the right arm to the top of the left shoulder, so as to present the appearance of a shoulder belt (*balteus*), which should lie as it does here, easily across the breast, and not be drawn so straight and tight as in the earliest manner (shown by the left-hand illustration on page lvi), nor yet so loose as in the Greek style exhibited by the right-hand woodcut (*nec strangulet, nec fluat*) on the same page. Lastly, as the end of that side which was first put over the left shoulder would have trailed upon the ground and impeded the motion of the wearer, in consequence of the great length of the entire piece of drapery, a part was drawn up from underneath this belt, or upper *sinus* (4), and turned over it in a small round fold, termed *umbo*, which thus kept it at a proper level.

The *toga prætexta*, worn by free-born children of both sexes, as well as the chief magistrates, dictators, consuls, prætors, and ædiles, kings, and some priests at Rome and in the colonies, was like the ones already shown, except that it was ornamented with a broad border of purple.

The *toga pura*, or *virilis*, was made of white wool, without ornament or colour, and worn usually by men.

The illustration below on the left hand shows the *toga picta*,* or toga ornamented with embroidery, originally worn by the consul at his triumph, but under the empire by the consuls generally, and prætors when they celebrated the Circensian games. The figure represents the consul in his character of president of the games holding up a handkerchief (*mappa*) as a signal for the races to commence.

* *Toga picta*, or embroidered *toga*.

† *Palla* as worn by the ladies of Rome.

†*Palla.*—Though not quite identical with the Greek *palla*, still the dress worn by the ladies of Rome was similar enough to it to justify its being called by the same name. The woodcut above on the right hand shows the priestess Livia with a *palla* on. The undermost garment, which comes close up to the throat, and has sleeves looped down the fleshy part of the arm, is the under tunic or *stola* (see illustration to *stola* on next page) ; over this is seen the *palla*, with its back and front edges fastened together by clasps upon the shoulder points, while a large veil (*amiculus*) is finally thrown over the whole, in the manner stated by Ovid, Met., 14, 262, and implied by Livy, 27, 4, " *pallam*

pictam cum amiculo purpureo," where the diminutive expresses fineness of texture. The skirts of the *palla* are concealed by the outer drapery, so that its actual length cannot be ascertained, but it probably did not reach much below the knee, so that it might not hide the flounce (*instita*) of the *stola*, the lower edges and plaits of which are seen over the feet and on the ground. In addition to this the lady wore a chemise (*tunica intima*) next the skin.

Stola, the female robe which constituted the characteristic feature in the attire of a Roman matron, as the *toga* did in that of the male sex. It was a tunic made very full, and sometimes with long sleeves; at others with short ones fastened down the fleshy part of the arm with clasps, but put on as an

Stola, the female robe corresponding to the *toga* of the men.

indumentum over the chemise (*tunica intima*), and fastened with a double girdle (*succincta*), one under the breast and the other over the hips, so as to produce an ample display of small irregular folds (*rugæ*) when compressed by and drawn through its ligatures. Thus far the *stola* does not materially differ from the outer tunic usually worn by the Roman ladies. But what constituted its distinguishing feature was an appendage

termed *instita*, sewed on under the girdle (*subsuta*), Hor., Sat. i.,
2, 10, and trailing behind so as to cover the back half of the
feet (*medios pedes*) from the ankle bones (*talos*). The figure on
page lx. is supposed to be Veturia, the mother of Coriolanus.
The *instita* was not a circular flounce added all round to the
tunic, but a long breadth or scarf, hanging behind and conceal-
ing the heels or half the feet.

Tunica.—The ordinary and principal under garment of the
Greeks and Romans of both sexes, corresponding very nearly
in its general form, use, and character with the *shirt*, the
chemise, the *frock*, or the *blouse* of modern times.

1. (Χιτὼν ἀμφιμάσχαλος, *colobium.*) The ordinary tunic
of the male Greek and Roman consisted of a plain woollen
shirt girded round the loins, and reaching to the knees or
thereabouts, with two short sleeves which just covered the deltoid muscle, or upper portion of the arms as far as the armpit
(μασχάλη). The working population wore it in their daily

Ordinary plain woollen tunic.

pursuits, as the above woodcut shows; but the upper classes,
and, indeed, most others on festivals and holidays, when they
were dressed in full attire, had either the *toga* or some garment
over it if Roman, and the *pallium*, or some other Greek gar-

ment if Greek, which of course in the annexed figures hides most of the under vest or tunic. The figure on the left is supposed to be Aristides with the *pallium* over his tunic, and on the right a Roman with his *toga* outside his. These two articles

Figures representing Aristides on the left, with his *pallium* over his tunic, and a Roman on the right with his toga over it.

constitute the complete attire usually worn by the great mass of the free population in ancient Greece and Italy, and are as intimately connected as the shirt and coat of modern times.

Tunica, or χιτών, with *only one* short sleeve.

2. A tunic (χιτὼν ἑτερομάσχαλος) made with *only one* short

sleeve covering the deltoid muscle of the left arm as far as the
armpit, as shown by the figure at the bottom of page lxii, which
represents a young slave going to market with a purse in one
hand and a basket in the other.

3. (Ἐξωμίς, *exomis.*)* A tunic which only covered the left
shoulder (ὦμος), leaving the right one entirely exposed, as shown
by the figure on the left below. It was often made of fur, and
commonly worn on the stage, by the labouring population,
slaves, artists, and even females addicted to the chase or war,
as by Diana and the Amazons.

* Tunic called *exomis.*   † Tunic called ἐπωμίς.   ‡ The *slit* tunic.

4. (Ἐπωμίς)† A tunic worn by the females of Greece, so
called because fastened with brooches on the top of each
shoulder at the point where it joins the collar bone. It was
of wool, and fastened by a girdle worn low upon the hips. See
the middle woodcut.

5. (Σχιστὸς χιτών.)‡ The *slit* tunic, which was only sewed
close up from the bottom on the left side, leaving a long slit on
the right for the purpose of allowing free action to the limbs,
and through which the greater part of the thigh would be seen
in active exercise. It was usually fastened by brooches on the

shoulder, as in the middle figure, one of which may be supposed
to have come undone in the right-hand figure.

6. *Tunica manicata*, or *manuleata* (χιτὼν χειριδωτός, or καρ-
πωτός).   A tunic with long sleeves reaching down to the hands
or wrists, like the French *blouse*.   In the early age long sleeves
were not worn by the male population either of Greece or
Italy, nor generally by females, but they were afterwards adopted
as a luxury from the foreigner, and became very common.

Tunic with long sleeves down to the hands or wrists.

The figure is supposed to represent the *pædagogus*, or children's
attendant, in the celebrated group of Niobe; and he was of

* *Tunica talaris.*   † Hercules as a tragic actor.

course a slave and foreigner, who taught the Roman children Greek, as a French *bonne* might teach English children French.

7. *Tunica talaris* ($\chi\iota\tau\grave{\omega}\nu$ $\pi o\delta\acute{\eta}\rho\eta\varsigma$). A tunic with long skirts reaching down to the ankle joints, commonly worn in early times by both sexes of the Ionian colonies, and in use at Athens until the time of Pericles. It was sometimes very full and loose over the arms, as in the case of the figure of a female on the left, and sometimes reaching down to the wrists, as shown by the example on the right of a tragic actor† in the character of Hercules (see page lxiv). The Romans considered this tunic as extremely unmanly, and never adopted it as part of their male national costume.

8. *Tunica muliebris.* A woman's tunic, generally longer and closer than those worn by men, and fastened by a girdle imme-

Tunica muliebris, or woman's tunic.

diately under the bosom, instead of round the loins. The middle figure on page lxiii shows the tunic of the Dorian women, which is an exception to the usual style ; that of the Ionian women is shown by the left-hand figure of the two on page lxiv, and the example above shows the same article with a half-sleeve reaching nearly to the elbow, and having a long slit

e

on the outside, the edges of which are connected at intervals by
a set of studs or brooches, so as to leave a series of open loops
between them.   The article on *stola* shows the principal tunic
of the Roman lady.

9. *Tunica interior* and *intima*.   The under and undermost
tunic.   Both sexes were in the habit of wearing two tunics, and
persons of delicate constitutions sometimes would put on as

The under and undermost tunic.

many as four, in which case the outer one is *the* tunic (*tunica*),
and the under one *tunica interior*, or *intima*.   The above
illustration shows a figure in two tunics very distinctly

Figure reclining clad in the *tunica interior*.

Figure of a Greek female
taking off the *tunica interior*.

marked, the under one with long sleeves and a skirt which
reaches halfway between the knee and the ankle ; the outer one
with short sleeves and a skirt which terminates at the middle of
the thigh, and a girdle round the waist, which compresses both.
But the ordinary kind of tunic worn next the skin by women
was made with short sleeves, and rather loose round the neck ;
very much like a modern chemise, as shown by the examples
at bottom of page lxvi, the one on the left from a Roman bas-
relief, and the one on the right representing a Greek female
taking off her chemise.

Another sort of tunic, called *recta* * (ὀρθοσταδίας) was sometimes worn, woven in one piece all round like our stocking,
which filled in to the waist, and took the form of the figure
without requiring any girdle to keep it adjusted to the person,

* *Recta,* or tunic woven in one piece.

as was necessary with the common tunic, which was made of
equal width from top to bottom.   It consequently hung down
in straight (*recta*) folds from the neck to the feet, as the
annexed figure of Ceres shows.

The expression *tunicatus* corresponds often with our phrase
" in his shirt," as opposed to *togatus,* " in his coat ;" so the
phrase *tunicata quies* means either the ease and independence
of country life, as in dishabille, or the reverse, indicating

that a person is obliged to lay aside his toga to work in his tunic.

So in Horace, Ep. i., 7, 65, of the lower classes, whose daily occupations compelled them to wear a tunic, only without the toga.

SATIRE I.

ERRATA TO BOOK I. OF THE SATIRES.

Page 5, two lines from bottom, after " *Rome*" read " *to answer to his bail.*"

Page 7, Note 3, for " *bushels*" read " *pecks*," and " *six thousand*" for " 25,000" in text.   Three lines lower, for " *me*" read " *I.*"

Page 8, eight lines from the bottom, after " *heart*" read " *and when at home.*"

Page 9, omit the word " *Horace*" to the paragraph.

Page 17, line 12, omit the word " *at.*"

Page 57, line 9, for " *fame*" read " *fane.*"

Page 64, line 2, omit the word " *up.*"

cockcrow knock at his door, says, " Happy husbandmen!" Another, dragged from country seat to Rome, declares that those alone are blest who live at Rome.   The

that a person is obliged to lay aside his toga to work in his tunic.

So in Horace, Ep. i., 7, 65, of the lower classes, whose daily occupations compelled them to wear a tunic, only without the toga.

SATIRE I.

This Satire is directed against the habit of finding fault with fate, and the envy of others' condition, that was then so prevalent among men, and declares the cause of this habit and envy to be the practice of amassing money without spending it; and of deluding one's self with the idea of enjoying old age and wealthy ease at some future time, that never really comes. The Augustan age was one of foppery rather than crime.

Horace. How is't, dear Patron, that no man lives happy in that lot which or fixed choice has given him, or chance thrown in his way, but praises those who follow opposite pursuits to his?

" Blest are ye merchants," says the soldier, now worn out in limb by hard campaigns. And yet the trader, when the [1]fierce winds toss his bark, says, " Warfare is to be preferred to this."—[2]Well, pray why not? They meet in battle's shock, and in brief space comes speedy death, or gladdening victory.

Again, the man who's skilled in precedents of equity and written law, when clients at cockcrow knock at his door, says, " Happy husbandmen!" Another, dragged from country seat to Rome, declares that those alone are blest who live at Rome. The

[1] The south winds were rough and fierce.

[2] Horace supposes an objection to be made, and answers it.

other cases of this kind—so numerous are they—[1] would stop the most persistent argument.

[1] Literally, are able to tire out Fabius, who was a Roman knight, remarkable for pertinacity in philosophical argument.

To save my taking up your time, just hear the issue of all this. If any god were but to say, "Well, here: I'll see your wishes carried out; for you, who were just now a soldier, shall turn merchant; you, just now a barrister, shall take up farming life; come, change your places, pass away; you from this side, and you from that. [2] Come, come, I say, why do you linger there?" They would not care to change; and yet they may be happy, if they will. What reason is there to prevent the king of heaven from swelling out [3] both cheeks with rage, and vowing that henceforth he'll lend no kindly ear to prayers they make? But that I may not treat this lightly, just as one who treats of sportive themes,—although what does prevent one telling truth in playful mood, as often tutors give their pupils cakes caressingly, to make them care to learn their A B C?—yet still I say, to drop all jest, let me search out the graver truth.

[2] Eia is a particle expressing impatience.

[3] Implying the strength of his anger.

The man who works the heavy earth with his hard plough: the cheating innkeepers [4] one sees: the soldier and the merchant too, who reckless speed o'er every sea, say that they bear their toil with this intent, that when they're old, they may retire to ease and safety, when they've gained security from want;—just as the tiny ant, so diligent,—for

[4] "Hic" is like our use of the words "one sees" or "you have."

it's a case in point, say they—drags with its
mouth whate'er it can, and adds it to the
heap it's piling up, for it knows well what
times may come, and guards against them
well.   And yet this ant when—as some poet
says,—[1]"Aquarius makes dull the ended
year,"—both stays within its hole, and carefully enjoys what it acquired before ; while
you nor summer's blazing heat, nor winter's
cold, nor fire, nor sea, nor sword, would
move from keen pursuit of gain ; nay, nought
would stay you, could you but prevent your
class outstripping you in wealth.   And pray,
why love you so with fear to hide in
stealthily dug hole enormous mass of silver
or of gold ?

The Miser. Because, were one to spend it,
it would dwindle to a [2]paltry sum.

Horace. Yes, true; but if you don't buy what
you really want, what honourable use is there
in mere accumulation ?   E'en suppose the produce of your threshing-floor comes up to [3]five-
and-twenty thousand sacks of corn, yet still,
through this, you'll not be capable of eating
more than me ; as, if you were to carry, as
perhaps you might, upon your laden back,
surrounded by your slaves, a net-bag full of
bread, you still would get but just as much
as one who carried nought.   Or, tell me,
what 't would matter to the man who lived
on just so much as nature could not do
without, if he owned [4]sixty or six hundred
acres ?

[1] A parody of some epic poet's line.
Literally, creeps forth to no place.

[2] The "as" was about a penny in value.

[3] Centum milia modiorum, sc, 100,000 bushels.

[4] Jugera—rather more than half-acres ; "aret" means ploughs by means of his servants, *i.e.*, owns.

The Miser. I can't tell; but still 'tis joy to take from a large store.

Horace. And yet, if you let us take just the same from smaller store, why should you praise your barns more than our lesser bins? 'Tis just as though you wanted but a ¹cask, perhaps, or wine-glass full of water, and still were to say, "I'd rather take ²with ease from some large stream than at some pains get just the same from this small spring that flows close by; and so it is that the ³rough flood bears off and hurries on together with the bank all whom too great abundance gratifies. Yet he who only wants the little that one cannot do without, nor drinks from stream disturbed by mud, nor loses life in the rough flood. But some one argues :— many men, misled by wrong desire of fame, say no sum is enough, because we all are rated by the money we possess. What would you do with them? Why, bid them live a wretched life, since they act thus of their free will; as wretched as, at Athens, some rich miser was, who (as they say) was wont to thus despise what people said of him :—

"Aha! the Public hiss, but in my heart I say I'm right, directly that I gaze upon the coins in my strong-box." As says some poet, this is thirsty Tantalus who tries to catch the water as it rolls off from his lips. 'Well, why that laugh? but change the name, and then the story's told of you: you sleepless gloat o'er bags of money gained from every

¹ Literally, urna=three gallons; and cyathus, 1/12 of a pint.

² Dé implies easiness, and ex difficulty.

³ Aufidus was remarkable for the swiftness of its current.

Horace here anticipates, and answers an objection the miser might put forward.

An epic line slightly altered.

⁴ Horace was going to add, "and you are like Tantalus," but is interrupted by the miser with a derisive laugh at his quoting so stale a story as that, worn threadbare by the philosophers of the day.

source, and yet you're forced to touch them
not as though tabooed, or else you feel but
such delight in them as painting gives the   Very unsubstantial.
sense.   Pray don't you know the good of
money to you, or the use it is? You may
buy bread and herbs, your pint of wine, and
more, all else, which if our nature lacked, it
would feel pain.   Or, pray, is this your joy?
To dread thieves' villany, the firing of your
house, or lest your slaves should steal your
stores and run away? I'd ever pray to be
extremely poor in ¹blessings such as these.   ¹ Ironical.

    Horace. But if your frame be seized with chill,
and then get racked with pain, or if some other
accident confine you to your bed, then have
you friends to sit close by the couch, to get
the poultices, to beg the doctor to restore
your strength, and give you back to loving
child or relative?

    Not so: your wife don't want you to be   Horace replies to his
well and strong, nor yet your son; your   own supposition.
neighbours and acquaintances, aye, all the
world detests you heartily.   And, pray, are
you surprised that since you value money
more than all besides, none give the love you
don't deserve? Nay, should you think to
bind your kindred to you, and keep them
your friends without expense, you'd miserably
waste your toil, as all those would who tried
to teach a ²wretched ass to trot (like horse)   ² Asellus: the diminu-
obedient to reins upon the plain of Mars.   tive, among its several
                                               meanings, expresses con-
In fine, be there some limit to your search   tempt.
for gain, and since you have more than you

had, why, feel less dread of poverty, and
now begin to stay your toil, since you have
gained what you once wished to gain, lest
you should do as several have done before,

¹ Ummidius was no-
body in particular.

¹Ummidius for instance (and the story is not
long); he was so rich, he had to count his
sacks of gold, and yet so mean, he never
dressed aught better than a slave, and used
to dread until his latest day, lest want of
life's bare necessaries should o'erwhelm

² Like Clytemnestra,
a daughter of Tyndarus,
who killed her husband
Agamemnon.

him. ²But a freedwoman, the bravest of all
Tyndarus' line, cleft him in twain with her
(stout) axe.

The Miser. Pray, then, what do you bid me

³ Mænius was a great
profligate; Cassius No-
mentanus spent £56,000
in gluttony and de-
bauchery.

do ? Live like to worthless ³profligates, or
like the glutton and the rake ?

Horace. Ah! now you hesitate not to compare two cases diametrically opposite. I do
not, when I say, " Don't be a miser," bid you
turn out an abandoned scamp and worthless
wretch.

Tanais was a freedman
of Mæcenas ; nothing
further was known of the
father-in-law of Visellius.

There surely is some difference between
the eunuch and the ruptured man. I now
go back unto the point from whence I first

⁴ "Nemo ut avarus"
for " neminem avarum."
This construction is found
rarely even in Cicero and
Nepos, and again in
Satire iii. line 115, of this
book.

set out,⁴ I mean that no one miser is himself
content with what he does, but rather praises
those who follow opposite pursuits, and pines
with jealousy because his neighbour's goat
has teats more filled with milk than his, and
does not (as he ought) contrast his own lot
with the lot of all those poorer men, but ever
tries to pass now this, now that man in the
race for gold. So, as he hurries on, a richer

man is always in his way, just as the poet
Virgil says,—" When now the hoofed horse
swiftly drags along the car from barriers
let loose ; "—just so, I say, the charioteer
drives close upon the heels of steeds that
now outstrip his own, nought caring for the
'man once passed, who's riding in the ruck.
And so it is that seldom can we find a man
to say he has lived happily, and to quit life
as sated guests can quit the feast, well pleased
with all the time he spent in it.

But stay, I've said enough, nor will I write
another word, lest you should think I'd robbed
²blear-eyed Crispinus' shelves of books.

A parody of Virgil's
Georgic, i., 542.

1 'Auriga,' not 'equus'
is understood.

² Horace was himself
slightly blear-eyed, but
forgot his own small de-
fect in satirizing the glar-
ing one of Crispinus.
Crispinus was a garrulous
Stoic philosopher. To
rob his shelves of books
would mean to imitate
his garrulity.

SATIRE II.

A satire written against every kind of excess, and to show the general inconsistency of men.   The main argument is contained in line 24.

AND so the [1]guilds forsooth of female flute-players, the vagrant quacks, the ragamuffins, ballet-girls, and [2]toadies too,—yes, they and all like them are sad and terribly distressed because [3]Tigellius the singer and the music-master's dead.   And certainly he patronised them well.

[4]Yet here's a man, who, through a fear the world should say he is extravagant, would never give a needy friend enough to keep cold hunger from the door.   Yet if you ask a third the reason why he wickedly [5]spends all that splendid property his grandfather and father left, by buying all the dainties that he can with borrowed means, he answers, 'Tis because [6]I do not care to be thought mean and pusillanimous.   And so the spendthrifts praise him, while the misers blame.   Fufidius the banker, rich in land, rich too in money placed at interest, fears lest he should be called both an abandoned scamp and worth-less wretch.   [7]Sixty per cent. he wrings out from his principal, and just as men are reck-

less in their course, so he more fiercely grinds
them down.   He hunts up all the bonds of
young men ruled by angry sires, who, now
sixteen years old, have donned the manly
garb. Who does not cry out, " O great
king of heaven," on the instant he hears
this?

    Well, true; yet surely on himself he spends
a sum commensurate with what he gains?

    Not so. You'd scarcely credit how un-
kindly he will treat himself,—indeed, so
much so, that the father whom the [1]comedy
of Terence represents as living wretchedly,
when he had scared his son away, did not
torment himself aught worse.   Suppose a
man were now to ask, " What means all
this?" I then should answer thus, " In
trying to avoid one vice, fools run into its
opposite." [2]Malthinus struts along with
garments trailing on the ground, yet there
are men who walk with dress raised even to
indecent height, supposing it good [3]taste.
Rufillus smells of aromatic lozenges; Gar-
gonius as strong as any goat. There is no
happy mean. Some men would ne'er go near
a girl unless the border of her neat-hemmed
gown hid foot and ankle too; yet others only
look at those who practise lowest prostitution.
As once a noble left a house of evil fame, the
Censor Cato's splendid words ran thus :—
[4]"Go on in virtue's course, for right it is that
when foul lust has once inflamed the blood, our
youth should go to such resorts, and so keep

The Lætorian law forbade any one younger than twenty-five years of age from concluding a money transaction by post-obits.

A supposed apologist speaks here.

[1] The Self-Tormentor was a comedy of Terence, in which the cruelty of the father Menedemus drove the son Clinia into Asia to be a soldier, and where the father was wretched in consequence.

[2] An effeminate character.

[3] Facetus means rather "elegans" than "ridiculous."

[4] Minima de malis eligenda sunt.

[1] Cupiennius was a great rake and friend of Augustus.

[2] A parody of Ennius' lines—"Andire est operæ pretium procedere recte Qui rem Romanam Latiumque augescere voltis."

[3] A clever lawyer, not very chaste himself.

[4] Servius Tullius divided the people into five classes. He wittily applies this division to the freedwomen, who represented, to a great extent, the demi-monde of our day.

[5] Salustius was a nephew of the sister of Salust the historian.

[6] Origo and Arbuscula were celebrated actresses and hetæræ of the day.

clear of all adultery." Yet [1]Cupiennius, that lover of the white-robed matron, says, " I would not care to be praised thus." [2]'Tis really worth your while, all ye who do not wish adulterers to thrive, to learn how utterly they are distressed, and how their pleasure's marred by many pangs,—how seldom, too, it comes, and often is surrounded by rough risks. One man has thrown himself from some housetop ; another has been flogged to death with scourge ; a third has met with a fierce band of thieves, as he runs hurriedly away ; a fourth has had to pay a good round sum to stay the mutilating knife ; a fifth has been debauched by vilest slaves. Indeed, e'en this occurred :—some man deprived th' adulterer of power to err again. The town said, "Legally ;" but [3]Galba said, "Not so (it should have been a fine)." And yet how much more free from risk the intercourse with those of [4]lower rank,—I mean the freedwomen ; for whom [5]Salustius shows quite as mad a love as the adulterer for married dames. Yet if he would be merely kind and generous, so far as means and reason would suggest, and as he can discreetly be, he might give quite enough to them, and yet not bring disgrace and ruin on himself. But, no ; he soothes his conscience by this fact alone, delights in this, and lauds himself for it, and says, " I touch no neighbour's wife." As once Marsæus, he who loved [6]Origo so, the man who squandered land and personalty too upon an actress, said, " I ne'er intrigued with others' wives."

If not, you do intrigue with actresses and courtesans, and from them your good name gets greater ill than does your property. Or is it quite enough for you to shun the class or rank, instead of what in each case does the harm? To lose one's fair repute, to waste the means one's father left, are ills where'er they be. What matters it if you go wrong with [1] married lady or with [2] ordinary girl? In Fausta's case, one [3] Villius, jocosely called " Dictator's son-in-law," misled, poor wretch, by that one sobriquet, paid penalty enough, —aye, more too than enough,—mauled as he was with fist, attacked with sword, and e'en shut out of doors while [4] a more favoured swain was in the house. Well, now, suppose his mind made passion's organ see these ills, and speak to him like this—" What want you, pray? Do I e'er ask you for a woman sprung from mighty consul, nearly hid in her long robes, when I am stung by lust?" What answer would he make? He'd say, " The girl is born of noble sire." Yet how much better, how opposed to this your trifling, the advice that nature gives, so rich in her own stores, if but you cared to regulate them rightly, and to cease from thus confusing good with ill. Or think you that it matters not should you go wrong through your own fault, or through the force of cir-

1 "Oblimare," as "limus," mud makes meadows unproductive for a time, so the prodigal cripples his property.

2 Married women wore the long gown and wide over-dress, fastened by two brooches; the female slaves and ordinary women wore the toga, or plain long dress.

3 Sextus Villius Annalis had debauched Fausta the daughter of Sulla so often. that he was ironically called Sulla's son-in-law.

4 Longarenus was a more favoured lover, and he set some highwaymen upon Villius.

cumstance ? So, then, lest you should rue
it, give up this pursuit of married dames;
for thence you will derive more toil and woe
than you will reap enjoyment from success.
Nor are the dainty married lady's limbs,
though pearls and emeralds adorn them,
though they equal thine, [1]Cerinthus, aught
more delicate or straighter built,—nay, oft
the ordinary woman's are to be preferred.
Besides, [2]she wears her beauty set off by no
adventitious aid, shows openly her charms,
boasts not of good points she may have, nor
makes them prominent, nor tries to hide her
blemishes.

See what our nobles do when buying
horses : they examine them when covered
with a cloth, lest (as will happen), if a generally
comely form should rest on weakly legs or
faulty hoofs the shapely flanks, the head so
neatly turned, the arching neck, should whet
the buyer's wish to buy ; and this they rightly
do. So don't you gaze on beauties of a
woman's form with eyes as keen as Lynceus
had, while her deformities you look upon
with vision blinder than notorious Hypsæa's
was. You say, " Oh, what a splendid leg !
what graceful arms ! And yet she has too
lean a back, too long a nose, thin flanks,
splay feet. You could see nothing but a
married woman's face, for she, unless she be
most [3]shameless of her sex, conceals all else.
And should you try to gain forbidden views
of charms thus fenced about with dress (that

[1] Cerinthus was an exquisite, celebrated by Tibullus.

[2] The ordinary woman.

Literally, the fact of the flanks being well-formed.

[3] Catia was notoriously immodest.

dress it is that fires your mind), then many
hindrances you'll meet,—her eunuch retinue,
the chair she rides in, those who dress her
hair, the whole dependent crowd, the robe
that flows down to the ankles, and the close-
embracing cloak, and much besides that
would not let you have clear view of all her
form. [1]As for the freedwoman, there is no
hindrance here; for you may see her in her
gauze-like dress, as though she were quite
nude, and find that she has no misshapen
leg, nor ugly foot; then with a glance at her
side's dimensions you could gauge. Or would
you wish a trick played off on you before
I've shown my wares? [2]Here the adulterer
will hum these lines,—"Though oft the
hunter course the hare through the deep
snow, and yet cares not to take it up when
shot or killed." And will then say, as apposite, "My wish is like to his; for it speeds
by what all may have alike, and tries to
catch what cheats pursuit."

But, pray, do you expect that all your
griefs, your passions' ebb and flow, your
grave anxieties, can be scared from your
breast by paltry lines like these? And is it
not far better worth your while to search out
what the limits are that nature gives to our
desires, what 'twould reck not though it
lacked, and what it could not bear to have
withheld from it; far better too to separate
the true coin from the dross? Pray, when
your throat is parched with thirst, do you

[1] Altera is a nomina-
tive absolute for "quod
ad alteram attinet."

[2] The adulterer, instead
of answering, quotes from
an epigram of Callima-
chus, then often sung.

B

seek cups of gold? or, when you're hungry,

[1] The rarest delicacies. do you spurn all but the turbot or the [1]peacock's flesh? or, when your lustful passions rise, though plenty are close by at once to rid you of love's stings, would you prefer to be

[2] The particle "num" distraught by lecherous desire? [2] Not you;
requires a negative an-
swer in English.   not I;—indeed, I love an easy yielding
   Pavo, the peacock, and
rhombus, the turbot, were flame.   And Philodemus says that she who
both great delicacies.
   Philodemus was an cries, "Well soon; but give me more.   Yes,
Epicurean.
                   if my husband leave the house," is fit but
for the worn-out priest of Cybele; while she
who wants no heavy price, nor lingers when
she's bid to come, is fit for him.   Let her
look bright, be straight in limb, be so far
elegant as not to care to look more tall or
pale than her own form and face allow.
When such a woman I embrace, I call her
[3] Ilia and Egeria were by the [3]noblest ladies' names, or any name I
the names of noble ladies.
                   like; nor do I fear, whilst I am there, her
husband should come hurriedly from country
seat, the door be broken in, the dog bark
loud, the shaken house re-echo with the din,
the woman, deadly pale with fright, jump
from the bed, her maid and confidante say,
[4] Faithless slaves were "Woe is me!" and fear lest her poor [4]legs be
so punished sometimes.
                   broke; the wife detected, fear lest she should
[5] The woman could le- [5]lose her dowry; and I dread lest I be killed
gally lose part of her
dowry if taken in adul- outright.   One has to run away half dressed
tery.
                   and with bare feet, to save one's purse, one's
body, or one's name.   'Tis fearful to be
                   caught, and that I'll prove, though stupid
Fabius was an absurd
Stoic philosopher.   Fabius himself be judge.

SATIRE III.

A Satire written against those who see their neighbours' vices far clearer than they do their own, and also against the Stoics' theory that all crimes are equal.

ALL singers have this fault, that, in a party of their friends, when asked to sing, they never are inclined; while if they wish, and are not asked, they never will leave off.

[1]Tigellius, [2]of world-wide fame, [3]who would do most things for a price, had this defect; and him Augustus could not move when-e'er he asked him thus,—[4]" Tigellius, I pray you, by my father's patronage and by mine own, to sing ; "—though if he were inclined himself, he'd keep on giving[5] drinking songs[6] all through the dinner-time, now in the lowest key, and now in that which shrillest sounds upon the lute's four strings. Consistency in him one could not see; he'd often run like one who fled away from foe, and then, again, he'd often slowly walk as Juno's [7]sacred basket-bearers do. He often kept two hundred slaves, and often only ten : at one time boasting of his friend the noble or the prince, and all that's great, and then, again, he'd

[1] The singer of the day.
[2] Ille is ironical.
[3] "Sardi venales" was a proverbial expression. A Sardinian would do nearly anything for money.
[4] The actual words Augustus used, instead of the oblique narration.

[5] "Io Bacche." Words occurring in drinking songs.
[6] The Roman dinner began with eggs and ended with dessert.

[7] I. e., with slow and solemn tread.

[1] "Mensa tripes"— say, "Give me a [1] table plain in form, a shell
made after the fashion
of the Delphic tripod, of to hold clean salt, a dress, though coarse it
an humble kind.
be, which may keep off the cold." Yet had

you given to this thrifty man, so satisfied

[2] Decies centena millia with humble means, [2] ten thousand pounds, a
HS, or sestertiorum, is
the full phrase, and means few days after that he would not have a
ten times a hundred
thousand sesterces, or penny in his purse; he'd keep awake at night
twopences.
till break of morn, and snore out all the day.

He outdid all in inconsistency. Now, if

some one should say to me, "Well, how

about yourself? Have you no faults?" I

[3] "Immo" implies a should reply, [3] "I don't mean that; for I have
polite dissent from what
has been said, and gene- others, and I dare say not so bad as yours."
rally introduces an
emendation.   [4] As once a spendthrift slandered in his
[4] Mænius was a noto-
rious profligate, men- absence [5] Novius the miser, some man cried,
tioned in Sat. i., line 104.
[5] Novius may be the "Ho there! do you know nothing of your-
man who is satirized in
Sat. vi., line 124.   self; or do you think to cheat us all as

though we knew you not?" "Not I," re-
/
plied the profligate, "I find excuse for what

I do *myself*."

A foolish and excessive self-love this, and

worthy of a stern rebuke! But since, like

blear-eyed men with eyes smeared over with

the salve, you see your faults so dimly,

why this keen perception of your friend's

defects, as keen as eagle's sight, or Epidaurus'

snake's? Yet, on the other side, it happens

that they too in turn search out your faults.

[6] Horace probably [6] Suppose a man be rather passionate, and
means himself.
not quite suited to the nice taste men of

modern times evince. He might be ridi-

culed because his hair is badly cut, his coat

hangs slovenly, while the loose shoe can

scarcely keep upon his heel ; yet still he's a
good citizen—indeed, he cannot be surpassed in this—still he's your friend, still
wondrous power of mind lurks 'neath this
rough outside,—in fine, just [1]test yourself,   [1] A metaphor from
and see if nature, or bad practices, perhaps,   shaking a thief.
have e'er implanted any vice in you ; for,
as you know, the weeds do grow apace in
fields not duly worked, and must be burned
to stay the harm.   But let us hasten to discuss this first,—that ugly blemishes the girl
he loves may have are all unnoticed by the
lover, or that their mere presence gives him
joy, as [2]Hagna's wen delights her [3]swain.   [2] Hagna is a name de-
And oh that in our friendships too we made   rived like our Agnes.
the same mistake, and that a generous justice   [3] Nothing further is
stamped the foible with a term approved by   known of Balbinus.
all !   Indeed, as fathers do not feel disgust at
any bodily defects their children have, so we
should feel none at our friends'.   To put a
case, some father says his squinting son has
but a pretty cast ; again, all those who have
a child absurdly small, like Sisyphus, that
offspring of untimely birth, call him " dear
little chick ;" another, with those inward-
turning toes, they term a " Varus," or in
lisping tones call [4]" Scaurus " one who scarce   [4] Varus and Scaurus
can stand on ankles out of shape.   So, then,   were names of noble
suppose a man lives rather niggardly, let him   families.
be called but careful of his means ; suppose
another shows bad taste, and talks in boastful
strain too much, he (doubtless) only wants to
show a genial wit to friends.

[1]Yes, but his bearing is too insolent, and he is much too plain in speech. Then let him be supposed to be an open and a truthful character. Yes, but he is too passionate. Well, then, let him be classed with men of spirit ; and, methinks, 'tis this that makes us friends, and keeps us friends when made. But we change what is really virtue into vice, and fain would sully the unblemished casket of morality.

[2] The indicative is often used by Horace to express a supposed case.

[2]Suppose a man of honesty dwells in our set, he's far too spiritless for us, we call him " dull," or " dense ;" perhaps

[3] Literally, presents his side exposed to no evil plotter understood).

another shuns all snares, and gives [3]a chance for no malignant hand to deal a blow, because he lives with men among whom revels envy's tooth, and the false charge is rife ; yet him we call a double-dealing, cunning rogue, instead of a shrewd, careful man. Again, suppose some one speaks what he thinks too openly, or acts (as oft, dear Patron,

[4] Libenter. Freely—because he knew that Mæcenas would not mistake frankness, even if gauche, for deliberate annoyance.

I have [4]freely shown myself to you) so as to interrupt annoyingly with the first words that come into his mouth one who may possibly be reading, or wrapt in deep thought, we say, " 'Tis clear the man lacks common sense." Ah me, how rashly do we ratify an unjust law that tells against ourselves ! For no one in the world lacks faults, and he's the best who's influenced by the most trifling ones. A dear friend, as is fair, would weigh my good points 'gainst my bad, and turn the scale to the more numerous good qualities, suppose there be more good ; if he should care to be beloved himself, and on these terms, he shall be placed in the same scale. [1]Let him who fain would not offend by his gross faults, look over his friend's [2]slighter weaknesses ; for right it is that one who claims excuse for his mistakes should give the same in turn.

[1] The future is elegantly used as a mild imperative.
[2] Literally, by large boils and small warts.

In fine, since nor the fault of rage, nor those defects besides that cling to us poor foolish men can be completely rooted out, why does not philosophic reason use the weights and measures suitable, and, as the several cases need, so check the wrong with punishment ?   If any one should crucify a slave for feasting on the partly eaten fish, or on the soup now nearly cold, when bade [3]to clear away, he would by men of sense be called more mad than [4]Labeo.   And yet how much more mad, how much more wrong, to act like this !—Suppose your friend has made some slight mistake, which should you not forgive, you would be thought morose and stern, yet you both hate and shun him as a debtor hates and shuns [5]exacting usurers ; for he, poor wretch, when the sad [6]settling day has come, unless he can fish out from some or other source the interest or principal, just like a captive has to hear, [7]with neck stretched out as if to bear the blow, [8]the wearisome description of the man's own life. Suppose a friend in wine has slightly outraged decency, or has thrown down a plate once held in old [9]Evander's hands,—

[3] Literally, to take away a dish.

[4] Labeo punished a slave very severely for a trifling fault.

[5] Ruso was a usurer, and writer of wretched biographies.

[6] The first day of the month.

[7] I. e., for the victor to slay him.
[8] I. e., The man's autobiography.

[9] Horace laughs at the excessive reverence then displayed for antiquity.

should he for this be less endeared to me?
or if, in hunger, he has seized a fowl served
up in front of me in my part of the dish?
If so, what should I do, suppose he has
turned out a thief, or has betrayed some
[1] trust, or failed to keep his word? The
Stoics, who think crimes are all well-nigh
alike, are quite perplexed in testing this their
theory; for common sense, morality, and
even interest, that is so nearly the prime
source of justice and of equity, is quite
opposed to it.

[2] When savage men crawled forth upon the
scarce-formed earth, like brutes, unsightly,
not possessed of speech, they fought for
[3] mast and lairs with nails and fists, and then
with clubs, and so, as time went on, they
used the weapons that experience had later
forged, until they found out words and terms
with which t'express cries showing each sen-
sation; then they soon began to give up
war, build towns, and lay down laws to
check the thief, the highway robber, and
adulterer. For woman was the foulest cause
of war long previous to Helen's time, but that
race perished with their deeds unsung. For
them, as brute-like, they indulged in lawless
love, the stronger ever slew, as in the herd
the bull. You must admit, if you but care to
read the world's first history and calendar,
[4] that right was introduced through dread of
wrong. Nor can (as Stoics say) unaided
Nature separate the unjust from the just, as

[1] Fide is the old dative for fidei.

[2] "Animalia." This word is used to show that man did not much differ from the brute.

[3] Acorns.

[4] The Stoics held that justice was a natural vir-tue, not a necessary in-sitution.

she removes the bad from good, what we
should shun from what we ought to seek ;
nor will their theory prove this—[1] that one
who has but trampled down young cabbages
that grow on neighbours' garden-ground, does
wrong as great and quite the same as one
who has sacked temples of the gods by night.
Let there be some fixed rule t'inflict due
punishment on crimes, so that one need not
chase with scourge armed with dread iron
points one who needs but the [2]milder lash.
For since you say that each case is alike,
and threaten (would but men make you their
[3]king) to check with just the same restraint
theft, highway robbery, great crimes and
small, I have no fear lest you should chasten
with the lighter rod one worthy of severer
punishment. Since, as you say, philosophers
alone are rich, good cobblers handsome,—
ay, and kings,—why want to gain what you
already have ? Here [4]he replies,—" You do
not know what says [5]Chrysippus, founder of
our sect. 'Tis this,—'Philosophers ne'er make
themselves or Greek or Latin shoes, yet still
philosophers are cobblers.' "

Tell me how.

" Why, just as, though [6]Hermogenes sing
not a note, he is a first-rate singer and
musician ; or as shrewd Alfenius, although
he'd parted with all tools belonging to his
trade, and shut up shop, was the best artisan
in ev'ry kind of work, and so a king."

And yet, O mightiest of mighty kings,

[1] " Tantandum ut peccat " is for " Eum tantumdem peccare."

[2] A leathern strap with which slaves were punished for smaller offences.

[3] Ironical ; the Stoics said that the philosopher was everything great and good.

[4] Some Stoic.

[5] Although Zeno was the real founder of the Stoic system, yet Chrysippus was often called so.

Horace.

The Stoic.
[6] Not the same Tigellius as mentioned in Sat. ii.
Alfenius Varus was a cobbler at Cremona, who came to Rome, and obtained eminence as a barrister and consul.

Horace.

the wanton street-boys pull you by the beard,
and if you do not check them with your stick,
you're jostled by the crowd that hems you in,
and, wretched man, you have to break a
bloodvessel with shouting and with scolding
them.   In short, while you, though king you
be, [1] go to the [2]farthing baths to bathe, and
not a soul attend you there except the absurd
Crispinus, my dear friends will pardon any
wrong that I, no [3]Stoic, may have done, while
I, in turn, shall gladly bear their failings, and,
although a nobody, shall live more blest than
you a king.

[1] Ibis and sectabitur are really futures.

[2] Quadrans was about a farthing, or less in value.

[3] Stoic is sapiens; ergo, stultus is no Stoic.

SATIRE IV.

Horace wrote this Satire to defend himself from the detraction of those who tried to take away his reputation as a poet, on the ground that he ignored the artificial style of writing then so much in vogue, and used too much freedom in satirizing others. He quotes the best writers of comedy in former times as having used the same licence without reproof.

THE poets Eupolis, Cratinus, Aristophanes, and [1]other comic writers of old times, would with great freedom satirize all those whose character deserved to be so accurately drawn, since they were villains, thieves, adulterers, cut-throats, or otherwise notorious. Now, on the writers I have named, Lucilius, so full of wit, with keen perception, though rough in the structure of his lines, entirely depends; has imitated them, with but the metre changed or rhythm. Yet, surely, he was wrong in this, that he would often, as though quite a feat, read to his slave [2]to copy down two hundred lines an hour with sportive easiness. As he rolled incoherently along, there were some lines one fain would take away; besides, he was verbose, and [3]shirked the toil composing gives,—that is, composing as one should, for I care nought for quantity.

[1] Such as Pherecrates and Epicharmus.

[2] Puero, a manu. Poets had a slave as amanuensis.

[3] Literally, was slow to bear.

1 Crispinus was a gar-
rulous Stoic philosopher.
The words—"For the
least sum I like to stake,"
imply that Crispinus felt
so sure of victory, that he
would stake much more
than his adversary if
necessary.

Behold, the prating [1]Stoic dares me now
to try my skill with his, and that, too, for
the smallest sum I like to stake.   He says,
" Take, if you will, your tablets,—let a place,
and time, and umpires be assigned us,—let
us see which of the two can write the more."

Thus I reply :—The gods have blessed me

2 The mind gives us
the ideas to express in
words.

much in making me possess a [2]mind of poor
and trifling powers, that but seldom clothes its
thoughts in words ; while you, as you prefer,
use speech that sounds like wind shut up in
goatskin bellows, ever struggling to get

forth.   E'en [3]Fannius thinks he is blest, because a bookcase, with his precious works

and portrait of himself, is [4]offered him unasked ; while no one reads the lines I write,
who shrink from indiscriminate recital, for
the reason that, as most men merit blame, so
there are some who hate this style of mine.
Just pick me any one you will from out the
general class of men.   He is afflicted (you
will find) with avarice or hapless thirst for
power.   Another is distressed with mad desire
for married women's love ; a third with love
for boys ; a fourth the sheen of plate at-

5 Albius was not re-
markable for anything
else.

tracts ; [5]a fifth beholds with rapt amaze
bronze statues ; and a sixth goes trading

6 Literally, from the
rising sun to that with
which the western clime
grows warm.

from the [6]east e'en to the west,—nay, more,
speeds headlong through disastrous hindrances, like dust by whirlwind gathered up,
in terror lest he lose some portion of his

property, [7]or fail to make it more.   And all
such men fear lines like mine, and hate the

[1]satirist. [2]" He's dangerous," say they, "flee far from him. Can he but raise a laugh at what he says, to suit himself, he will not spare his dearest friend ; and will be glad that each child, and old woman too, as they come back from bakehouse or from public fount, should know whate'er he may have [3]carelessly scrawled on his manuscript."

Come, now, just hear a few words on the other side. And, first, I will withdraw my name from out the ranks of those to whom I'd give the term of " bard ; "—and really one ought not to say, " It is enough to give a line six feet," or think all those true poets who, like me, write what is more like prose. Give him the proud distinction of this name, who has real genius, whose thoughts are more inspired, whose mouth will, no doubt, utter noble sentiments. And 'tis for reasons such as these that some have questioned whether comedy be poetry or not ; because in comedy the language and the subject-matter both lack fire and force,—indeed, it is mere prose, but for the metre's law. [4]But Plautus says, the father, hot with passion, storms because his spendthrift son, through mad love for a harlot mistress, will not wed a richly dowered wife ; storms, too, because he's drunk, and (what's a dreadful stain upon his character) goes revelling with torches lit before nightfall.

[5]And would [6]Pomponius, were but his father now alive, hear words aught gentler in their tone than those (you say the father used)?

[1] They assumed that every one who wrote at all wrote satires.
[2] Oxen given to tossing had hay bound round their horns.

[3] Semel. Shows that he did not revise.

[4] Horace here supposes some opponent to say this, and refutes him. The argument is this :— We have instances every day of fathers angry with their sons, as Plautus describes, so that is not sufficient by itself to make comedy poetry.

[5] Answer to the supposed opponent.
[6] A dissolute and extravagant youth.

¹ Imaginary opponent. ¹ He certainly would not.   ² So, then, 'tis not
² Horace.
                                   enough to end a line in words devoid of
                                   style, if, when one took away the metre, any
                                   one you please would storm with rage, just
                                   like the father in the comedy. Were you to
                                   take away from these lines I now write, and
³ Literally, the fixed those Lucilius once wrote, the ³pauses, limits,
pauses and the rhythm.   and the rhythm ; then make the word that's
                                   first in order last, and place the last before the
                                   first, you would not find the bard's true ele-
                                   ments when sundered thus, as you would find
                                   them if you so deranged ⁴such poetry as this,
⁴ Lines of Ennius.   —"When fell dissension brake the iron doors
                                   and gates of war." Enough of this. At some
                                   time hence I will discuss the question whether
                                   satire be true poetry or not; but now I'll
                                   only talk of this,—I mean the justice or in-
                                   justice of the hatred felt to this my style of
                                   writing.   Sulcius and Caprius, those fierce
                                   informers, stalk about, both very hoarse with
                                   pleading, bearing accusations in their hands,
                                   both a great source of dread to highwaymen;
                                   but all who live as they should live need
                                   care nought for them both.   Though you be
                                   like to Cœlius and Birrius, the highwaymen,
                                   I am not like to Caprius or Sulcius, why
                                   should you dread me then?   And may no
                                   printer's shop nor column for advertisement
                                   have book of mine, for common people's
⁵ Not the same as Ti- dirty hands or ⁵music masters' to defile. Nor
gellius Sardus.   do I read my works to any but my friends,
                                   and only that when forced,—not in whatever
                                   place you will, or to whatever audience you

please. Yet many men read out their works
e'en in the open market-place, and many at
the bath. No doubt, the place, arched in,
suits well the reader's voice. And this is
joy to those vain men who never care to
learn if they do this with utter want of taste,
or at untoward times. [1] But some one says,
" You love to injure men's repute; malicious,
as you are, you do this purposely." [2] Whence
got you this reproach to cast on me? In
fine, are any of those men with whom I've
lived the author of this taunt? He who
disparages an absent friend, who fails to
speak in his defence when others blame, who
tries to make men loudly laugh, who aims at
being thought a wit, who can frame tales of
what he never saw, who cannot keep a secret
trust, is a malignant character ; beware of
him, ye honest citizens. One oft may see
four guests at dinner seated on the Roman
[3] couch, among whom one will make jests
both refined and coarse, on all except the
host, and him as well, when drunk,—when
Bacchus, who brings out the truth, unlocks a
man's real thoughts. Yet you, who hate
malignant rascals so, think this man courteous and witty, and but free in speech. And
do you think it virulence and spite in me,
if I have laughed because Rufillus smells
absurdly of the aromatic lozenge, and Gargo-
nius like any goat? And yet suppose, when
you are by, some mention has been made
about [4] Petillius Capitolinus' theft, no doubt

[1] Some imaginary op-
ponent.

[2] Horace.

[3] The triclinium was
composed of three
couches, called lectus
imus, medius, summus,
on each of which never
more than four sat in
good society.

[4] Stole a crown belong-
ing to Jupiter Capitolinus,
when he was governor of
the Capitol, but was ac-
quitted out of regard for
Augustus, whose friend
he was.

you would defend him, as you're wont, in
words like these,—" Capitolinus, certainly,
has often dined with me, and been my friend
e'er since I was a boy, and has done much
for me at my request, and I am glad that he
lives safe at Rome ; yet, still, I wonder how
he *did* escape that trial talked about so
much."

Horace replies.

This is the virus of malignant hate,—
sheer malice this. And that my works and
heart be free from such defect, I promise, first,
as I do promise, too, whate'er I can with truth,
about myself, if in my satires I have made
remarks too free, or possibly made too severe
a jest, grant me the licence, and excuse it ; for
my dear good father trained me to do this
through showing me each several vice, by
quoting cases of indulgence in the vice, that
I might shun the same. When he encou-
raged me to live with thrifty care, and be
content with what he had amassed for me,
he'd say, [1]" Of course, you see what a bad
life young [2]Albius lives ; how poor Barrus
is ? Good reason there to stay a man's
desire to spend his father's property." And
when he checked my wish for some disgraceful harlot's love, he'd say, " Don't you be
like Scetanus." Then, again, to save me
from adultery, when I could well indulge
a love less criminal, he'd say, " Tre-
bonius, caught in the act, enjoys no good
repute. Philosophers will give you reasons
showing what is better to be shunned,

*The future is ele-
gantly used as an impe-
rative.*

[1] Nonne. Expects as-
sent to the question.
[2] Nothing further was
known of Albius, or
Barrus.

what better to be sought; but 'tis enough
for me, if I can but observe the good
old rules the ancients gave; and while
you need a guardian, keep your life and
reputation free from harm, and then, directly
that your time of life has given you more
strength of limb, and firmer mind, you'll
float (in life's wide sea) without a swim-
ming-belt." So, by his words he trained
me when a boy; and if he bade me choose
some course of action, he would bring before
my notice one of the grand [1]jurymen, and
say, "You have a precedent for acting
thus." Or was there aught he told me
not to do, he'd ask me this,—" What? Would
you doubt if this be shameful or against
your interest to do, when more than one
man is notorious for it?" A funeral next
door dispirits the intemperate and sick, and
makes them less indulgent through a fear
of death. And so another's ill repute will oft
deter young minds from vice. For through the
training I spoke of, I'm free from vices that
bring ruin on a man, and only influenced by
small defects that one may well excuse, and
e'en from them, perhaps, long life, th' advice
of candid friends, my own reflection, will
take much away; and I do not neglect my
duty when I go into my study or walk in the
colonnade, for then I muse like this,—" Yes,
that is better. I shall lead a purer life if I
do so. Again, if I do that, [2]my friends will
gladly meet me. Ah! a certain man was

C

Literally, you will swim without a cork. The amplification seems necessary to express the idea fully.

[1] The judices selecti were 360 men chosen by the Aurelian law from among the senators, knights, and tribunes, to try criminal cases.

[2] Literally, I shall meet my friends dear to them.

very wrong in what he did ; I wonder if I e'er shall, unacknowledged to myself, do aught like that." Such are th' unuttered thoughts I have, which in some leisure hour I sportively jot down on manuscript. And that is one of those defects one may excuse,— which, if you will not overlook, the numerous clubs of bards will come to aid[1] me (for we far outnumber you), and as the Jews compel their proselytes, so we will make you join this wide-spread set of ours.

[1] Such as Virgil, Varius, Aristius.

SATIRE V.

In this Satire Horace imitates Lucilius, who made a journey from Rome to Capua, and then to Sicily. The time taken in travelling was fifteen days, and the distance travelled about 390 miles. Mæcenas, Virgil, Plotius, and Varius accompanied the poet, but not on the first part of the way. Although a state mission, it rather resembled an excursion. It refers to the treaty of Tarentum, made between Octavianus and Antony.

Modern names are used for two reasons:—First, because they will be more familiar to the non-classical reader, and probably to the classical not much less than the ancient ones ; second, because they are more manageable and euphonious.

THE JOURNEY FROM ROME TO BRINDISI.

First day's journey, from Rome to Aricia, now La Riccia, a town in Latium. 16 miles.

LA RICCIA first gave me shelter in its humble inn, when I'd left mighty Rome.

The Roman mile was 142 yards less than ours.

Second day. From La Riccia to Forum Appii, now Borgo Lungo, near Treponti. 20 miles. 36 from Rome.

[1] A rhetorician, far the best the Greeks then had, went too.

Then Borgo Lungo took us in,—a place too full of sailors and of cheating innkeepers.

We idly made two journeys [2] of the road from Rome to Borgo Lungo, though it is but one for active travellers ; [3] nor is this

Journey by night and up to 10 o'clock a.m. next

road of Appius so bad for those who take their time. [4] Here I

[1] Longe doctissimus is the language of compliment, as Heliodorus was almost unknown.

[2] Hoc iter means the 36 miles from Rome to Borgo Lungo.

[3] The Appian road, by which they came, led from Rome to Capua, and was continued from thence by Trajan to Brindisi.

[4] I. e., one feels the fatigue less than those who travel fast.

refuse all nourishment to save my drinking water of the vilest kind, and wait in no contented mood till all who, like myself, were going by boat, had dined.

[1] Even now the water is so bad at Borgo Lungo, that travellers will not stay longer than they can help.

day, down a canal 17 miles long, to the temple of the goddess Feronia. Traces of the canal still remain, and of a tower near Terracina, called now Torre otto Faccia.

[2] But soon, as says the bard, 'gan night spread o'er the earth its pall of shade, and then the slaves and bargemen heaped abuse like this on one another's heads. [3] A slave says, " Here, land where I am." But soon the boatman cries, " Ho there, you're packing crowds on board ; hold hard, we want no more." And so an hour slips away, while fares are taken and the mule yoked to the towing-rope. The tiresome gnats and frogs that love the marsh drive sleep away ; while now, well drunk with bad, flat wine, the bargeman and a passenger sing of " the girl they left behind them." At last the passenger is wearied, and begins to sleep ; and then the bargeman idly lets the mule go out to graze, and ties the rope fast to a stone, and snores reclining on his back. And now day just began to break, when we saw that the barge made no headway, until an angry passenger leaped out upon the shore and beat the head and loins of mule and bargeman too, with willow club. We scarcely [4] disembarked at last by ten o'clock. [5] We wash our hands and faces in thy fount, Feronia ; then, after lunch, we slowly travel

[2] A parody of a line of Ennius.

[3] Some slave guarding his master's luggage requests the boatman to land where he is. The boatman complies ; but such a crowd rushes on the boat that he cries out, Trecentos, &c.

[4] The Romans reckoned from six a.m. to six p.m.
[5] The language is rather bombastic on purpose.

Third   day.
From 10 o'clock
a.m.   Distance
from Feronia to
Terracina 3 miles.
20 miles from
Borgo Lungo. 56
from Rome.
three more miles, and come to
Terracina's walls, reared high on
cliffs that gleam afar. Mæcenas
was to meet us here ; [1]Cocceius,
too, that best of men, both sent
as deputies to treat of matters of grave moment, both well qualified to reconcile friends
once estranged.   Here, as my eyes were
sore, I dressed them with black salve. Meantime, arrives my patron, and with him Cocceius and Fonteius Capito, a perfect gentleman, as dear a friend as Antony then had.

[1] Cocceius Nerva, the great-grandfather of Nerva, afterwards Emperor, helped to reconcile Antony and Augustus.

Fourth   day.
From Fundi, now
Fondi, a Latin
town, 13 miles
from Terracina,
69 from Rome,
on to Formiæ,
now Mola di
Gaeta.   12 miles
from Fondi. 81
from Rome.
We gladly passed through
Fondi, where Aufidius,[2] "the
purblind," was the mayor, and
well we ridiculed the honours
won by that mad "quondam"
clerk ;—his white robe edged
with purple, senator's rich dress,
and pan of burning coals. Then, wearied out,
we stayed all night in the Mamurræ's town,
where Varro gave us beds, and Capito found
food.

[2] Of course, " Luscus " is really a cognomen, but there may be a jest meant in its application here. Even Mæcenas was content with the augusti-clave, a less richly adorned dress, which made the bustling pom-posity of Aufidius more ridiculous.
Lucius Licinius Terentius Varro Murena. Mæcenas married his sister.
An ironical allusion to Mamurra and his descendants. He was a Roman knight, engineer to Julius Cæsar in Gaul, and afterwards satirized by Catullus for his luxury, and called " decoctor Formianus."

Fifth   day.
Through Sinu-
essa, now Bag-
noli, a town in
Latium, 18 miles
from Mola di
Gaeta, 99 from
Rome, on to the
little villa near
the   Campanus
pons, now"Ponte
Ceppani," 3 miles
from Bagnoli, 102
miles from Rome.
Next morning dawned much
more agreeably, for Plotius and
Varius and Virgil met us at
Bagnoli, and than them the
earth has ne'er produced more
frank and honest men, nor men
to whom another was more
dear than me.   Oh, what kind
greetings then there were ! what heartfelt joy !
I never could while of sound mind compare

aught to a pleasant friend. The little country
house that stands near the Ceppani Bridge
gave us a bed, [1] the state purveyors found us
fire and salt.   From this place, in good time,
our mules laid down their packs
at Capua.   Mæcenas goes to
play at tennis, I and Virgil go
to sleep; for tennis does not suit
sore eyes and weak digestion.
Then Cocceius' well-appointed
home, that stands just past the
Caudine Taverns, shelters us.

And now, my Muse, fain would
I that you give a brief description
of the wordy war between Sar-
mentus the Buffoon and Messius the [2] Cock,
and tell us too the lineage of both these
men, who then began the fray.   Well, then,
the Oscans formed the [3] noble line of Messius.
Sarmentus is e'en now a slave.   Sprung from
such ancestry, they met in strife.   Sarmentus
first says, " Why, I vow you're like an un-
tamed horse."   We laugh, and e'en "the
Cock " himself says, " Well, I take the chal-
lenge," and then gives his head a toss.
Again Sarmentus cries, " Had that wart not
been cut from out your brow [4] how terrible
you'd be ! since though so sadly maimed, you
threaten thus."   For a foul scar had marred
the hairy temple on the left side of his face.
Then he made many jests upon his strange
[5] disease, and on his face ; he begged that
he would show by dancing [6] Polyphemus'

[1] " Parochus " was an officer whose duty was to furnish to government officers, when travelling, indispensable necessaries —such as fire and salt.

Sixth day. From Capua, 22 miles from "Ponte Ceppani, 124 from Rome, to Cocceius's villa, near the Inns of Caudium or Caudine Forks; near what is now called Monte Sarchio, 21 miles from Capua, and 145 from Rome. Account of the quarrel between Sarmentus and Messius, down to line 71.

A parody of Homer's " Iliad," bk. ii., line 484.

[2] The term "cicirrhus" is the same as the German Gackhahn.

[3] Ironical.   The Oscans, a Campanian tribe, were notorious for their vices.

[4] Literally, what would you do !

[5] Elephantiasis ; a disease the Campanians suffered from.
[6] A very ungainly movement.

wooing, for he would not need a [1]mask or
stately tragic buskin with that scar. The
Cock made many smart replies to this. He
said,[2] "Pray have you, as you vowed you
would, now consecrated to the household
gods your chains?[3] although you are a clerk,
your mistress' right of ownership is quite as
good; in fine, why did you ever run away,
when but a [4]single pound of meal was quite
enough for you, so lean a manikin?"
With such amusement, we quite pleasantly
prolonged that meal. Straight from the
Inns of Caudium, we bend our
steps to Benevento, where the
host, as with officious zeal he
turns some thrushes most absurdly lean upon the spit, was
nearly burnt himself! for, as the poet says,
[5]"Out fell the fire, and soon the flames strayed
o'er the crumbling kitchen floor, and onward
sped to play around the roof." And then
you might have seen the eager [6]diners, and
the slaves who feared the scourge, snatch at
their dinner in the fire, while all tried hard
to quench the flames.

And, next, Apulia began to
show its hills we knew so well,
—hills the Altino chills with nipping cold, which we had never
passed had not Trivico's inn
close by afforded shelter for the
night, though plagued with
smoke that brings the tears into

Seventh day. From Cocceius' villa to Beneventum, now Benevento, 12 miles from the Inns of Caudium, and 157 from Rome.

Eighth day. From Benevento to Trivicum, now Trivico. Distance not mentioned. It was a town on the borders of Campania.

Ninth day. From Benevento to a villa near Trivico.

[1] I.e., the scar was better than any mask.
[2] Giving the man's actual words, instead of the indirect narration.
[3] A parody of the custom of youthful nobles at Rome, who offered their (bullæ) ornaments to the household gods at the age of sixteen and a half years.
[4] Strong, able slaves used to eat four pounds of meal a day.
[5] A parody of two lines of Ennius; perhaps purposely clothed in rather bombastic language.
[6] The guests eager to prevent the loss of their dinner, and the slaves eager to save themselves from a beating.

Velle. Means here rather the attempt to execute the wish.
The Altino was an easterly wind.
Torret refers to the nipping effect of the cold upon the herbage.

one's eyes, because the fire is fed with damp boughs that still have their leaves left on. Here I, fool that I was, sit up till midnight waiting for a girl who fails to come; but sleep surprises me thus bent on love, and dreams portray th' embraces I had meant to give and take. From this place we ride quickly on for four-and-twenty miles in jaunting-cars, intending to re- main at a small town that I can scarcely name in verse, but which one easily may indicate by telling features of the place.

Tenth   day. From the villa near Trivico to Equus Tuticus, now Castel Fran- co, a town in Samnium,   22 miles from Bene- vento, 177 from Rome.

Here water, cheapest of all things there are, is actually sold; the bread, however, is extremely good, so that a travel- ler who knows what he's about will carry on his back a basket of the same still further on the road. [1]For at Canosa bread is full of grit, and it's a place that is not better off for water by a single jug than Castel Francois, and it was founded by brave Diomede. Then Varius in sorrow quits the [2]place and quits his weeping friends. And next we came to Ruvo, wearied out, like men who've traversed a long way made softer than it ought to be by rain. The next day gave us finer weather, but the roads were worse quite up to Bari's town, so full of fish and fishermen.

Eleventh   day. From   Castel Franco to Canu- sium, now Cano- sa. 84 from Be- nevento, 261 from Rome.

Twelfth   day. From Canosa to Rubi, now Ruvo. 24 miles from Ca- nosa, 285 from Rome.

Thirteenth day. From Ruvo to Barium, now Ba- ri. 22 miles from Ruvo, 307 from Rome.

[1] " Qui locus " refer to Canosa.

Canosa.

And then Fasano, built beneath the ban of fountain
[1] nymphs, gave food for laughter
and for jest, by its mad wish to
make us think that [2] frankincense without
the aid of flame will melt upon the threshold
of some fane.

Let any superstitious Jew
think so, but I could not, for I
know now from Epicurus that
the gods pass their time free
from care, and that it is no threatening rage
of theirs that sends down from the heaven's
lofty dome whatever natural phenomenon we
see. Brindisi was the end of my long story
and our journey too.

[1] *I. e.*, it had no pure water.

[2] Pliny, in his Natural History, says that a certain stone was shown at Gnatia, which had the power of setting fire to wood.

SATIRE VI.

Horace wrote this Satire to defend his reputation from the jealousy of those who asserted that he had stolen into favour by a lucky chance, and for the purpose of gaining wealth and power.

DEAR Patron, you do not, as most men do, sneer at, with cold disdain, all of ignoble birth like me, from freedman father sprung, because of all the Lydians that ever dwelt in Tuscan realms, not one is nobler born than you; nor yet because upon the mother's and the father's side you've ancestors who once led mighty armies to the field. Now when you say it makes no difference from what parentage one be sprung, provided that[1] one be no slave, you then hold this correct opinion that, before th' ignoble sway and reign of [2]Tullius, full often many men, sprung from low origin, have both lived honestly and been raised to the highest offices of state.

And then, quite contrary to this, you well know that Lævinus, son of that Valerius by whom proud Tarquin once was

[1] Slaves were not admitted to the rights of citizens; Horace was the son of a freedman, and so escaped any bar of such kind.

[2] The mother of Servius Tullius was a captive.

(Probe nosti) you well know is understood out of the words, "persuades hoc tibi vere." Publius Valerius Lævinus was so abandoned and dissolute that he never got higher than a quæstor in rank.

The argument is that Lævinus indeed be worthless if the people who generally

feel an ignorant
excess of rever-
ence for high
birth and title,
found such fault
with him.
driven from his realms and
fled, was never thought a whit
more of for his high birth; for
e'en our public, whom you know
so well, who foolishly so oft give high distinctions to unworthy men, who so absurdly are
the slaves of mere repute, who stare with
blank amaze at monuments inscribed, or
statues and wax pictures hung in halls; e'en
they, I say, placed the bar sinister against his
name.

[1]Well, what should I and those who think
like me do, men whose thoughts are so
opposed to vulgar views?   For e'en suppose
the public should prefer to give distinction
to Lævinus (of that proud descent) [2]than to
the parvenu; and e'en suppose the [3]rating
officer were to degrade me from the House
were I not found to be of free-born parentage,
he would do what I well deserved; since
I should then have higher aims than nature
meant I should.

[4]And yet, to tell the truth, as sings the
epic bard,—" In glittering car alike enslaved,
the low-born and the noble glory draws."
And Tillius, what good to you to wear again
the senator's rich dress you had to lay aside
and be elected a commanding officer?
You're envied more than when you held no
office under government; indeed, the moment
that each foolish man has bound around his
leg the shoe-tie made of soft black leather,
and let flow down from his chest the senator's

[1] Nos implies, I and all who think like me.

[2] Decius Mus was of plebeian origin, and is quoted to represent a class.
[3] The duty of a censor was to regulate the public morals, and rate the citizens.

[4] An epic line from an unknown poet.

Tillius is quoted as an instance of this universal and absurd desire for glory; he was degraded from the Senate as a follower of Pompey, and restored after Cæsar's death.

broad stripe, he hears at once such questions as—Who is the man? and what's his origin? Just as all those who are afflicted by the mental error Barrus is (that exquisite), I mean the wish to be thought handsome, and to make the girls, where'er he goes, quite anxious to learn each particular, what sort of face, for instance, legs, and teeth, and hair he has. So one who vows, if he but be returned, that he will guard his country-men, his city, empire, country, and the temples of the gods, makes all men try to learn, and ask what is his origin, and ask if (as may be) he be disgraced by mother of low birth.

"Sura" strictly means the calf, but by synec-doche may be put for the whole leg.

Like members' pro-mises before elections.

¹"And do you dare, you son of some base slave, to hurl down the Tarpeian rock, or hand to public executioner your countrymen?"

² Well, but my colleague Novius is one degree below myself in rank; for he is what my father was.

³ And pray, on this account, do you think you are one of our great noblemen? Besides this, Novius will shout so loud that he will drown the clarions' and trumpets' sound, e'en if two hundred wains and three large funerals met in the open market-place. No doubt this power of voice attracts us. ⁴ Now I talk once more about myself, sprung from a freed-man father (as men ever say), whom all carp at as sprung from freedman father; now because I dine so oft with thee, dear Patron, but in days gone by, because, as a command-

1 Some one of the peo-ple is supposed to say this to an officer of go-vernment, perhaps a tribune.

2 The tribune replies. —Horace may mean himself secretly. Novius was a freedman, Horace the son of a freedman, therefore of better blood.

3 One of the people replies.

Paullus and Messalla were great nobles. The funerals at Rome were always attended by trum-peters, cornet players, &c.

4 Horace speaks here.

ing officer, I once led a brigade into the
field. This is unlike the former case, for
with no justice could whoe'er you please, as
they might possibly the honour of command,
grudge me your friendship too, when you're
so careful in selecting those who merit it,
and who are far removed from that bad habit
of place-hunting. I can't say I'm lucky in
this point, that I gained you as friend by
accident, for 'twas no chance that threw me
in your way, for Virgil, best of men, some
time ago, then Varius told you my character.
When first I saw you, after speaking a few
words in broken tones,—(for diffidence that
checks the speech prevented me from saying
more),—I did not tell you I was sprung from
noble sire, nor that I rode around some
country-seat on horse of purest breed, but
told you who I really was ; you made brief
answer, as you're wont, and more than eight
months after that, you asked me once again
to see you, and then bid me rank among
your friends. I greatly valued this, my
pleasing you, who sift true virtue from what's
base, through no high birth, but through my
purity of life and heart. But if my character
be sullied by more venial defects and those
but few, and be in other points upright,
—as though, to put a case, one should find
fault with trifling blemishes occurring here
and there upon a handsome person,—if no
man shall fairly charge me with the fault of
avarice or meanness or bad company, if I be

Saturium was near Tarentum, and was famed for its breed of horses.

pure and guiltless, and to praise myself, live dear unto my friends, my father was the cause of this, who, though but poor with small estate, cared not to send me to the village[1] school, to which boys, though the sons of doughty captains, used to go with book-bag[2] and with writing tablet hung on their left arm ; and on the 13th or 15th of every month paid their school bills,—but had the spirit to take me to learn accomplishments which any gentleman of property, or member of the House might get his children taught. All those who'd seen my well-appointed dress and slaves attending me, as custom is in[3] a great town like ours, would think that means for such expense came from some fine ancestral property.[4] Then he himself, a guardian of the highest character, attended me as I went round to the Professors' lectures. And, in fine, he kept me chastely free from all immoral deeds, nor that alone, but even slander's slur ; and purity like this is virtue's greatest ornament. Nor did he fear lest any one should blame him, if at any time I were to choose some humble calling as a crier's, or that of collector of the salt-fish revenues, which he himself once plied ; nor should I have complained, but now, through that the greater praise is due to him, and gratitude from me. Were I not mad, I ne'er should feel regret for having such a father, and on that account shall not defend myself like very many men

[1] Flavius was the village schoolmaster.

[2] Out of the several interpretations this seems the most satisfactory.

Æra, the small sum paid for tuition ; octonis is used because the Ides fell on the 8th day after the nones.

[3] Literally, among a great nation or people, but the wealth of the nation was at Rome.

[4] Instead of the usual pedagogue.

Qui honos means pudicitia, chastity.

who vow that 'tis no fault of theirs they have
no sires of noble birth and wide-spread fame.
My words and inward thoughts are much at
variance with theirs ; for just suppose that
nature bade men live their lives again from
some fixed year, and bade them choose,
according to caprice, whatever parents they
might severally wish to have, still satisfied
with mine, I would not care to choose the
highest officers of state for mine, mad,
doubtless, as most men would think, but
sensible perhaps in your view of the case,
because I cared not to endure without experience, the burden of such tedious distinction. For, at once, more ample means
would have to be acquired by me, more
compliments be paid; nay, I must then take
one or two companions with me to prevent
my going alone into the country or abroad,
more common slaves and hacks be kept,
and carriages be drawn along. While I may
ride, if I but care, e'en to Tarentum, on my
humble mule, the loins of which my wallet,
and the sides the rider galls. Yet none
will charge me with the meanness they will
charge you, Tillius, with, when upon the
road to Tibur; five slaves only follow you
(though high state officer you be), and carry
with them cooking-pots, and basket for the
wine. And yet, distinguished member of
the House, I live with greater comfort than
you do in this and countless other ways.
I take a meditative stroll where'er I please ;

Œneid, vi., 882, armus
generally means should-
ers, but rarely, as here,
sides.

I ask the price of vegetables and of corn;
I often saunter through the public market-
place and cheating-circus at the close of day.
I watch the prophesying dream expounders;
then I go off home to eat my meal of leek
and chick-pea, and meal cakes; my dinner's
served up by three slaves, a slab of plain
white marble holds two glasses and a ladle;
a cheap saltcellar stands by, a cruet and
wine-bowl of common earthenware. And
then I go to sleep, nor think with anxious
care that I must rise betimes, or visit the
law courts where [1]Marsyas (though ugly and
of stone) shows by the upraised hand that he
detests th' expression of the younger Novius'
face.   I stay within my study until ten
o'clock; then at eleven I go for a walk,
or when I've read or written something that
may please me as I meditate, I dress myself
with oil, but not with that mean filthy Natta
does, when he has robbed the lamps.   But
when the sun's now keener rays have bid me
weary go to bathe, I shun the Campus
Martius, and game of ball.   Then after
a slight lunch, yet quite enough to save
my passing through the day with empty
stomach until dinner-time, I take my ease at
home.   Such is the life of those who are not
bound in sad ambition's grievous thrall.
With such a system, I console myself that
I shall live more pleasantly than if I were
the grandson, son, or nephew of some [2]petty
officer of state.

[1] There was a statue of Marsyas in front of the Rostra where pleaders used to meet, and bail be given, and usurers also carried on their business here. Marsyas was a statue of the satyr of that name, and the jest is, that though Marsyas (as a satyr) was ugly enough, yet he deprecated the usurious chicanery of the younger Novius by holding up a hand with a gesture of disgust, and so Novius must have been hideous.

[2] The quæstor was such officer.

SATIRE VII.

An account of a noisy piece of litigation that took place in the Court of Marcus Brutus, the deputy-governor of Asia, between Publius Rupilius, who enjoyed the sobriquet of "Rex," and a certain Persius,* of Clazomenæ, a city in Ionia.

No doubt 'tis quite well known in every chemist's, every barber's shop, how Persius, half Roman and half Greek, repaid the malice and the spite of one Rupilius, an outlaw, surnamed "King." This Persius was rich, and lent large sums of money at Clazomenæ, and had a vexing lawsuit with "the King;" a stubborn fellow was this Persius, and one who could surpass "the King" in rancour; boastful too, and passionate, and of such virulence of speech as to [1]entirely outstrip our cleverest buffoons in loud abuse. I now say more about "the King." When they could make no compromise—and you must know that all between whom falls out bitter strife, contend with fierceness in proportion to their bravery;

Apothecaries and barbers' shops were the places for gossip. It was a very common thing to suffer from blear or sore eyes; those who did would go to the chemist's, and gossip there.

[1] White steeds were proverbially the fastest.

* Persius was descended from an Asiatic father and Roman mother, and was a banker and general agent.

D

indeed, between the brave Achilles and great Hector, Priam's son, so deadly was the feud, that nought but death's last stroke could sunder them ; and all because consummate valour was possessed by both ; while, if two cowards quarrel, or a strife spring up between two men who are no match, as once with [1]Diomede the Lycian Glaucus fought, the duller of the two retires, and sends a voluntary gift ; [2]I say, since they could make no compromise,—these two, Rupilius and Persius, when Brutus was the governor of fertile Asia, fought, a pair so aptly pitted 'gainst each other, that no gladiators e'er were better matched. ([3]Like soldiers to a battle-plain) they fiercely rush into the court, a fine sight both.   Then Persius begins the case ; the bench of judges laugh ; he loudly praises Brutus and his friends in court ; styles Brutus, " Asia's sun," and styles his retinue, " health-giving stars," " the King " alone excepted, for he said that he had come like that dog-star so [4]hated by the husbandmen ; in fine, he poured along his torrent of abuse just like some wintry flood, [5]where few trees grow on its steep banks.   But then Præneste's son in answer hurled at Persius, as he rolled on with fluent bitter jest, coarse gibes from [6]vineyard picked, a rough vine-dresser[7] he whom none could beat, to whom full oft a passer by, though he should cry in angry tones, [8]" Cuckoo !   Aha !   you're late," had been obliged to yield.

[1] Iliad, vi., 234.

[2] The repetition seems necessary to remove the effect of the long interpolation.

[3] Ironical.

[4] Because it parched their crops.

[5] Literally, whither seldom is brought the axe.
He was a native of Præneste.
[6] The language of the vineyard corresponded to our Billingsgate.
[7] Rex.
[8] Husbandmen pruned their vines and did other work in spring before the cuckoo came, and to cry " cuckoo," was a reproach to idle ones who neglected theirs until the cuckoo had come.

¹ Literally, drenched with Latin vinegar.

² The Greeks were much more polished and witty than the Romans; to suppose Græcus a mere repetition of the idea conveyed by the word "hybrida" would be pointless.

Marcus Brutus was supposed to be descended from L. Junius Brutus, who removed Tarquin.

Here Persius, now smarting with ¹this caustic Latin wit, cries out with all a Greek's quick ²repartee, O Brutus, as you're wont to kill our Kings, I ask you here in heaven's name, why don't you kill this King? For surely 'tis a task that well belongs to you.

SATIRE VIII.

In this Satire Priapus, a rustic deity once worshipped by the people of Lampsacus, and by the Romans after, as a guardian-god of gardens, complains that the Esquiline hill was infested by the magic rites of sorceresses, and scares them away.

Priapus speaks.

I ONCE was but a fig-tree log, a useless block, when he who carved me, doubtful whether he should make a stool or garden-god, preferred that I should be the god. So, then, I was the god, great source of terror both to thieves and birds; for my right hand together with the symbol of productiveness I show, keeps thieves in check, while on my head a reed stuck up scares off the birds so mischievous, and will not let them settle on the pleasure-grounds Mæcenas laid out but the other day. (Ere that,) the slaves would place the corpses of their fellow-slaves thrown out from narrow cells beneath the earth in common coffins to be carried to this place. This used to be the usual place of burial for all the lowest classes in the town; and would

Pantolabus and No-mentanus were then alive.

have been for Gripeall, the buffoon, and for the spendthrift too.

This pillar here marked out 1,000 feet 300,000 square feet.
towards the public road, 300 more towards
the fields, and on it were[1] these words :— 1 That is, it was given
" This ground for burial does not pass to the in perpetuity to the public.
heirs as property."   But now, one may well The oratio recta is given here.
live upon the Esquiline quite free from pest,
and take a walk upon a sunny terrace, where
but a few days ago the melancholy passers by
beheld the fields disfigured by men's whiten-
ing bones; although the thief, the fox, and
vulture that are wont t' infest this place, do
not distress or trouble me so much as do
those hags who, with their incantations and
their drugs, distract men's minds, for by no
means can I destroy them or prevent their
picking bones up from the ground, and baleful herbs; directly that the moon, as she
[2]rolls on her course, has shown her lovely 2 "Vaga Luna." So in Virgil Æn. i. 742. " Er-rans Luna."
orb.

Why, I myself beheld Canidia, as with her
sable robe tucked up, with feet all bare and
hair unkempt she stalked on shrieking with
the [3]elder Sagana; and pallor had made 3 Sagana had a younger sister.
both revolting to behold.   They then began
to [4]scratch the earth with nails, and rend in 4 To make a hole for the blood.
pieces a black lamb, by biting it; the gore
was poured into the hole, so that from thence
they might draw forth the shades,—the spirits
meant to answer them.   There was an image, Canidia was the woollen image, the false lover was the waxen one.
too, of wool, and one of wax ; the greater
one of wool to hold the lesser one in check
by punishment.   The waxen one stood like
a suppliant, as though 'twas doomed to die

By burning, torture, or the cross.

(like slaves) a miserable death. The woollen image called the witches' goddess to its aid, the waxen called the Fury that avenges blood, and then you might see snakes crawl forth, and hell-hounds stray about, and e'en the moon herself blush and conceal her face behind the huge gravestones. And if I do not tell the truth, may birds heap insults on my head, and may that [1]debauchee called by a woman's name, and Julius his paramour, Voranus, too, the thief, annoy me in the way God's images detest. But why tell each particular? how, speaking in alternate strains with Sagana, the spirits wailed in sad, shrill tones, and how by stealth they hid within the earth wolf's beard with tooth of spotted snake, and how from waxen image fiercer blazed the flame, and how, no unavenged spectator, I showed detestation of the cries and deeds of these two hags. For, fig tree though [2]I was, I made a noise so natural and loud, as sounds a bladder when 'tis burst, that they ran off to Rome. Then with loud laughter and with merriment you might behold Canidia's false teeth drop out, and Sagana's high tête of hair and magic plants, and their charmed lovers' knots [3]upon their arms, fall to the ground.

[1] A Roman knight so effeminate that his name was changed from Pediatius to Pediatia. Julius was a lover of his. Voranus was a freedman of Quintus Lutatius Catulus.

[2] The fig-tree wood was not dry perhaps and split with the heat, making the sound that scared the hags away.

[3] Threads of different colours to chain the affections with.

SATIRE IX.

A Satire showing how Horace was annoyed by men of bad taste, who thought themselves poets and critics, and tried to gain Mæcenas' favour.

Horace. IT happened that I took a walk upon the [1]Sacred Road, and, as I'm wont to be, was wrapped up in some speculative trifling thought, when some one, whom I know by name alone, ran up, and shaking hands, said, "Best of men, how do you do?" I answered, [2]"Tolerably well just now, and wish you all success." Then, as he followed me, I took him up with this remark,—[3]"Can I do aught for you before I go?" But he replied, "You know me well, I am a man of letters."

"Oh! then I shall think the more of you," said I. Then trying very hard to get away, at one time I would walk on faster, at another stop, or whisper something to my page, [4]when beads of perspiration stood upon my terror-stricken brow. Then muttered I, as he kept prating of whatever came into his head, such

[1] A favourite walk.

[2] The phrase Wish you all success is a mere frigid form of politeness.

[3] A usual form of leave-taking.

[4] Literally (by humorous exaggeration), flowed down to the bottom of my ankles.

as the rows of streets, the town,—[1]Bolanus, blest indeed were you in having that quick temper. But when I persistently made no reply, he said, "You sadly want to get away; I've seen it long, but 'tis no use, for I shall stay on to the end; I'll follow you where'er you go from here." Here I rejoin, "There's no use in my taking you out of your way, I want to go and call on some one you know nothing of, he's ill in bed across the [2]Tiber, near to the late Cæsar's park." But he replies, "I've nothing much to do, and I'm an active man, I'll go with you as far as that."

Then like a miserable ass, in stubborn mood, when a too heavy burden has been put upon his back, I drop my wretched ears, (and say no more).

Here he begins again: "Unless I'm much mistaken, you'll not value your friend Viscus more, or Varius, than me. For who can write more lines, or who more quickly, than myself, and who can dance with more lithe grace. And then I sing in such a style that e'en our [3]greatest singer may feel envious." Here was a chance of interrupting him, and so I said, "Have you a mother or some relative to whom your safety's dear?" "Not one," said he, "I've laid them all to rest."

How blest are they! I answer, now I'm [4]left (for you to lay to rest). Pray kill me now: for o'er my head impends [5]a miserable fate which erst when she had shaken her

[1] Bolanus was a mad, passionate fellow, who soon told those he did not like what he thought of them, and so rid himself of them. Bolanus was a surname of the Vellii, from Bola, a town of the Œqui.

[2] Julius Cæsar gave it to the people.

[3] Hermogenes was the son of Sardus Tigellius mentioned in Satire iii., line 3, and the Sims Reeves of the day.

[4] I suppose you'll weary me to death by talking, as you did them.

[5] Mock heroic.

prophetic urn, a Sabine fortune-teller pro-
phesied to me. This boy, said she, no baleful drug, no sword in war, no pleurisy, con-
sumption, no, nor crippling gout shall kill,
but him a prater shall destroy sometime ; so
then, if he be wise, let him flee far from those
who talk too much directly that he has
reached man's estate. We now had come
to [1]Vesta's fame, and it was nine o'clock, and
then he was obliged to answer to the plaintiff's call, or lose his caution money. Here
he said, [2]Now do, dear sir, stay here awhile.
But I replied, [3]Nay, by my life, I cannot play
the advocate, nor know I aught of common
law ; besides, I am in haste to reach, you
know what place. Well, let me see, said he,
what shall I do, give you up or my case?
Oh, give up me I beg, cried I. But he
replied, Oh no, I won't, and once more led
the way ; I followed, as 'tis hard to strive
when overmatched.

He here resumed the conversation thus :—
" How stand you with your Patron now? [4]he
is accessible to but few men, and has a
shrewd discrimination ; none have shown
more tact in their high station. You would
have a powerful aid, a man who could play
second to your first, if you but cared to
recommend myself ; why, by my life, you'd
soon supplant them all." Here I replied,
We do not live there in the way you think,
there is no family more free from, more
opposed to ills like these ; it never does me

[1] Between the Capitol and Palace.

[2] Like our judgment by default.
[3] Literally, may I perish if I do.

Si me amas, if you love me, was a usual formula of polite re-quest.

[4] Like yourself and Virgil.

any harm because some man is wealthier or
better read than I, for each has there his
proper place.   Indeed, said he, you tell me
something strange, in fact, what's scarcely
credible.   Yet so it is, said I.   Then, he
replied, you make me all the more desirous
to be on closer terms with him.   To this
I answered, Just conceive the wish, your
merit is so great you'll take the citadel by
storm, and he is easy to persuade, and therefore he makes difficult the first approach
to him.   Said he, Oh, I shall do my duty,
I will bribe his slaves, I won't give up.   If
on the day on which I call, he says he's not
at home, I'll choose my times, I'll meet him
at the crossings of the streets, nay, I'll escort
him home ; you know life gives man nought
without some toil.   As he kept trifling thus,
A clever grammarian. quite unexpectedly my friend [1]Aristius met
us, a man I loved, and one who knew the
fellow well; we stopped.   He asked me
whence I came, and whither I was bound,
and answers the same questions put by me.
I then began to pull and pinch his arms,
which seemed without all feeling, and to hint
by nod or wink that he should rescue me.
But, with malicious wit and smile, he feigned
Literally, anger be- not to perceive my drift ; then anger rose
gan to inflame my heart
or liver ; the ancients within my heart, and I exclaimed, " You
thought the liver was
the seat of passions more certainly said more than once that you would
than we do.
talk with me of something privately."   But
he said, " Oh, yes, I remember, but I'll tell
you at a time more suitable than this, to-

day's [1] a most important Jewish feast, would
you deride the circumcision rite?" Here
I replied, "I have no scruples on that
score." "Ah! but I have," said he, "I don't
possess your strength of mind, I think as
most men do; [2] excuse me, pray, I'll tell you
at another time." Here muttered I, To
think that this day should have dawned
so black upon my head! The rogue ran off,
and left me like a victim ready for the sacrifice. At last, by chance, the plaintiff met
him, and in a loud voice cried, "You villain,
whither are you bound?" and then to me he
said, "Here, do you [3] witness the arrest?"
I gladly went through the required form. [4]
He dragged him into court; on both sides
followed noisy crowds; and so my patron-
god preserved me from this "bore."

[1] A holiday or feast held by the Jews, perhaps on the 30th day of the month.

[2] The future is used elegantly as an imperative.
"Surrexe" for surrexisse.
Literally, under the knife (of the priest).

[3] The witness turned the tip of his ear to be touched by the summoner.
[4] Vero, literally indeed, has more meaning here, and shows the readiness with which Horace complied.
Apollo was the guardian and defender of poets.

SATIRE X.

This Satire is a defence of opinions expressed in Satire IV., which opinions had been unjustly found fault with by some antiquaries who over-estimated the merit of Lucilius.

It also shows with great taste and wit how unable men are to form a right judgment, who praise an ancient poet to excess merely from an aversion to a contemporary. It also contains several rules for poetry.

The first eight lines are not found in most MSS., or translations, and though they bear the stamp of antiquity to a certain extent, were probably written by some grammarian or commentator.

LUCILIUS, I'll prove by evidence that Cato the [1]philologist can give, who so supports your style, who tries so to correct rough lines, how full of faults you are ;[2] and this he does more gently in proportion as he is superior, and is a better critic far than he is, who, the best grammarian of all our knights, in boyhood was [3]severely warned by whip and wet rope's end, that there might be a man to play the champion for ancient bards against these [4]modern sneers. But to return. Well, yes, I did say that the lines Lucilius composed were often roughly made, for who

[1] A grammarian and poet in the time of Sylla.

[2] "Facit" is the ellipsis. "Hoc"—"quo"— are for the more usual— eo—quo.

[3] Exhortatus is used passively, no other instance is found.

[4] Literally, our disdain.
Illuc may refer to the 4th Satire of this book.
Literally, ran in rough feet.

defends Lucilius so foolishly as not to admit
this? and yet this very bard is praised by me
in the same work for having satirized the
town most wittily; yet though I grant him
this, I would not grant him all that's excellent besides; for if I did, I should admire as
perfect poetry the farces of [1]Laberius.

It is not then enough to make your audience laugh loud,—although there is some
merit in this point as well,—you must be
terse besides, to make your clauses rhythmical,
and save their being hampered with long
words that but oppress the weary ear.
Again, you must employ a style, at one time
grave that shows the character of orator
or poet, as the case may be, and then,
at other times, a sportive vein that well
describes a polished wit who keeps his power
in reserve, and weakens it on purpose; and
the satire's jest will generally solve all matters
of great moment with more spirit and success
than declamation's gravity. [2]Those authors
of old comedy were popular through this;
in this [3]are models for our use; whose works
Hermogenes the exquisite has never read,
nor has that [4]miserable wretch who apes his
style, who has been trained to sing nought
else but [5]Calvus' or Catullus' lines.

[6]Well, true; yet he achieved a great success
in using Greek as well as Latin words.

O ye so late to learn, how can ye think
aught hard, or worth your admiration, that
[7]Pitholeon of Rhodes could do?

[1] A Roman knight who was compelled to act his own farces.

[2] Eupolis, Cratinus, and Aristophanes.

[3] Through the merits mentioned from lines 9 to 15.

[4] "Iste" implies contempt. The man's name is not known.

[5] Amatory poets.

[6] An apologist for Lucilius says this.

Horace.

[7] A very mediocre satirist.

Apologist. Yet still, a Latin style agreeably mixed with Greek words is pleasanter, as if the rough Falernian be blended with the softer Chian[1] wine.

1 " Nota" corresponds to our "brand" and seal.
Horace.

I ask you if you mean this only when you write light lines, or also when you have to speak in some defendant's almost hopeless[2] case. Although our greatest orators were pleading hard in their own tongue, would you, forsooth, like some [3]half-Greek, half-Oscan from Canusium, forgetful of your fatherland, prefer to mingle phrases borrowed from abroad with your own tongue? Why, when I, [4]Roman though I am, began to write Greek lines, the shade[5] of Romulus appeared when midnight's hour had struck, when dreams come true, and with such words forbade; "you would not more absurdly carry coals to Newcastle, than you would act, if you preferred to overfill Greek authors' crowded ranks." While that bombastic [6]Alpine bard (as he is called) describes the death of Memnon in his wretched lines, or tells laboriously of the source the Rhine flows from, I treat of lighter themes, not meant to be recited loudly in the Muses' temple, subject to our critic Tarpa's praise or blame, nor meant to have a run upon the stage.

Fundanius, you best of all men in the world, can with good taste tell sportively your comic tales in which a cunning courtesan and slave cheat some old man, as Terence tells us in the Andria; while [8]Pollio

2 Satire iv., line 94.

3 Canusium was an Apulian town, its inhabitants spoke Greek and Oscan.
Literally, country and father.

4 Mare citra—*i. e.*, born in Italy.
5 Serio-comic.

6 Marcus Furius Bibaculus of Cremona was called Alpinus from a line in his description of the waging of the Gallic war by Cæsar; he wrote a tragedy called Æthiopedes, in which Achilles plays Memnon, a mythical king of Æthiopia, who went to aid the Trojans; Bibaculus also wrote a bombastic account of the Rhine in his history of the Gallic war.
7 A comic writer after Menander's style.
Davus was a usual name for a slave.
He and Chremes are characters in the Andria of Terence.
8 Caius Asinius Pollio was a great literary character.

describes kings' deeds in the Iambic Trimeter; again, the fervid [1]Varius, far better
than all others, builds the bold heroic lines;
and last, the Muse that joys so in the fields,
has given gentle elegance to [2]Virgil's pen.

'Twas this satiric verse that I, when [3]Varro
Atacinus tried and failed, could write with
more success though still inferior to [4]him
who introduced the style, nor should I dare
to try to rob him of the crown that sits
so gracefully upon his brow.

Still I did say that what he wrote rolled
turbidly[5] along, just like some torrent stream
that often bears with it more that requires
taking out than keeping there. And come
now, critic as you are, do you find no fault in
great Homer's works? And does Lucilius,
with all his taste, make no change in the
style of tragic Accius? And does he not
decry the lines of Ennius, which are not
dignified enough, when he speaks of himself
as one no better than the bards he blames?
And what prevents me, too, when I read
what Lucilius once wrote, from asking whether
his rough genius, or the rough nature of the
subject-matter, would not let him pen more
polished lines, or lines that ran more smoothly
on (than those a man would pen) if satisfied
with this alone, I mean the writing something
in hexameters, he were accustomed to strike
off two hundred lines before his breakfast, and
two hundred more when he had dined, like to
the genius of Tuscan [6]Cassius, more wild than

[1] Varius was a tragic actor.

[2] The Bucolics and Georgics were then published, and he was engaged on the Œneid.

[3] Varro was a satirist, called "Atacinus" from the "Atax," now the "Aude," a small river in Narbon GauL The others are unknown, unless one be Særius Nicanor, a satirist of Sulla's time.

[4] Lucilius introduced the style.

[5] Literally, that he flowed on muddily, (bearing) presenting to our notice more that ought to be taken away, than that which ought to be left.

[6] Cassius was a satirist who wrote so much that his books and shelves were sufficient form his funeral pyre.

some swift flood, for he, they say, was burnt
on pyre built up with his shelves and books.
Suppose, I say, Lucilius has both good taste
and wit, suppose besides he is more polished
than most authors are who write an inartistic
style of verse, untried by Greeks; more
polished, too, than [1]Andronicus, Novius,
Pacuvius, or Plautus; still suppose Lucilius
had been reserved by fate for our own times,
he would erase much from his works; would
cut out all that might seem needlessly spun
out, and as he formed his lines, would often
scratch his head in angry thought, and bite
his nails down to the quick.   [2]Ofttimes erase,
if you intend to write what may prove worth
a second reading, and don't try to gain the
admiration of the mob, but be content with a
choice few to read your works.   Or would
you madly wish that poetry of yours should
form heart lessons in some third-rate schools?
Well, I would not; for " 'tis enough that
gentlemen should give me their applause,"
as once [3]Arbuscula, despising others in the
theatre, said boldly, when hissed off the
stage,—What?   should the wretched slander
of [4]Pantilius touch me; should it distress me
that [5]Demetrius backbites me when away, or
that some silly [6]Fannius, the singer's parasite,
should try to injure me?   May Plotius[7] and
Varius my patron, Virgil, Valgius, Octavius,
approve of what I write; and fain I would
that Fuscus, best of men, and both the
Visci gave their praise; and with no thought

[1] More ancient poets.

[2] The upper end of the
" stilus" was broad, and
used for erasing its marks
on the waxen tablet; the
lower end was sharp, and
used for writing.

[3] A fashionable actress.

[4] A wretched poet
called "Cimex," because
his satire was as coarse
and biting as the insect
of that name.
[5] Demetrius aped Ti-
gellius.
[6] Fannius was a toady
of Tigellius.
[7] The best poets and
critics of the day, and
his friends.
Fuscus Aristius was a
clever grammarian.
The Visci, two knights
of senatorial rank.

of courting favour, I may mention you too,
Pollio, and you, Messalla, and your brother, *Publicola   Messalla*
and you, Bibulus and Servius, and also you, *Corvinus, and Quintus*
Pedius Publicola.
impartial Furnius, and many more ; but them, *"Simul his," together*
with these.
though men of letters, and my friends, I pur- *Caius Asinius Pollio,*
a tragic poet, historian,
posely omit, and trust that these my lines, *and orator. Vide line 42.*
Servius, a philosopher,
whate'er their merit be, will suit them all ; *son of Servius Sulpicius,*
the consul.
for I shall feel chagrin if they don't please as *Caius Furnius was an*
impartial historian.
well as I expect they will.   But you, Deme-
trius, and you, Tigellius, I bid go sing your *There is a "double*
entendre" in the word
sentimental trash among the seated ladies *"plorare," which means*
to sing effeminately, or
whom you teach. *to go to perdition.*

  Go, slave, and quickly write this next in
order in my book now done.

SATIRE I.—BOOK II.

Horace pretends to ask Caius Trebatius Testa, an eminent barrister, what he ought to do, as some one had threatened him with an action for libel. Trebatius advises him either to give up writing, or describe the exploits of Augustus. The poet disclaims ability for such undertaking, and avows his intention of satirizing none but those who have assailed him unprovoked.

Horace. Some think that in my satires I am too severe, and nearly libellous ; the rest consider all my writings spiritless, and that a thousand lines a day like mine could be composed as easily as yarn is spun. Trebatius, advise me legally what now to do.

Trebatius. Don't write.

Horace. What ! not compose, say you, a single line ?

Trebatius. I do.

Horace. Well, 'pon my life, it would be best; but I can't sleep.

Compare the same use of "poteras" in line 16 for "posses."

Trebatius. Let those who want sound sleep do as [1] I do, dress well with oil, and thrice swim o'er the Tiber's stream, and have a skin full of good wine at night's approach ; or, since so eager a desire to write impels you 'gainst your will, dare to describe the ex

[1] Trebatius was fond of swimming and good wine.
Such forms as "transnanto" and "habento" were common in legal language.

ploits of Augustus the indomitable, for doubtless you will gain rich guerdon for your toil.

Horace. Respected sir, my powers are not
a match for my desire : indeed, not any
one you please can well portray a Roman
army on the march, all bristling with the
javelin, or Gauls' death-agony upon the spear-
point broken in the wound or wounds the
Parthian inflicts while gliding off his horse.

Trebatius. And yet as erst the wise Lucilius portrayed the younger Africanus, so you
might have drawn Augustus, just, high-souled,
and brave.

Horace. Oh, I shall do my duty when a
proper time shall come, and Flaccus' words
will fail to gain Augustus' ears unless the time
be suitable ; for if you pay him awkward
flattery [1] he spurns you, safe from all attacks.

Trebatius. And how much better this than
to assail in biting lines Pantolabus the rake,
and spendthrift Nomentanus, when men each
fear for themselves and hate the satirist, though
unattacked !

Horace. What should I do ? The [2]buffoons
dance directly that the fumes of wine have
[3]mounted to their brains, and all the lamps seem
doubled. [4]Yet Castor takes delight in steeds,
while boxing Pollux loves ; there are as many
different pursuits as men alive ; and so, as
once Lucilius, [5]superior to both of us, wrote, I
too love to write hexameters. Lucilius, in
times gone by, used to entrust the secrets of
his heart to books as though to trusty friends,

The "pilum" was the national weapon.

An allusion to the contrivance of Marius, who substituted for one of the two iron pins with which the shaft of the javelin was fastened to the head, a wooden one, so that when the javelin struck on the shield of the enemy it should break instead of being able to be used for hurling back, or even pulled out from the wound.

[1] Metaphor, from horses kicking back upon awkward grooms.

[2] Milonius, a buffoon, is quoted to represent the class.
Confer. Persius, Sat. i., 12 : "Quid faciam? Sed sum petulanti splene cachinno."
[3] "Millia" is understood before "capitum."
[4] Literally, born from the same egg ; an allusion to the myth of Leda and the swan.
Argument : — If brothers differ, how much more should those who are no relations !
[5] *I.e.*, in property and birth ; he was Pompey's great-uncle.

and ne'er would go to any other aid if
[1]good or bad luck had befallen him; and
this is why the whole life of the ancient
bard is known as well as if portrayed in
pictures such as shipwrecked sailors offer
to some god. I imitate this poet, doubtful
whether I am of Lucanian or of Apulian
descent, for now Venusia's sons dwell close
upon the confines of both countries, sent,
as the old story runs, for this, when now
the Sabines had been driven out,—to stay an
enemy's incursion on the [2]Romans through the
space untenanted, in case Apulia, or else Lucania, should wage aggressive war with them.
And yet this pen of mine shall make no
unprovoked attack on anything that lives, and
like a sword in scabbard cased shall guard
me; and pray why should I attempt to draw
it while I'm safe from all molesting highwaymen? [3]O Jove, great sire and king, grant
that this weapon may be laid aside and wear
away with rust, and that none may assail me,
eager as I am for peace. But he who shall
have once provoked me—'twill be better that
he touch me not, I cry—shall rue it, and, become notorious, shall be the theme of jest
through all the town.   .

Th' informer [4]Cervius, when he's provoked,
is wont to threaten those he hates with prosecu-
tion and the voting urn: Canidia will threaten
all her foes with poison that Albutius once
killed his wife with: [5]Turius, with signal loss
of any case tried when he's judge. How

[1] The verb "contigit" implies good fortune; "accidit," reverse.

[2] "Romano" = "Romanis," a use common enough in Livy and other writers.

Argument: — He strikes terror, as it were, into the hearts of his enemies by intimating that he is descended from those brave Venusians who were sent to protect the colony by force of arms, if necessary, and that he inherits their bravery; but avows that he also adheres to their custom of attacking no one aggressively.
[3] He parodies a line of Callimachus, showing that this is not to be taken as sober earnest.

[4] A petty advocate and informer.

[5] A corrupt judge of that time.

men deter the foes they hate, each with the
power he is most gifted with, and how the
laws of nature order it, learn now by reasoning
with me like this.   The wolf with tooth
attacks, the bull with horns : why so, unless
by instinct bid ?   Entrust his long-lived
mother to the spendthrift [1] Scæva's care ;
[2] affection's hand will work no deed of blood ;
and yet, no stranger this, than that the wolf
attacks none with his heels, nor ox with teeth :
—for baleful hemlock will take the old lady
off, when honey has been poisoned with its
juice.   To save all needless taik—if calm old
age await me, or if death be hovering round
with sable wings,—if rich, if poor, at Rome,
or, an chance shall have willed it so, in
banishment, whate'er the tenor of my life
shall be, I still will write.

Trebatius. My dear young friend, I fear
you'll not live long, and I'm afraid lest some
one of your influential patrons should withdraw his patronage.

Horace. How so? pray, when Lucilius once
dared to be the first in writing verses framed
according to this style, and to drag off that
specious cloak in which men severally walked so
fair before their fellows' eyes, though base at
heart, —was [3] Lælius,—was Africanus, who derived his well-earned name from crushing Car-
thage by his arms,— annoyed by genius like
his, or felt they pain whene'er [4] Metellus was
attacked, or [5] Lupus thoroughly lampooned ?
And yet he took the leading public men to

task, the public, too,[1] through every class alike; and, sooth to say, he spared but virtue and its friends. But Scipio so brave in war, and Lælius so gently wise in state, were wont to trifle in his company, and sport with playful ease, until their humble meal was cooked, directly that they had withdrawn themselves from this life's busy stage into their own retreats. Whate'er I be, though far below[2] Lucilius in means and genius, yet Envy must perforce confess that I have ever lived among the [3]great, and when she tries to fix her tooth on some weak place, will strike against what's hard and firm, unless, most learned barrister, you do not quite agree with this.

Trebatius. Oh yes, I quite approve. Yet still, that you may be advised and on your guard, lest, as may happen, ignorance of sacred law should bring some trouble on your head, I tell you that there is a [4]court and verdict too, in case a man shall have composed against another verses that are bad because they're libellous.

Horace. Yes, true; if any one have written verses that are bad because they're weak; but how if any one shall have composed lines, good according to Augustus' view, and shall be praised by him for them, or if one have lampooned those worthy of reproof, deserving none [5] himself?

Trebatius. The magistrates will smile, and give their votes with lenience, and you will be set free and leave the court without a fine.

[1] *I. e.*, through all the thirty-five tribes, — a periphrasis for the whole people.

[2] Lucilius was of equestrian origin, and granduncle to Pompey the Great on the mother's side.

[3] Such as Augustus, Mæcenas, and Pollio.

Trebatius employs the legal word "diffindere," not in the sense of making a matter stand over for further consideration, but in its ordinary sense of rejecting or altering.

[4] The *lex Cornelia* is referred to.

Horace pretends to misunderstand Trebatius's use of the word "mala."

"Integer ipse." Horace does not imply that he is free from all faults, but from such as he would then be satirizing.

SATIRE II.—BOOK II.

Under the character of a Roman countryman, the poet recommends a more frugal style of living than that which prevailed among the luxurious inhabitants of Rome, and also cautions men against erring in the other extreme, as some did.

————————

Horace. Good friends, learn, not surrounded by bright gold and silver plate, or marble tables, when the gaze is dazzled by th' excessive glare, and when the heart, inclined to choose the false, rejects the better course, but here, ere tasting food, discuss with me the nature and extent of good there is in living in a humble way ; and these are not my words, but rules a countryman Ofella gives, who, though belonging to no sect, is a philosopher possessed of healthy common sense.

A friend puts this question.

Why this ?

Horace. I'll tell you if I can. All those whose sense of truth high living once has spoiled, but feebly search for right. When you have coursed the hare, or when you're tired with breaking in a horse, or if the [1]Roman hunting weary you, accustomed as you are [2]to live like Greeks effeminately, then, if the swift tennis-ball attract you,—while the inte-

[1] He contrasts the Roman hunting and riding with the Greek dicing and game of hoop.
[2] The construction is thus :—" Seu pila velox (agit te), molliter austerum studio fallente laborem (lude pila,.

rest you take makes you delightfully forget the rough exertion of the game,—why, play at tennis; or if quoits be more your fancy, cleave the yielding air with the hurled quoit. Then, when your toil has forcibly removed disgust, ere tasting food or drink, refuse, if then you can, all common food, drink nothing but the primest 'honey mixed with richest wine. Suppose your butler has gone out, or that the sea keeps safe its fish through louring storm; no matter, bread and salt will well appease so good an appetite. And whence gained this, think you, or how? The greatest pleasure is not found in food that's dear and savoury, but all depends upon yourself. Get relish to your food by hard exertion, for nor oyster, no, nor rich red mullet, nor the Alpine grouse, will give delight to the pale glutton bloated with excess. Yet, were a peacock served upon the table, scarcely could I drag you from it, and suppress your wish to whet your appetite with it in place of common food, misled as you would be by specious show, because a bird that's rare is sold for a great price, and makes a splendid show with tail of varied hues:—as though that were aught to the point. Pray, do you eat that plumage that you praise so? No. Pray, has the bird such beauty cooked? No. Yet you'd rather eat its flesh than that of fowl, although they are the same. 'Tis clear that you're misled by mere outside, that differs so. Well, granted :—but whence do you get

The Romans every day took strong exercise before the undeviating custom of bathing. One of the most favourite exercises was the game of ball, which was then played by adults in various ways, and is now in Italy. Horace here refers to the "pila" or smaller ball, something like our tennis-ball, and not to the "follis," a sort of football.

The quoit was made of stone, brass, or iron, and thrown by the help of a thong put through a hole in the middle of it. The shape was round and broad, or square.

1 The honey of Hymettus was the sweetest, and the Falernian wine the richest. The allusion is to the "mulsum," or mead, which was taken as a sort of whet or antepast.

The construction is thus :—Patet te deceptum imparibus formis (vesci or (vesci cupere) carne hâc magis (quam carne) illa.

the nice taste to decide if this pike gasping (on the shore) was [1] caught in Tiber's stream or in the sea,—if it swam through rough floods betwixt the bridge of piles and of Fabricius, or nearer to the river's source in Tuscany. You praise a mullet, madman that you are, that only weighs [2] three pounds, which you're obliged to cut into small bits to give each guest a taste. I see, it is appearance that attracts ; and since that's so, what good is there in loathing those long pike ? No doubt you loathe them so, since nature has bestowed on them too large a bulk, and on the mullet but small weight. The appetite that's ever cloyed despises common food.

Yes, but I could have wished to view a fish of wondrous size stretched out at length on some large dish, says Gluttony, that e'en [3] voracious monsters might well suit.

O come with all your forces, ye south winds, and taint these gluttons' dainty food. [4] Nay, there's no need:—for the wild boar and turbot too, although quite fresh, are stale enough to them, since such distressing plenty cloys the feeble stomach, so that, sated as it is, it rather fancies radishes or elecampane dressed in vinegar. Although not yet is all plain food excluded from our nobles' boards, for even now the common egg and dark preserving olive have their place. [5] Not very long ago, the table of Gallonius the auctioneer was quite notorious for having on it served a sturgeon whole !

[1] Pike were thought better of when caught after a storm, or when wearied with making their way against an adverse stream.

[2] *I. e.*, an unusually fine one. Domitian's celebrated mullet weighed six pounds, and was thought miraculous.

[3] He refers to the Harpies, described by Virgil, Æneid iii. 210, and following lines, as devouring and defiling the food of Æneas and his followers. *At* is a particle of indignation here.

[4] Corrects himself, and reflects that all food alike is flavourless to them.

Eggs and olives were eaten at the commencement of the dinner ; the latter were supposed to be provocative of appetite.
The dark olives were supposed to be the best for preserving.

[5] Eighty years before, in the time of Lucilius.

What! did the ocean not breed turbot then as now?

[1] Yes, but the turbot then was safe, and safe the stork in unmolested nest, until the ex-mayor Rufus showed you how to cook them both. So now-a-days, if any one have solemnly affirmed that sea-gulls roasted are good food, the [2] noble youth of Rome, so quick to learn the wrong, will listen to his words. But, [3] as Ofella thinks, mean living will not be the same as moderate, and surely useless will it be for men to shun one fault, [4] if they be so turned by another from the right as to become depraved. A certain miser, who e'en now is called "the Dog" because he really is so dirty, lives on olives spoilt by being kept five [5] times too long, and cherries that grow wild; nor will he pour his wine from cask to bowl until it's flavourless, and on his cabbage drops [6] himself with niggard hand—though liberal enough with the spoilt vinegar—from cruet made of [7] horn that holds two pints, such oil that one could never bear the smell; and this, although in fresh-fulled toga clad he keep the after [8] marriage feast, or birthday, or some other holiday. What kind of living, then, will the philosopher adopt, and which class will he imitate,—the gluttonous or miserly? [9] I am between two fires, as the proverb says.

Philosophers will so consult good taste, as never to disgust their guests by meanness, or unluckily go wrong in either style of life :—

1 The argument is, that the sturgeon was as much thought of then as the turbot now, only no fool had brought it into vogue.
Sempronius Rufus.

2 Ironical.

3 That is, I am commending a plain and moderate, not a mean style of living.

4 "Si te alio ita detorseris, ut pravus fias."

5 They would only keep a year

6 Lest the slave should put too much on.
"Instillat caulibus oleum cujus olei odorem."

7 *I.e.*, of the commonest kind.

8 The bridegroom gave a dinner on the day after the marriage, and the carousing was then renewed.

9 Literally, a wolf presses me on this side, a dog on that.

will ne'er, as he assigns their work, be harsh to slaves as old [1]Albutius once was; nor will they, like good easy Nævius, give greasy water to their guests to wash their feet in; this is flagrant want of taste. Now learn the nature and extent of good that plainer living brings with it. And first you'd have good health; for you may well believe how [2]bad for man is rich and varied food, when you think of the diet which, plain though it was, agreed so well with you in days gone by; whereas, directly you have mixed boiled meat with roast, shellfish with game, these dainties will turn into bile, and sluggish phlegm will cause derangement of the stomach. Do you see how pale each guest gets up from [3]dinner, where one scarce can tell which dish to choose? Nay, more; the body, burdened with th' excess of yesterday, weighs down with it the soul as well, and makes that [4]emanation of the godlike Essence grovel on the ground. The other when he has laid down to sleep his limbs refreshed as quickly as may be with food, gets up quite vigorous for the day's rule of work. Yet he'll be able at due times to change to richer food, if the returning year have brought a holiday, or if he shall wish to recruit his frame, now spare with living low, when, [5]too, he shall be growing old, and when the feeble stage of life shall need a gentler treatment; but, pray what addition will be made for you to that luxurious indulgence which, while young and strong you now anticipate, in

[1] Albutius used to threaten his slaves with death if they did not do his commissions exactly. He would flog his slaves before they had committed any offence, saying that he feared he should not have time after they had done wrong. He made a great show on a little.

[2] "Ut" = quomodo; "credas" is for "licet credere."

[3] Terence, Phormio, 2, 2, 28: "P. Cœna dubia apponitur. G. Quid istuc verbi est? P. Ubi tu dubites, quid sumas potissimum."

[4] He alludes to the Stoic doctrine, that our minds are emanations from God's universal mind. Pythagoras held the same idea.

[5] "Ubique" = et ubi.

case bad health or crippling age fall to your
lot?

The ancients praised a boar e'en if high-
flavoured, not because they had no sense of
smell, but, I believe, with this idea, that any guest
who might come rather late should eat it, tainted
as it was, more suitably than that the greedy
host should swallow it when fresh. Oh that
the earth in days gone by had brought me
forth to dwell among such demigods as these!
No doubt you have regard for fame, for[1]
words of fame fall on the ear of man more
pleasantly than song; well, know [2] that these
large turbots and expensive dishes bring with
them both great disgrace and loss.

Then, further, there's your [3] uncle's and your
neighbour's rage, yourself disgusted in your
heart, and wishing death would come, but all
in vain, since you'll not have a penny piece
to buy a halter with.

Yes, rightly, he replies, is Trausius the bank-
rupt blamed in words like those of yours, but I
have ample revenues, and wealth sufficient for
three noblemen.

Then is there nothing on which you can
spend your surplus income better? Why do
any suffer want they don't deserve while you
are rich? Why do the gods' time-honoured
fanes fall to decay? And why, insatiate wretch,
don't you mete out from those large stores of
wealth some portion for your fatherland which
should be dear? No doubt [4] on you alone will
fortune never cease to smile! O you doomed

[1] Quæ = quippe quæ.

[2] "Scito" is understood in thought.

[3] The ill-nature of uncles and step-mothers was proverbial.

[4] Ironical.

soon to be great source of laughter to your enemies when all your wealth is spent !

Now which of these two characters will have a surer self-reliance 'gainst reverse ? The one who has long used his haughty mind [1] and pampered frame to luxury, or he who, satisfied with humble life, and careful of his future lot, like a good general has well prepared for war in time of peace. And this I'll tell you, that you may more readily believe : — when quite a little boy, I knew Ofella did not spend his yet unstraitened means more lavishly than he does now they are curtailed. You might have seen him, with his flocks and sons, as a stout tenant farmer in the land the public officer assigned [2] Umbrenus, and his words were these,—" But seldom upon working days have I ate aught but greens and a smoked leg of pork. And if some friend I had not seen for long, or neighbour called, and proved a welcome guest to me when disengaged through rain, we then enjoyed—no fish conveyed from town, but fowl and kid, and after that a bunch of grapes that had been hung to dry, while walnuts and split figs made our dessert. And then we played a [3] game, and forfeits in it fixed the wine we had to drink or go without; and Ceres worshipped with the words, ' So rise with lofty stalk,' [4] smoothed out with wine the wrinkles of our anxious brows." Let fortune frown, and stir fresh tumult up, how much, pray, will it take from these advan-

[1] " Superbus " applies both to "mens" and "corpus."

[2] Umbrenus got Ofella's land in the division of conquered property : because he had served at Philippi against Brutus and Cassius.

[3] The game was probably one of dice, and the one who made a mistake had either to drink a bumper or go without wine when he wanted it.
[4] In the oratio recta the words would be "surge culmo alto."
For the passive use of "venerata" confer Virgil, "Æneid," iii., 46c.

tages?—how much less fat and strong, my
children, and my slaves, have you been since
this new resident came here? And I say
"resident," because nor him nor me nor any
one has nature fixed to be the owner of
the land in perpetuity. He turned me out,
and him profuse expenditure, or ignorance
of legal quirk, or certainly at last, his heir,
who's longer lived, will oust. The farm now
bears Umbrenus' name, and lately bore
Ofella's; 'twill belong in perpetuity to none,
but pass into the tenancy now of myself,
now of some other man. So, then, live
bravely on, and bravely stem adversity's
opposing stream.

SATIRE III.—BOOK II.

This Satire contains a conversation between Horace and Damasippus, a silly fellow, who, after losing all his property in trade, grew a long beard, and strutted about the forum in a philosopher's cloak, reciting the rules Stertinius, a garrulous philosopher, gave him. Horace represents Damasippus as intruding upon him in his Sabine villa on the festival called Saturnalia, which was held on the 17th of December and few following days, in memory of the good old times when men were all more equal, and lived an easy primitive life.

Damasippus. You write so seldom now, that you don't ask for ¹parchment four times in the year's whole length, emending all you have composed, and angry with yourself because, indulging as you do in wine and sleep, you tell in verse nought worth the mentioning. What will be done ? ²What, nothing ! Yet you fled to this retreat at the commencement of old Saturn's noisy festival. So then, in earnest, tell us something suitable to your professions : come, begin. You utter not a word. 'Tis no use blaming pens, and striking unoffending walls built 'neath the gods' and poets' ire. And yet you had the

¹ The writing on the wax tablets was transcribed on parchment.

² As Horace does not immediately reply, Damasippus answers his own question.

air of one who made us many splendid promises, if but your little country house had
sheltered you beneath its comfortable roof.
What good was it to pile [1]Menander's works
on Plato's, and to take forth such distinguished comrades on the road as [2]Eupolis, or
as [3]Archilochus? Are you preparing to draw
envy's teeth by turning [4]idle now? If so,
you'll be most wretchedly despised :—that
wicked Siren Sloth must be avoided, or whatever praise you've gained by your more energetic life must be surrendered with content.

Horace. [5]May heaven's powers combine
to find a barber for you, Damasippus, in
return for this your good advice; but by what
means came you to know my character so
well?

Damasippus. Why, after I lost all I had
on 'Change, I turned philosopher, and saw to
other people's business, when ejected from
my own by creditors :—for once, a virtuoso, I
would hunt out some bronze bath in which
that cunning [6]Sisyphus had washed his feet.
I'd notice too what might be carved in inartistic style, or cast in rather rough a mould.
Then, as a connoisseur, I fixed the value
of this statue at eight hundred pounds; I,
best of all men, could buy pleasure-grounds
and houses at a profit, whence all those who
thronged the streets at auctions called me
[7]Mercury himself.

Horace. I know, and am astonished that
you're rid of that sad aberration [8]of the mind.

[1] A Greek comic writer.

[2] An ancient Greek comic writer.
[3] The inventor of the iambic verse.
[4] Virtus = industria here.

[5] Horace here pretends not to know that Damasippus had turned philosopher, and therefore had grown the "philosophic beard," and so he jestingly expresses a wish that heaven would confer the greatest blessing it could on him by ridding him of his dirty beard.

[6] Sisyphus founded Corinth, and was the son of Æolus.

[7] There was a corporation of traders at Rome called Mercuriales.
[8] "Morbi purgatum" is a Greek construction for "morbo purgatum."

F

Damasippus. Nay, but in wondrous wise, a new disease of mind has rid me of the former one, as happens when distressing pleurisy or headache changes to a stomach-ache :[1]—as when the apoplectic men one sees turn boxers in a frenzy fit, and drive their doctors off.

Horace. [2]As long as you do nought like this to me, do as you will.

Damasippus. My dear sir, don't deceive yourself, both you and nearly all besides are mad and fools, if aught of truth Stertinius can [3]din into one's ears, from whose dictation I attentively wrote down these rules of wondrous worth, what time, to solace me, he bade me grow a "philosophic beard," and come back from the [4]bridge of suicides with cleared-up brow.   For when I, through my ruined state, would fain have veiled my head and leapt into the stream, he luckily stood by and said, [5] "See that you do not anything unworthy of yourself; it is false shame that tortures you, for you're afraid to be thought mad when all the world is mad. And first, I'll try to find the nature of this madness out, and if it prove to be in you alone, I'll utter not another word to stay your dying with stout heart.   [6]Chrysippus' sect and pupils say that all are mad whom vicious folly or the ignorance of truth drives blindly on. This philosophic rule applies to nations and to mighty kings, and all but the philosopher. Now listen to the reason why all those

---

[1] "Cor" = os ventriculi: "trajecto" is a medical term.

[2] Horace speaks ironically, the Stoic seriously. There is an ellipsis of the words, "in me fiat :" "esto" is the third person.

[3] The verb "crepat" conveys an idea of reiteration and a loud voice.

[4] Built by Fabricius the consul : used like our Waterloo might be for suicides.

[5] "Cave faxis" = cave ne facias ; faxis being the old form for facias or feceris.

[6] "Chrysippi porticus" was a colonnade at Athens, where Zeno and his followers taught.

who've called you 'madman' are as mad as
you. As in the woods, when some mistake
drives from the beaten track men vaguely
wandering, one goes off to the right, another
to the left,—they make the same mistake, but
in quite opposite directions ;—so think that
you're mad, and that the man who mocks
you is no saner than yourself, and a fit [1]laugh-
ingstock for boys." There is one kind of
folly that dreads what there is no cause to
dread, and so complains that fire and rock
and flood oppose its way in th' unobstructed
plain ; and there's a second sort quite opposite to this, and quite as mad,—I mean of
him who rushes through the midst of flames
and streams, though his dear mother, his
chaste sister, his relations, father, wife,
should cry a deep ditch here, a high rock
there, take care ; he'd [2]hear no more than
Fufius some time ago when drunk, as he
slept out the play Iliona, although two
hundred thousand voices cried out Catienus'
words, "I call thee, mother, mine." I'll
prove that all men are afflicted with a madness like to this. Here's Damasippus [3]mad
in buying antique statues, [4]while the man
who lends him money is of quite sound
mind. Well, yes, suppose he is. Yet if I
say to you, Here, take a sum, which you
can never pay me back again, shall you be
mad if you accept the sum, or more distraught if you refuse the "find" that fav'ring
·Mercury so sends? Draw up ten bonds

[1] Literally, drags a tail, *i. e.*, of paper or rags fixed on by boys.

[2] In the play Iliona, the actor Fufius fell asleep through wine, and Catienus, who acted the part of the ghost, could not wake him with the words, "Mater te ap-pello," so the whole audience shouted out the words of Catienus.

[3] According to the popular and erroneous idea.

[4] He supposes the creditor to be sane, but only to prove him as mad as Damasippus.

[1] Nerius was one of the chief money-lenders at Rome.

"Cicuta" (hemlock) was so called from his chilling, hard nature as a usurer.

[2] Proteus was a sea-god who had the power of changing himself into all kinds of shapes: he is described in the 4th Georgic of Virgil.

Anticyra was in the Maliac gulf, and the supposed cure for madness — "hellebore" — grew there.

Nothing further is known of Staberius.

[3] Arrius was a friend of Cicero, and gave a splendid funeral feast to his father.

framed by our [1]greatest usurer;—'tis not enough: then add a hundred obligations drawn up by Cicuta skilled in quibbles of the law: then add a thousand legal ties besides; yet still this rascal, like a second [2]Proteus, will escape the chains.

When, as he laughs excessively, you hurry him into the court, he will become a boar, anon a bird or stone, and when he will, a tree. Since to mismanage one's affairs bespeaks the madman, and to manage well, the sane; believe me, old Cicuta is more addle-headed than you when he tells his clerk to write a cheque for what you never can repay.

I bid you list to me, and now prepare to carefully attend, all you whose cheeks are pale through that pernicious quest of rank or greed of gain; all you whose passions are inflamed by luxury, or hearts distressed by gloomy superstition, or by any possible disease of mind; approach in order nearer me, while I explain that all are mad. The miser needs by far the strongest cure; I almost think philosophy intends Anticyra's whole produce for his use.

Staberius's heirs inscribed upon his tomb the sum he left, for had they not done so, they would have been obliged to give a hundred pairs of gladiators for the public show, a banquet suited to th' expensive tastes of [3]Arrius, and all the corn that's reaped in Africa. For said Staberius, "It was my will if right, it was my will if wrong, don't be

severe with me." Methinks the foresight of
Staberius anticipated this reluctance to adopt
the clause. What was his meaning, then, in
ordering his heirs to carve upon his tomb
the sum he left? Why, while he lived, he
thought that poverty was a great vice, and
guarded against nothing with more care ; so
that, if he had died, as possibly he might, less
wealthy by a single farthing, he'd have thought
himself less virtuous :—[1]for merit, fame,
and glory, all things human and divine bow
low before fair Money's power, and he who
has amassed this wealth will be distinguished,
brave, and just.

[2]Will he be a philosopher as well? Ay,
and a king, and whatsoe'er he will.

Staberius expected that th' inscription, as
though earned by merit, would prove a great
source of fame to him.

How widely different the Greek sage [3]Aris-
tippus acts! who in the midst of Libyan
deserts bade his slaves throw down the gold
because they made but little way, grown lazy
through the weight they bore. Which is the
madder of these [4]two?

[5]We cannot tell. An instance that in
trying to solve doubt but causes fresh, brings
no result. Yet, if a man should purchase
lutes, and having purchased, should at once
convey them all to the same place, although
addicted not to playing on the lute or any
other branch of the musician's art :—if one
who were no cobbler should buy paring-

[1] Stertinius says this ironically.

[2] Stertinius asks himself and answers.

[3] See page 195, Epistle xvii.

[4] Staberius or Aristippus.

[5] Stertinius here remembers that the theory of his sect was that one could not solve one doubtful matter by creating another, and gives up the comparison between the miser and the man who has no regard for money, and proves the miser to be the greater fool, by quoting instances so plain as to require no illustration.

knives and lasts, one disinclined to trade,
buy sails and gear for ships : why, men like
these would justly be by all called mad and
crazed.   And, pray, what difference is there
between such men and him who stores up
gold and silver coin, and knows not how to
use his gains, but fears to touch them just
as if tabooed ?

Suppose a man, long club in hand, should
ever watch stretched out at length by a large
heap of corn, and though the owner, and
though hungry, should not dare to touch a
single grain of it, but niggardly should rather
feed on bitter leaves; if he should drink
bad vinegar, although he keeps, stored up
within, a thousand, nay, three hundred thousand casks of Chian wine and old Falernian :
—nay, if a man, though eighty years of age,
should lie on horse-rugs, while his richly
broidered coverlets, the prey of moths and
worms, were rotting in his chests, no doubt
he would seem mad to very few, because
most men are just as mad. Old man, detested
by the gods, pray, do you guard this wealth
so that your son, or possibly a freedman
as your heir, may squander it ? or is it lest
you come to want ?   Nay ; for how small the
sum each day's expense will take from your
whole wealth, suppose you do begin to dress
your cabbages, and head, defiled with un-
combed scurf, with better oil ! When very
little is enough, why falsely swear, and filch,
and rob where'er you can ? Pray, are *you*

sane ? If you began to stone the public and the slaves you purchased, young and old would all alike cry out that you were mad : though as the common people think you're in your right mind when you kill [1]your wife by strangling, and your mother by the poisoned bowl.

[1] Avarice often ends in murder and matricide.

Perhaps you'll say, [2]Why not ? or say, you do not this at Argos, or that you don't kill your mother with a sword, as erst Orestes did when mad :—or do you think that he went mad when he had done the deed of blood, and was not driven mad by Furies ere he had imbrued the sharp sword in his mother's throat ? Moreover, from the time Orestes was supposed to be of unsound mind, he certainly did nought that one could find fault with : he ne'er attempted to attack his friend or sister with a sword : he but reviled them both by calling her a Fury, him whatever term his hypochondria suggested to his mind. [3]Opimius, who had so much, though really poor in gold and silver, stored within his house ; who drank " vin [4] ordinaire " on holidays, and mere spoilt wine and water poured into the cup with [5]common ladle upon working days, was seized once with a grievous fit of lethargy, so that his heir in joy and triumph skipped about among his coffers with his keys. But him his faithful doctor with prompt energy raised up like this :—he ordered that a table should be placed close by : the bags of money emptied

[2] Stertinius ironically supposes the following defence on the part of the man who kills wife or mother :—I who have only committed a crime of every-day occurrence at Rome, where murderers and poisoners dwell, I who *deliberately* killed my mother, am not to be compared to Orestes who slew his mother with the sword of violence, and at a place (Argos) where the crime was rare.

[3] Nothing more was known of Opimius.

[4] The Veientan wine was a poor wine of the claret kind.

[5] The most ordinary ware was from Campania.

on it, and that several should come to count
it out; so he restored the man, and said
besides these words :—" If you don't guard
your own, your greedy heir will soon make
off with all this wealth."

Not, surely, while I live?

Well, then, that you may live, rouse up,
do this.

What do you mean?

Your veins will make no blood to keep
you up thus weak, unless some strong support
should aid your failing appetite.

What, do you hesitate?

Come now, take this rice gruel.

At what cost?

Oh, very small!

Yes, but how much?

Well, sixpence.

O what misery! what matters whether I
come to my grave through some disease, or
through such theft and robbery?

[1] Who then is sound in mind?

All those who are not fools.

And what about the miser?

He's a madman and a fool.

And if a man be not a miser, is he therefore sound in mind?

Oh dear no, not at all.

[2] Why, Stoic, pray?

I'll tell you.

If one patient's stomach be all right, (suppose
that [3] Paget said so,) is he therefore strong, and
will he leave his bed of pain? The doctor

1 Stertinius again puts
questions, and answers
them himself.

2 He addresses himself
in the vocative.

3 Craterus was a distin-
guished physician em-
ployed by Atticus.

will say No, because he is attacked by pleurisy or Bright's disease. Suppose a man be nor forsworn nor mean : then let him slay a [1]pig in honour of his fav'ring household gods ; yet still suppose he hunt for place and be unscrupulous : then let him sail off to [2]Anticyra at once. For, pray, what matters it if you throw all you have into some fathomless abyss, or ne'er enjoy your gains ? 'Tis said that [3]Servius Oppidius, a man of wealth and good old family, gave at [4]Canusium to each of his two sons one of the farms he had, and dying, called the youths to his bedside, and said these words :—

When, Aulus, I had seen you carry carelessly your dice and nuts, give them away and play with them, and you, Tiberius, count them with anxious brow and bury them in holes, I then was terribly afraid, lest madness quite opposed in kind should influence you both : lest you, Tiberius, should imitate the [5]miser ; and you, Aulus, prove a prodigal.

So, then, entreated by your hearths and homes, take care, you Aulus, lest you squander, you Tiberius, lest you increase too much the sum your father thinks enough, and nature fixes limits to. Nay, more, that longing for renown may not excite your minds, I'll bind you by an oath : whichever of you two shall e'er be e'en the [6]lowest officer of state, let him be infamous and be accursed. You'd squander all your property in largesses of peas, and beans, and tares, so that with

[1] The usual monthly offering which the insane were not allowed to offer.
[2] To get hellebore to cure his madness.

[3] Servius Oppidius was a Roman knight.

[4] Canusium, now Canosa, was in Daunia.

[5] Nomentanus, Sat., I., i., 102.
    Cicuta, Sat., II., iii., 69.

[6] The offices of edile and prætor opened the avenues to the highest preferment.

flowing dress you might strut in the circus, and have statues made of bronze, stript of your land, you madman, and the personalty too, your father left, so that, forsooth, *you*, like the cunning fox that aped the noble lion once, might gain th' applause [1] Agrippa gains.

Soldier. Great Atreus' son, why do you say men must not wish to bury [2] Ajax now?

Agamemnon. I am a king.

Soldier. Then I, your humble subject, ask no more.

Agamemnon. Besides, my order is quite fair, and if I seem to any man unjust, I let him with impunity express his thoughts.

Soldier. Most mighty king, may heaven grant that after taking Troy you may lead home your fleet! Shall I then be allowed to ask and answer [3] questions as the lawyers and their clients do?

Agamemnon. Oh yes! ask on.

Soldier. Pray, why does Ajax, son of Telamon, the bravest man next to Achilles, famed for having saved the Greeks so oft, through whose strong arm so many youthful warriors fell on a foreign field, unburied rot, that Priam's people and their sovereign may exult o'er him denied a tomb?

Agamemnon. When mad, he slew a thousand sheep, declaring loudly that he killed renowned Ulysses, Menelaus, and myself.

Soldier. And, godless man, pray, are you sound in mind, when 'you in Aulis place your

[1] Agrippa, afterwards consul, gave a most magnificent theatrical entertainment to the people when he took the office of edile.

A supposed conversation here takes place between Agamemnon and one of his common soldiers, who probably really represents the Stoic philosopher.

[2] Ajax, son of Telamon, was a Greek hero who contended with Ulysses for the possession of the arms of Achilles, and when Ulysses obtained them he went mad and killed himself. The Greek tragedian Sophocles has a tragedy on the subject.

[3] He humorously compares the king to a barrister.

[4] Agamemnon offered his daughter Iphigenia in Aulis to appease (as he supposed) Diana's wrath, and gain a fair wind for his weather-bound ships.

child that should be dear, just like a calf
before the altars, and then sprinkle sacrificial
meal upon her head?

Agamemnon. What means all this?

Soldier. Why, how was Ajax mad when
with his sword he killed the sheep? He did
no violence unto [1] his wife or child, and though
he cursed the sons of Atreus much, he did
no harm to Teucer, nay, nor e'en Ulysses.

Agamemnon. True: but I appeased the
gods with blood on purpose to set free the
ships fast bound upon the hostile shore.

Soldier. But surely with your own blood,
madman.

Agamemnon. With my own, but I'm not
mad.[2]

He who shall form ideas that don't agree
with truth, and are confused through the
disturbance in men's minds that guilt will
cause, shall be esteemed deranged, nor will it
matter whether he go wrong through folly or
through rage. When Ajax slays the un_
offending sheep, as *you* say, he is mad:
and when you perpetrate a crime to win an
empty name are you right in your mind?
and is your heart free from all fault when
it's upheaved by passion's tide? Suppose
a man should take about a pretty lamb
in a sedan, get ready clothes for it, and
maids and gold, as for a daughter, call it
Rufa or Pusilla, and intend that it should be
the bride of some brave man, the magistrates [3]
would take all legal rights away from him,

[1] Tecmessa and Eurysaces.

[2] End of pretended dialogue.

[3] The prætor's duties corresponded very much with those of our own magistrates.

and the administration of his property would pass to his sane relatives. And-what of him who gives to death a daughter, like a brute and speechless lamb? Is he in his right mind? Ne'er say he is. So, then, where there is vicious folly, there the greatest madness dwells. The criminal will be distraught, and round the man whom specious fame has dazzled, the war-goddess who exults in blood will ring her thunders and send mad. Now come and join me in my censures upon luxury and prodigals, for well philosophy will [1] show that foolish spendthrifts are insane. The moment that some man received a [2] quarter of a million pounds his father left, he issued orders by his slaves that fishmongers and fruiterers, that poulterers, perfumers, and that godless mob that dwell in street Turarius, that sausage-sellers and buffoons, [3] cheesemongers, oilmen, and the dealers in both [4] fish and flesh, should on the morrow all come to his house.

What then took place? They came in crowds. The pander was the spokesman, and said this :—" Whatever I or each of these men have at home, think that your own, and send for it at once or else another day." Just listen to the kind young man's reply : " You sleep in hunting-leggings cased in the Lucanian snow, that I may dine upon a boar ; and you catch in your drag-net from the stormy sea, the fish I eat. I am not worthy,

[1] Vinco for evinco, to prove, is rarely found in prose.

[2] The talent was worth about £250.

[3] " Velabro :"—there was a marsh once at the bottom of the Aventine hill, where commodities were carried in barges (veho), and afterwards a street for cheesemongers, &c.

[4] "Omne macellum." The abstract is put for the concrete, the shambles for the dealers.

[5] He turns first to one, and then another tradesman.

idle as I am, to have all this: away with it!
Here, take eight thousand pounds, you take
the same, and you take thrice as much from
whose house runs your wife so oft when called
by me."

The actor Æsop's [1] son drew from [2] Metella's
ear a splendid pearl, and melted it in vinegar,
so that, forsooth, he might gulp down at
once eight thousand pounds; and how was
he less mad than if he had thrown that same
precious stone into a swiftly running stream,
or the great sewer of the town? The sons
of Quintus Arrius, those brothers of such
[3] wondrous worth, true twins in trifling and
rascality, and love of all that's bad, were wont
to buy up [4] nightingales at an enormous price.
And in which class should they be ranked?
Should they be marked with white, as sane,
or black, as though insane? Again, all
grown-up men, whom building baby-houses,
yoking mice to go-carts, or the game of odd
and even should delight, would be affected
with insanity. If now philosophy shall prove
that lawless love is still more childish e'en
than this, and that it makes no difference
if you should [5] play at working in the dust
as erst you played when three years old, or
suffer anxious grief through fondness for a
courtesan; pray would you do what [6] Polemon
reformed once did: would you give up those
implements of luxury, the shoe-socks, elbow
cushions, comforters, as he is said, though
drunk, to have by stealth torn off the

[1] Æsopus was a cele-brated tragic actor.

[2] Metella was divorced from Cæcilius Lentulus Spinther, on account of her amours with Dolabella.

[3] Ironical.

[4] The nightingale was prized as much as the modern "ortolan."

[5] Pretending seriously to build forts, and moats, and castles.

[6] An effeminate and luxurious Athenian youth.

1 They wore them on
both the head and neck.
2 Xenocrates. The
story is that as he was
reeling drunk through
Athens, he heard Xeno-
crates teaching philo-
sophy close by, and went
to mock him, but was ultimately convinced by his
arguments, and became
quite a reformed cha-
racter.

garlands from his neck, when he was repri-
manded by the sober words of the [2] philosopher?

When you reach fruit to children in a
pet, they will refuse. Suppose you say
to one, My [3] darling, take it: it says, No, I
won't, but wishes for it, if you give it not;
and, pray, what better is the
lover of a courtesan when shut
out from her house, who asks
himself if he shall go to or
shall keep away from that place
whither he quite meant to go
again, though not sent for; and
clings close to the door that he
pretends to hate? What, shall I
not approach, says he, now she,
unasked, invites? or should I rather think
of ending all my pain? She shut me out,
now calls me back; what?—should I go?
No, not if she implore me to. Hear now
a slave much wiser than his lord: "My
lord, a thing that knows no bounds or
plan will not be treated by restraint and
plan. In love there are these ills: war
first, then peace; and if a man should
try to fix upon some settled system for
himself all this that is well-nigh as fickle as
the weather, and rolls on as blind chance
guides, he would effect no more than if he
tried to act the madman with some plan and
bounds. What?—when you pluck the seeds
from [4] Picene apples, and feel joy if haply you
have hit the ceiling, are you sane? What?—

3 Among the
various meanings
of the diminutive,
reproach and an-
ger find no place;
while that of en-
dearment is com-
mon   enough.
With us the term
dog is not used
as an endearing
one, even in such
phrase as "Aha!
you young dog!"
although there is
no anger in such
phrase.

4 Lovers used to place
the moist seeds of fruit
between the first fingers
of each hand, and jerk
them out: if they hit the
ceiling, it was a lucky
omen.

when you utter [1] lisping lovers' words with aged mouth, how are you less mad than the man who builds the baby-house? [2] Add bloodshed to your foolish love, and with a sword stir up the fire. Pray, when but lately [3] Marius leapt off a rock, when he had struck down Hellas, was he frenzied, or will you acquit the man of madness, and condemn him on the charge of crime, affixing, as men do, to things, [4] terms nearly similar?

There was a [5] freedman's son, an old man, who, though sober,—in the morning,—would with hands washed with religious care, run up and down the streets, and [6] pray like this: "Save me alone, and 'tis not much I ask, save me alone from death; for surely it is easy for the gods." The man was sound enough in [7] ear and eye, although an owner of a slave like him would, when he tried to sell, not warrant him as sound in mind, unless he loved lawsuits. [8] Chrysippus classes all these superstitious men as well among the fruitful family of mad [9] Menenius. "O King of heaven, who dost bring upon men and remove from them dread pain and sickness," cries the mother of a child that has been ill for full five months, "if but the ague leave my son, [10] upon the morning of the day on which you may proclaim a fast, he shall stand naked in the Tiber's stream." Suppose some chance or doctor's aid have raised the sick child from his deadly peril, then the crazy mother will stick him upon the chilly river's bank,

1 The words are supposed to be struck back by the roof of the mouth, and the sound so weakened.
2 He now describes more heinous crimes as a worst phase of madness.
3 Nothing further was known of Marius and Hellas, whom he loved and killed.

4 Called "*homonyma*" in the Stoic teaching.
5 He now mentions the absurd superstition to which the lower orders were subject, and chooses the freedman's son to represent his class.
6 Men who were going to pray used to wash their hands.

7 *I. e.*, in body. Men selling slaves used the words "sanus (est) corpore et animo," he is sound in mind and body.
8 Chrysippus, a great Stoic philosopher.

9 Menenius was a madman of the day, known to every one.

10 A hint at the Jewish and Egyptian rites which began to be in favour at Rome, a prominent feature of which was bathing in rivers.

so bring the fever back, and prove his death,
affected, pray, in mind with what disease?
Of course with superstition.

This, then, the defence Stertinius, fit to
be called the [1] eighth wise man, gave me, his
friend, so that I should not with impunity
hereafter be attacked. The man who shall
have called me mad shall be called so himself as often, and shall learn to look at his
own faults that hang, as [2] Æsop says, upon his
back that he can't see.

Horace. O Stoic, after all your loss, may
you sell whatsoe'er you buy at more than
what you gave, [3] but on condition that you
tell me with what sort of folly you think
I am mad, since there's more kind than one?
For I think I am sound in mind.

Damasippus. What, when [4] Agave carried
in her hands the head of her unlucky son,
cut from the neck, did she herself think she
was mad?

Horace. Well, I admit that I'm a fool, let
me allow the truth, and even mad; but only
tell me clearly this: with what disease of
mind you think me labouring.

Damasippus. Then listen:—first you build;
—I mean you vie with [5] bigger men, although
you are from top to toe scarce two feet high,
and yet you laugh at [6] Turbo's mien and gait
when clad in arms, as too ambitious for so
small a frame: though how are you the less
ridiculous? Pray, is it right that you as well
should do whate'er your patron does, although

[1] As wise as the cele-
brated seven wise men.

[2] An allusion to Æsop's
fable, in which our
neighbours' faults are in
a bag in front, our own
in a bag behind.

[3] "Sic" implies this.

[4] Argument:— One of
the chief characteristics
of madness is the igno-
rance of the fact of being
mad.
Agave was the
mother of Pentheus, king
of Thebes, who denied
that Bacchus was a god,
and was therefore killed
by his mother, who was
a Bacchanal.

[5] We use the phrase
"bigger men" for more
wealthy.
He alludes to Horace's
Sabine villa, and, per-
haps, a portico he was
building.
[6] Turbo was a dwarf
and gladiator.

you are so different from him, that *you*, so low,
should vie with *him* so high in rank ?   The
young ones of a frog, when by the old frog
left, were trampled down by a calf's hoof, and
when one had escaped, it told the dam how
that a mighty beast had crushed its brother
frogs. Then asked the dam, How great was it?
and swelling out her skin, said, Surely it could
not have been so great as this ?   The young
frog answered, Half as great again. Well, surely
not so great ? then asked the dam.   Then
said the young one, You will never equal it,
although you burst yourself. This simile is
nearly suited to your case.   Then add your
scribbling verses, that is, feed the flames with
oil : for if a single man be sane who writes,
then you will be sane too. I mention not
your ¹dreadful temper.

¹ Especially   against
careless slaves.

Horace. There now, stop.

Damasippus. I speak not of your style of
living that exceeds your means.

Horace. Come, Damasippus, keep yourself
to your affairs alone.

Damasippus. Nor of your countless passionate amours.

Horace. O greater madman, prithee spare
one who is not so mad as you.

G

SATIRE IV.—BOOK II.

This Satire is written with the purpose of separating men who made gluttony their chief pleasure, from the true followers of Epicurus, one of which
Horace himself professed to be to some extent.

Catius Miltiades was a freedman of Catius Insuber, mentioned by Cicero,
Ep. ad Famulos, 15, 16, 1 ; a writer on the art of cookery, and the laughing-
stock of all Rome.   He professes to have received, as if from an oracular
shrine, some rules for gastronomy of paramount importance to life, and the
satire is increased by the fact that most of Catius's rules run counter to
received custom in eating and drinking.

"Catius" is not the
vocative, but implies—
"hic homo in quo Catium
agnoscere nobis vide-
mur." The ellipses are
"venit" and "tendit."
[1] The mnemonic art was
known to ancient orators
and philosophers.

Anytus, Meletus, and
Lycon, were the accusers
of Socrates. Anytus was
a leather-dresser, who
had long entertained a
personal enmity against
Socrates, because he
blamed his avarice in
depriving his sons of the
benefit of learning.

As Catius sees that
Horace does not want to
talk of anything else, he
is glad to tell him the
rules, and so to fix them
on his own memory.

Horace. And whence comes Catius, and
whither is he bound?

Catius. I cannot stay to talk ; desirous as
I am to fix connecting [1]memory links to some
new rules, so excellent that they surpass what
Socrates, Pythagoras, or learned Plato wrote.

Horace. I know I'm wrong for interrupting
you at so inopportune a time, but prithee,
with your wonted kindness pardon me ; and
you'll soon recollect the little you may now
forget, be that due to a natural or artificial
power, for you are wonderfully gifted in both
ways.

Catius. Nay, but my very purpose was to

recollect them all as matters of a subtle sort,
and told in subtle language too.

Horace. Pray tell me the man's name;
and tell me too if he be Roman or a foreigner.

Catius. The rules themselves I'll tell in
philosophic style from memory; their author's
name shall be suppressed :—

" Be sure and send to table [1] eggs of oval
shape, for they have better flavour and are
whiter than the round, and oval ones are
closer in consistence too, and keep unmixed
the [2] male yolk they contain. The broccoli
that grows in well-drained fields is sweeter
than that is that [3] grows round Rome ; nought
is more tasteless than the produce of a garden
that's not drained enough. Suppose a guest
has paid an unexpected visit at the close of
day, to save the fowl from proving tough
and disagreeable to taste, I will [4] instruct you
now to souse it in Falernian :—this wine
will make it tender. Truffles and mush-
rooms from meadows are the best ; one does
not well to trust in [5] other sorts. That man
will live a healthy life who after [6] lunch shall
eat ripe mulberries culled from the trees
before the mid-day sun. [7] Aufidius did wrong
to make the whet of honey mixed with
strong Falernian, since we should give the
hungry stomach nought but what is mild ;
with milder mead one would far better whet
the appetite. Suppose you want a pill, the
mussel common shell-fish, and low-growing
sorrel-plant, but mind, with some white Coan

[1] Eggs always appeared
with the first course of a
Roman dinner.

[2] Pliny, "Nat. Hist.,"
10, ? 74, " Feminam
edunt, quæ rotundiora
gignuntur, reliqua ma-
rem."

[3] Because of the many
fishponds and streams.

[4] "Doctus eris"= doce-
bere or " docetor a me."
" Malum responsare "
may be compared with
" perfidum ridere," or
" canere indoctum."

[5] *I.e*, such as grow in
marshes.

[6] The plural "prandia"
may imply the necessity
of the habit of doing so
daily.

[7] Aufidius was not
known, unless he was the
man who first took to
fattening peacocks.

wine. will set you right. The waxing moon
fills out the slimy shell-fish with both juice
and size, but few seas are productive of the
richest kinds. The giant mussel from the
Lucrine lake excels the Baian purple fish ;
the oyster at [1]Circeii grows, sea-urchins near
Misenum's cape ; Tarentum in wide-opening
scallops prides itself.

"And yet, not any one you please should
rashly arrogate skill in the *bon vivant's* art ere
he has tested well the subtle [2]philosophic sys
tem flavours have. Nor is't enough to be the
first to bear off from some dear fishmonger's
shop the fish he has, although you do not know
which fish sauce suits, and which, when fried,
the sated [3]guest will soon begin again to eat.
The boar of Umbria fed too upon the holm
oak's mast, bends by its weight the large
round dishes of the man who shuns insipid
meat ; for the Laurentine boar is bad to eat,
coarse-fed on sedge and reeds. The vine
don't always give us [4]kids well fit for food.
The connoisseur will try to find the shoulders
of the hare that ever is with young. Ere my
nice taste came in, none studied and found
out the qualities of fish and fowl and season
for their use. The skill of some produces
nothing but new kinds of sweets. By no
means is't enough to give one's whole attention to one point, as though a man should
carefully provide for this alone, I mean that
his wine should be good, though careless
with what sort of oil he dress his fish. If

[1] Circeii, a town of Latium. Misenum, a town
in Campania.

[2] "Ratio," a philosophical system, is purposely
used because Catius
thought gastronomy and
philosophy nearly syno-
nymous.

[3] The guests used to
lean on the left elbow,
and raise themselves
slightly as they dined,
and when sated used
to recline on the cushion
or pillow.

[4] Because of the bitter-
ness of its leaves : kids
that feed in the lawns
and groves are the best.

you shall place the [1]Massic wine beneath clear
skies, whatever thickness there may be, will
be refined by the night breezes, and the
bouquet that affects the head will leave the
wine : but it is spoilt, and loses its full flavour
if strained through a linen bag. The connoisseur who mingles the [2]Surrentine wine
with dregs of the Falernian, successfully collects the sediment with pigeon's egg; for then
the yolk sinks down, and rolls with it all
foreign substances. Restore the sated zest
for drink by fried prawns, and by Libyan
snails, for [3]salad rises on the stomach that is
bilious after wine; it rather needs to be
refreshed and roused by ham or by smoked
sausages; nay, it would e'en prefer all highly
seasoned [4]dishes that are brought when
steaming hot from filthy eating-house. 'Tis
well worth while to thoroughly find out the
qualities of sauce, both simple and compound.
The [5]simple kind is made up of sweet olive
oil, and 'twill be suitable to mingle this with
rich new wine and tunny brine; that same
which the Byzantine salting-jars are strongly
flavoured with. When this has been well
blended with chopped herbs, and boiled, and
stood to cool, and has been sprinkled with
the saffron of Cilicia, [6]complete the compound
sauce with oil the berry of [7]Venafran olives
yields.

"The Picene apples are inferior to those
of Tibur in their juice, and this I tell you,
for they are superior in look. The grape

[1] The Massic was a rich Campanian wine.

[2] Surrentum, now Sorrento, a maritime town of Campania.

[3] Really lettuce. The Romans used to eat salad with vinegar to diminish the power of the wine at the end of their dinner; but remember that the satire often consists in Catius's disregard of acknowledged custom.

[4] So Suetonius tells us that Vitellius used to do.

[5] The simple sauce is olive oil, new wine, and tunny brine. The compound is the above with the additions mentioned.

[6] Literally, "add besides," the future being used imperatively.

[7] Venafrum was a city in the extreme north of Campania.

¹ Nothing is known of the Venucula. The Alban grape was a common kind.

they call ¹'Venucula' will do for storing up in jars; the Alban you would more correctly dry in smoke. 'Tis found that I first placed by every guest in clean small plates this Alban grape and apples, lees of wine and caviar, white pepper and black salt, well dusted o'er it with a sieve. It is a dreadful error to spend five-and-twenty pounds in the fish mart, and then to cramp the fish so used to room on much too small a dish. It causes great disgust, suppose a slave with hands made greasy as he licks the soup or sauce he stealthily secretes, has touched a cup; and so it does, suppose unpleasant sediment

² Literally, how great? understanding a reply denying the extent of the cost.

cling to the oft-used bowl for wine. ²How small the sum one has to spend on besoms, dinner-napkins, and sawdust! and yet, if they be not provided, 'tis a flagrant instance of bad taste. Is't possible that you sweep tesse-

³ They had floors of brick, four-cornered pieces of white and coloured marble, of real mosaic, and also of small diamond-shaped pieces or squares of marble. Their brooms were made of palms.

lated floors ³with dirty brooms, and cover purple ottomans with unwashed coverlets of chintz? forgetting that, in such proportion as these minor things cost much less time and money to provide, their absence is more fairly censured than the lack of luxuries that nobles' boards alone can have the fortune to possess."

Horace. Most learned Catius, appealed to by our friendship and the gods, remember that whithersoe'er you go, you take me to attend these lectures on good living; for however accurately you may tell them all from memory, you will not as the oracle's

mouthpiece give such delight as the philosopher himself could give.   Besides, there
is the man's own look and mien, which, blest
in having seen, you don't think much about,
because you've had the lucky chance, but I
feel [1] quite a strong desire to gain the power
of visiting those far-off sources of philosophy,
and getting golden rules for living happily.

[1] A parody of Lucretius, i., 926, "Juvat integros accedere fontes, atque haurire."

SATIRE V.—BOOK II.

This Satire contains, in a pretended dialogue between Ulysses and Teiresias, a blind soothsayer of Thebes, an invective against fortune-hunters, and a description of their various artifices.

----

[1] That is, his sufferings and safe return.

[2] By shipwreck and the suitors.

Ulysses. Teiresias, besides what you've [1]already told, at my request say by what arts and means I can regain the wealth [2] I've lost? Why do you laugh?

Teiresias. What! is it possible that one so shrewd as you is not content with getting back to Ithaca, and seeing once again your hearth and home?

Ulysses. O thou who ever tellest truth to all, thou seest how stript and destitute I come back home according to thy prophecy, and by the suitors all my best wines have been plundered and my cattle killed; and yet both birth and merit are more worthless than seaweed unless accompanied by means.

Teiresias. Well, since, to speak plain truth, you shrink from poverty, just hear a brief description of the means by which you may grow rich. Suppose a thrush, or some espe-

cial gift be made you, let it speedily be sent
to that man's house, where gleams the splendour of a handsome fortune, if but owned by
an old man. See that the rich man, who's more
worthy of your worship than the [1] household
gods, taste ere the household gods, your mellow fruit, and all the produce of your well-
tilled farm ; and though the man shall be
forsworn, ignoble, stained with brother's blood,
a slave who ran away, [2] still don't refuse to
walk upon the left side as a guard if he
should ask you to.

Ulysses. What! I walk side by side to
guard some dirty slave ! I ne'er demeaned
myself like that at Troy, aye rivalling great
Ajax or Achilles there.

Teiresias. Then you'll be poor.

Ulysses. [3] Well, I will bid my stout heart
bear this great disgrace, for erst I bore still
greater ills. Now, prophet, tell at once
whence I can quickly [4] gain this wealth, and
heaps of gold.

Teiresias. Indeed, I've told you, and now
tell again ; where'er you can, by cunning try
to get at old men's wills, and don't, if one or
two shrewd fishes have escaped the cunning
angler after nibbling off the bait, surrender
hopes because thus tricked, or give up your
profession. If a case of great or small
importance shall at any time be tried in
court ; whichever of the litigants shall be
both rich and childless, though a rascal,
though aggressive and unscrupulous he sum-

[1] Firstfruits of the produce were offered to the
household gods.

[2] He might request the
man to attend him when
he went out in public.
The left side was con-
sidered weaker, and more
exposed to attack; hence
the expression " tegere
latus."

[3] A parody of line 18 in
Odyssey, *v.*

[4] For the transitive use
of " ruo" confer Plautus,
" Rudens," 2, 6, 58, " Ibi
me corruere posse aiebas'
divitias ;" Virgil, Georgic
i., 105, " cumulosque
ruit male pinguis are-
næ."

mon into court a better man, go plead for him; despise the citizen who has a better reputation and more justice on his side, if he shall have a son or a prolific wife at home. Say, "Quintus," for example, or say, "Publius," —for ears refined do like a handle to the name, your merit has made me your friend. I know the law's uncertainty; I can plead cases; sooner shall whoe'er you please gouge out my eyes than mock or cheat you of a [1]penny piece :—my object this, that you lose nought, nor be laughed at. Bid him go home, and take care of his precious self; become his advocate yourself; [2]persist and persevere, though [3]Alpine bards shall make the glowing dog-star cleave the lifeless statues, or well filled with greasy tripe, they shall describe the wintry Alps bespattered o'er with hoary snow. Some one will with his elbow nudge a bystander, and say, Don't you observe his unremitting care, devotion to his friends, and active zeal? Then shoals of tunnies will swim in; your fishponds will increase. [4]Then, too, if any one shall have a weakly son whom he has both acknowledged and is bringing up in the possession of a splendid property; lest a too plain attention to a man who has no [5]wife should tell the world your views; by sedulous attention gently steal into the hope of being left a legacy; so that your name may be inscribed as next heir in his will; and that, if any lucky accident have proved the young man's death, you then may step

[1] Literally, "of a rotten nut," a proverbial expression for a trifle.

[2] The roughness of the words, "Persta atque obdura," themselves imply the pertinacity.
[3] Vide Sat., I., x., 36. Marcus Furius Bibaculus. Whether he give an absurd description of summer or winter; simply, whether it be midsummer or midwinter.

[4] Fathers who were willing to support their children used to take them up upon their knees, when lying on the ground; if not, they were exposed. Confer Virgil, "Æn." 9, 204, "Non ita me genitor . . . sublatum erudiit."
[5] "Cœlebs" here implies that the man either had lost his wife, or was divorced from her.

into his shoes. This venture seldom fails. Be
sure that you refuse, and put away from you
the documents of any man who shall have
handed you his will to read; but yet in such a
way, that by a side look you may quickly
catch the meaning of the second clause on
the first page. With swift glance read and
see if you alone be heir, or co-heir with some
more. Ofttimes a man who has turned clerk
instead of member of the [1] "Board of Five
Commissioners," will cheat the [2] eager raven,
and the fortune-hunter, like Nasica, will be
laughed at by [3] Coranus.

Ulysses. Are you mad, or do you mock
me purposely, by prophesying riddles such
as these?

Teiresias. Son of Laertes, whatsoever I
shall say [4] will either happen or will not, just
as I say; for surely great Apollo grants me
divination's art.

Ulysses. Yet still pray tell me, if you may,
the meaning of your words.

Teiresias. What time a [5] youthful warrior,
the dread of Parthians, a scion sprung from
great Æneas' stock, shall be renowned by
sea and land, the [6] stately daughter of Nasica,
who so hates to pay his debts in [7] full, will
marry brave Coranus, who will act like this
when son-in-law; he'll to [8] Nasica give his will
and say, " Pray read;" but he will oft refuse,
and then at last will take it, and will find no
legacy, but [9] ruin for himself and friends.
This further rule I give. Suppose, as possibly

[1] The quinqueviri were a board of five for any official function of an ordinary nature.
[2] As happened lately is implied.
[3] A wealthy man at Rome.

[4] Horace may purposely make the phrase ambiguous to show a disbelief in the art of soothsaying.

[5] A "juvenis" might be forty years of age, and have established a reputation as a warrior. Augustus is meant.

[6] The epithets "stately" and "brave" are both ironical.
[7] Solidum means the entire sum he had borrowed from Coranus.
[8] Literally, father-in-law.

[9] "Plorare," the *double entendre*, is to weep, and to go and be hanged.

may be, a mistress, or a freedman should be
ruling some old dotard; join their partner-
ship yourself, praise them, that when away you
also may be praised; this, too, does good,
[1] although 'tis far the [1] best to storm the citadel
itself. [2] Suppose some man insanely write
bad verses; praise them well.   Suppose, too,
he be fond of women; see that he don't
have to ask you; but unasked and readily
give your chaste wife to him—so much to be
preferred.

Ulysses. Do you think that can be?   Will
one so modest, so discreet a woman, whom
the suitors could not turn from virtue's paths,
be able to be thus seduced?

Teiresias. Yes, for the youthful band that
courted her came, very sparing in rich gifts,
bent not so much on love as on the cup-
board's stores.   Your wife is chaste thus far,
but if she once have learnt an aged lover's
ways, and shared the gain with you, she never
will be kept from it, no more than dogs from
a fat skin.   In my old age this circumstance
occurred, which I will tell you of. [3] At Thebes
a shameless woman was thus carried to her
grave according to her will; her heir bore
on his naked shoulders her dead body plen-
tifully greased with oil, to see, no doubt, if
she could [4] slip away from him when dead;
and this, I think, because he had stuck too
close to her while alive.   Be wary in your first
approach; don't be remiss, nor yet attentive
to excess.   A prater will disgust a peevish

[1] To take the old man by storm, as it were, through flattery.
[2] The student should observe the free use of tenses and moods for a supposed case in Horace.
[3] A story probably taken from some farce or popular jest.
[4] In which case the heir would have lost his inheritance.

and morose old man. You should not even
hold your peace unasked. Act like the [1]slave
in comedy; stand with your head bent [2]stiffly
down, like one most terribly afraid. Approach
him with complacent care; advise him, if the
air blow fresh, to cautiously wrap up his precious head; relieve him of the crowd by
thrusting them aside; lend an attentive ear
whene'er he cares to talk. Suppose he loves
incessant praise; then ply him, till with hands
upraised to heaven he cry, O stay! enough!
and swell his rising pride with fulsome flattery.
When he has freed you from [3]protracted slavery
and care, and wide awake, you shall have
heard this,— "Let Ulysses have a fourth of the
estate;" say now and then, "So! is my comrade Dama now no more? [4]Whence shall I
find a friend so brave, so true?" and if you
can a little, weep; you [5]may well hide your
face, that will betray the joy you feel.
Erect his tomb, that's left to your decision,
with no niggard [6]hand; the neighbours would
commend a splendidly appointed funeral.
Suppose, as possibly may be, one of your
fellow-heirs, now growing old, shall have a
nasty cough, then say to him, if he should
care to buy a farm or house belonging to
your share, "I sell it [7]you for anything you
like." But mighty Proserpine drags me away.
Long life, farewell.

[1] Davus was a general name for slaves.

[2] "Obstipus" implies the rigidity of a stake or block.

[3] That is, by his death.

[4] Confer Sat. ii., 7, 116. There is an ellipsis of "petam" or "parabo." "Illacrimare" is the imperative of the deponent verb.
[5] Est = licet.

[6] I. e., let it be made of marble, and carved in basso-relievo, and have an inscription.

[7] "Nummus" and "nummus sestertius" were used to express trifling value. Confer Cic. pro Rab., Post., 17, 45.
Proserpine is often described as sending and removing spirits. Confer Homer, "Odyss.," ii., 226, 632, et seq.

SATIRE VI.—BOOK II.

Horace had especially desired to be able to escape all business and care that prevented him from living as a philosopher should live, and, although he was partly able now to do so through his patron's gift, the Sabine villa and farm, yet he could not do so as often as he wished. This Satire, then, is written in praise of a country life, and against those who were either jealous of him, or incessantly importuned him to further their pretensions to poetic merit.

ONE of my wishes once was this: a plot of land of ordinary size, and that there should be there a garden, and a stream of running water, and a little wood besides.

The gods have been more generous and kind e'en than I wished. 'Tis well. I ask for nothing further, [1] Mercury, than that you make these blessings mine for life.

Since I have not increased my means by perjury or forging wills, and am not likely to diminish them by luxury, or idleness and want of care: since I don't utter foolish prayers like these : " O if that little nook would join my farm, which now so spoils its form ! O that some lucky chance would show to me a

[1] Maia's son. Maia was the mother of Mercury, and Jupiter the father. Mercury presided over open gains and business, Hercules over secret treasures : see last line of the page.

money-jar as erst to him who, with the trea-
sure he had found, bought the same field he
ploughed before as a day labourer, grown rich
by Hercules' kind help !"—since what I have
delights me grateful for the same, this is the
prayer I now address to you :—[1] weigh down
with fat the cattle for myself, their owner,
and all else I have with produce, but do
not weigh down my genius, and as you're
wont, still be my strongest guard.

> [1] The word "pingue" means heavy with fat as applied to the cattle, and heavy and coarse as applied to the mind. Cetera = fields, meadows, crops.

Well, then, when I've withdrawn me from
the city to my cottage on the hills, what
[2]better theme could I then find for these my
satires and plain style ?

> [2] I. e:, than the country.

There, nor the placeman's baneful race for
pow'r, nor the dispiriting sirocco, nor the
autumn's pestilence that brings the [3]cruel
death-goddess such gain, destroys my peace.

O thou whom we invoke at morn, or Janus,
if thou dost prefer the name, through whom
man regulates the day's first toils life's business brings, for so the gods have willed, be
thou my theme's exordium.   At Rome you
hurry me to bail some one.   You say, Come,
up, away, lest some one should oblige by some
such courtesy before yourself.   Although north
winds blow fiercely o'er the earth, or winter
[4]slowly drags along the snowy days upon
their narrowed course, you still must go.

> [3] An Italian goddess of funerals, called Libitina, in whose temple was deposited for every funeral a piece of money, and in which all that belonged to the appointment of funerals was kept.

Then after that, when I have uttered
clearly and distinctly [5]words that may bring
me some harm, I have to struggle in the
crowd, and roughly jostle loiterers.   With

> [4] The sun has much less distance to go round in the winter, and the day is supposed to be influenced by the sluggish cold and torpidity the season brings.
> [5] Some legal phrase, such as the phrase from Seneca, "Quocunque audivi, certa claraque affero." He would lose the bail if the defendant did not appear, as might be.

angry curses some one shamelessly assails
me thus :—What want you, madman ? What
are you about ?   You'd knock down all that
barred your way, if you were speeding back
to see your patron, thinking of nought else
but him.   This is delightful, this is sweet as
honey, I'll confess.   But still the moment
that I've reached the gloomy Esquiline,
then [1]endless business that does not belong to me annoys and hems me in, and
thus I think :—[2] " You know that Roscius
implored you to appear to give him evidence
to-morrow at the [3]prætor's court ere seven
o'clock.   And, Quintus, the official clerks
prayed that you would remember to return
to-day to see about a matter of unlooked-for
and great public interest."   And, asks another,
take care that your patron stamp these [4]docu-
ments with his own seal.   Suppose you say,
" I'll try ; "   " You can," he answers, " if you
will," and importunes you.

It is nearly eight years now since first
Mæcenas looked on me as one of his own
friends, but only thus far as to think me
one whom he might care to take up in
his carriage when he went upon a journey,
and to whom he would entrust such trifles
as,—" How goes the time ? " or,—[5]" Can the
gladiator Syrus, think you, beat Gallina ? " or,
—" The chill November morning air takes
hold of those who do not wrap up well,"—
and such remarks as well may be committed
to the ears of those who talk of all they

[1] Centum = sexcenta, 600, the usual indefinite number with the Romans.

[2] He says this to himself.

[3] The Puteal was so called from its resemblance to the mouth of a well. It was built by Scribonius Libo.
Roscius was a pleader. After the battle of Philippi, Horace was private secretary to a quæstor, but he is supposed to have sold the office soon after.
[4] Perhaps a state letter of recommendation, which the Emperor, sometimes by his deputy (Mæcenas), signed.

[5] As once the question, " Will Heenan beat Tom Sayers ? "
The epithet Thrax or Threx means gladiator.

hear. Through all this time, from day to day
(to use the people's words), [1] our friend was
more exposed to jealousy. If he, together
with Mæcenas, had gone to the theatre, or
played at tennis with him on the plain of
Mars, all cried alike, O fortune's favourite!
Suppose some sinister report spread from the
[2]Rostra through the streets, all those who
meet me question thus:—Dear sir, I ask
you, for you must know, since you have the
ear of government,—Have you heard aught
about the [3]Dacians? Not I, indeed, say I.
Then they reply, Ah! how satirical you
always like to be! When I rejoin: May
heaven destroy me if I've heard a word;—
another says, How now? Pray does Augustus
mean to give his army land he promised them
in [4]Sicily or Italy? Then if I vow that I don't
know at all, all wonder at me as a man of
quite unique reserve that none can penetrate.
And so unhappily I lose the day, and oft
repeat these longing words,—" Dear country,
when shall I see thee again?" When shall
I be allowed to drink in sweet forgetfulness
all life's cares, sometimes by reading ancient
lore, sometimes by the " siesta," by the
" *dolce far niente*" too? When [5]will that
common bean that old Pythagoras believed
akin to him, and with it, cabbages well
dressed with greasy bacon, be served up for
me? Ah me! those evenings and those
dinners, fit for gods, at which my friends and
I eat in the presence of my own hearth's

H

[1] Noster is humorously
put for " ego." Confer
German, unser Mann;
the common people
called him this.

[2] The " Rostra " was a
stage for speakers, and
the space around it, in
the Forum, was adorned
with the beaks of con-
quered ships.

[3] War was going on
with these allies of Mark
Antony.

[4] Sicily is called " Tri-
quetra " from its trian-
gular shape. The divi-
sion of land referred to
is that that took place in
the middle of the winter
after the battle of Actium,
when the Emperor went
to Brundusium to quell
a mutiny of the veterans.

[5] This is pleasantly
ironical, intimating that
although people gene-
rally might despise such
plain food, yet Pytha-
goras, the great philoso-
pher, did not. There is
also an allusion to the
idea of Pythagoras
which supposed the vital
principle of his father or
some other relative to be
in a bean.

gods, and feed my merry pert slaves born
at home with dishes that we've feasted first
upon.   Each guest, just as he fancies, freed
from foolish laws, drains glasses of unequal
size, though one with stronger head takes
potent draughts, another sooner feels the
gladdening influence with weaker ones.   And
so it is that conversation is struck up, but
not about our neighbours' country seats or
houses, nor about the dancing of Rome's
[1]ballet-masters, but we then discuss what
much more nearly interests ourselves, and
what to know not brings us harm : we learn
by argument if men be happy through their
wealth or virtues, what attracts us to form
friendships,—interest, or principle ; what is
the nature of the abstract good, and what
the greatest good ?   Meantime my neighbour
Cervius will tell us witty nursery tales, well
suited to the point.   For if one ignorantly
praise the [2]miser's wealth that breeds anxiety,
he thus begins :—Now once upon a time 'tis
said a country mouse did entertain a city
mouse in its poor hole, a well-known guest a
well-known friend ; industrious and thrifty of
its stores, the country mouse :—but still in
such a way as to sometimes relax its anxious
mind for hospitality.   In brief, it neither
grudged the stored chick-pea, nor oat with
its long husk ; it carried in its mouth a raisin
and half-eaten bits of bacon, and then gave
them to its guest because it wished, by
varying the food, to conquer the disgust

[1] *I.e.*, Lepos, a celebrated dancer of the day, in favour with the Emperor.

[2] Nothing more is known of him or Arellius, but that he was an avaricious neighbour.

showed by the guest, who scarcely touched
each tit-bit with its haughty teeth, although
the host himself ate spelt and tares, and left
his guest the richer food. At length the
[1]city mouse spoke thus: said he, "Dear
friend, what joy is it to live so hard a life
upon the mountain ridge with its rough grove
of trees ? Can you prefer a town's society to
the wild woods ? Come, start, take my advice, and go with me, since creatures [2]earthly
all possess by lot but transitory lives, and since
there's no escape from death for great or
small :—because of this, I say, dear friend,
while you've the chance, live happy in a
pleasant state, and well remember how short-
lived you are." When words like these prevailed upon the country mouse, he nimbly
leapt forth from his hole, and then they both
began their purposed way, because they
wished to steal beneath the city walls by
night. And now, as [3]sings the epic bard,
"the veil of midnight hid the sky"—when
both set foot in some rich noble's home,
where fabrics dyed with scarlet threw a brilliant lustre over ottomans of ivory, and many
courses were left from a banquet held the
day before, and were in baskets piled up
near to them. Well, when the host had
made the country mouse recline at length
upon a purple rug, he ran about like girt-
up slave, brought in the [4]courses one by one,
as servants would and did the waiting well,
first tasting every dish he brought. The

[1] The city mouse re-
presents the Epicurean
philosopher.

[2] Perhaps a parody o
Euripides, Alcestis, 782,
and following few lines.

[3] A parody of an epic
line, as in Sat., l., v., 9.

[4] "Continuat" — im-
plies that he took care
there should be no break
in the service.

country mouse reclining there, exulted in his change of lot, and played the boon companion in his happy state; when suddenly a dreadful creaking of some folding-doors made both leap from their seats; in fear they rushed through all the chamber, and half dead with fright made more hot haste, directly that the house with its high roofs rang with the mastiffs' barks.

Of course the country mouse said this after they had found shelter in the usual crevice into which the city mouse retired in such emergency.

Then said the country mouse, I want not life like this, and fare thee well; my wood and hole, safe as it is from treacherous surprise, will solace me with humble tares for food.

SATIRE VII.—BOOK II.

In this Satire Horace, by the mouth of a slave taking advantage of the licence allowed at the Saturnalia—a feast of three days' duration, from the 17th to the 20th of December, to commemorate the good old times when all men were nearly equal—represents the foolish Stoic philosophy of Crispinus. He also wittily describes the character and disposition of slaves. He probably also aims a side-blow at the habit then so universal in Rome as almost to include slaves, of trying to get a smattering of philosophy.

He also shows that men who are devoted to pleasure or luxury, carried away by excessive eagerness in any pursuit, misers or flatterers, are just as much slaves as those who are called so by name.

Davus. [1] I've been long waiting for an opportunity, and though I wish so much to say a few words to you, feel afraid because I am a slave.

Horace Is't Davus?

Davus. Yes, 'tis Davus, and he is a servant faithful to his master, honest, too, as far as is required,—that is, [2] he's not too good to live.

Horace. Come, then, since so our ancestors decided, take the licence that December gives, speak on.

Davus. Some men do glory in their vices with consistency, and have a settled plan ;

[1] Though Davus knows he has liberty to address Horace, he hesitates to make free use at first of a truce that so rarely occurred in the perpetual war between master and slave.

[2] Like our proverbial phrase, "That child is too good to live."

but many more are [1]changeable, adopting now what's right, now guilty of what's wrong.

One [2]Priscus, often seen to have three rings upon his fingers, often none at all, lived so irregularly that one moment he would wear

the [3]senator's broad stripe, another that the knights all wear. He'd leave some princely mansion where he dwelt, and suddenly hide in some hut from which a freedman of the better class could scarcely come out decently. He'd choose to live now as a rake at Rome, anon as a philosopher at Athens, born sub-

jected to the ire of all the [4]gods of change there are.

Again, a certain [5]dandy hired for daily wage, and kept a man to take the dice up from the board for him, and throw them in the box, when now the gout, he so deserved, struck all his finger-joints, and in proportion as he kept consistently to that same vice he was less wretched and less culpable than he, who,

[6]like a sailor, works with now too taut, and now too slack a rope.

Horace. You [7]rascal, will you not at once tell me the bearing of all this stale trash?

Davus. It bears upon yourself, I say.

Horace. How so, you scoundrel?

Davus. Why, you praise the happiness and character the people of old times possessed, and yet, if any god were to compel you to adopt their life, you would persistently refuse, because you either do not really think that what you talk so loud about is better, or because you are but a weak champion of right, and are entangled in the wrong, and vainly wish to draw your feet out of the moral mire. At Rome you long for country life; when in the country, fickle as you are, you praise up to the skies the town you've left. Suppose, as possibly may be, you are not asked to dine with any one, you laud your humble food so free from care, and just as though you went to see men, like a criminal to gaol, you vow you're fortunate, and gratify your self-love with the [1] thought that you have not to go and drink at some friend's house. But if your patron have, quite as an after-thought, invited you to come and see him at nightfall, with loud shouts then you cry—" Is no one going to quickly bring the [2] lantern-oil? Does any one attend?"—and rush about, as though you fled from foe. The [3] parasites and Mulvius curse you in language that I can't repeat, and go away. And just suppose [4] he says, " Well, I admit that I am fickle and attracted by my appetite, I sniff in gratefully the savour of good cheer; I'm weak, nay, if you wish, a glutton too." What?—would you, though you be the [5] same as I am, and perhaps still worse, aggressively assail me just as if you were superior, and hide your own defect though similar in specious words?

How if you're found to be more foolish than myself, though bought for [6] twenty pounds? Don't try to frighten me with that fierce look; restrain your hand and rage while

[1] Whereas he really gladly accepted all invitations.

[2] The Romans used small hand lanterns at night.

[3] Thus cheated of the dinner they expected.

[4] Mulvius, as the spokesman for the others.

[5] You pretend to be a friend of Mæcenas, whereas you really are his parasite, as I am yours.

[6] The drachma was equal to a denarius, and about tenpence in value.

I declare the truths Crispinus' porter told to me. You others' wives attract, a common woman slaves like me, which of us two the more [1]deserves the cross? When my fierce passions urge me on, whoe'er she be that gratified my wish, though wanton she may be, she still can let me go without dishonour or anxiety lest some more rich or handsome lover should possess her next. And are not you what you pretend to be, when, throwing off the tokens of your rank, the knightly ring and Roman dress, you leave your house like a base slave instead of an [2]appointed judge, while a coarse hooded cloak conceals your perfumed head? In fear you're introduced, and tremble in your inmost soul, while lust and terror hold alternate sway. What matters it whether you go, as gladiators go, sworn to submit to branding, scourging, or the stroke of sword, or—shut up in some filthy chest in which the maid, accomplice in her mistress' guilt, has packed you,—you're obliged to crouch with head and knees together drawn? Has not [3]the husband of the erring lady every right to kill you both? Indeed, a better right to kill him who seduced the wife. Nay, she don't [4]change her dress or leave her home, and is but passive in her guilt. Although the woman dreads you, and don't trust your promises of love, you still will wittingly put on the slavish yoke, and trust this raging master, lust, with all your property, your life, your person and repute. Perhaps you have

[1] Slaves were often crucified.

[2] Disguised in a coarse cloak with a hood, such as slaves wore. The 360 judices selecti were picked from the senators and knights and tribunes to decide capital offences.

[3] The husband could kill adulterers before the passing of the Julian law.

[4] As you do.

escaped ; no doubt you will then feel afraid,
and, through experience, will take more care?
Not you ; [1]you'll try to find another chance
of feeling the same fear, of running the same
risk of death, O you, so oft a slave ! Why,
what brute beast, when once it has burst
from its chains, and got away, perversely gets
itself chained up again?

You say, I am not an adulterer? And, by
my faith, I am no thief when prudently I
[2]pass by silver cups ; but take away the risk,
and when the barrier's withdrawn, my nature
will soon lawlessly display itself. Are *you*
my master, *you* subjected to such varied and
such powerful sway of circumstance and man,
you whom the [3]manumitting rod, though
thrice or four times it should strike you,
ne'er could free from miserable fears? Add
this besides, that bears upon the case no less
than what I've said, (for whether he who
executes another slave's commands be called
an under slave, as you are wont to say, or
fellow-slave as we declare), pray what am I
to you? In truth you, who rule me, are
but [4]another's wretched slave, and like the
wooden [5]puppet you are moved by strings
another pulls.

Horace. Who then is free?

Davus. Why, the philsopher who rules himself, whom neither poverty, nor death, nor
chains alarm, who can courageously check
his desires, and [6]fairly estimate the world's distinctions, one dependent on himself alone, as

[1] Davus here gets carried away by his words, and forgets that he was only telling what Crispinus's porter told him, and becomes more personal.

[2] *I.e.*, don't steal them.

[3] In the manumission of slaves the owner and a friend (assertor in liber-tatem), together with the slave, appeared before the city prætor ; the owner struck the slave with a rod, to intimate his own-ership, the friend pro-nounced this formula, "I declare that this man is free according to the Roman law." The own-er, as if yielding to com-pulsion, then said, "I am willing that this man should be free; let him be free, and go whither you will."

[4] *I.e*, a fellow-slave.

[5] Modern "marion-ettes."

[6] Like Cicero's "hu-manarum rerum con-temptio," which should not be translated "con-tempt for," as it means a proper or not undue ap-preciation of anything.

1 The ancients thought
a sphere the most per-
fect shape.
perfect as a [1]sphere, so that no outward matter can rest on the polished surface, one whom fortune aye attacks with crippled might. Pray can you in all this find aught that suits your case? Again, some woman asks you

[2] Really, £1,218 15s.

for [2]twelve hundred pounds or more, annoys you, drives you from the door, and drenches you completely with cold water, then she calls you back again; come, free your neck from this disgraceful yoke; come, say, I'm free! yes, free! You cannot; for a harsh taskmaster rules your mind, and plies you with the spur, though weary, and constrains you e'en against your will. Pray, how are you, you madman, when you gaze with

[3] Pausias was a cele-
brated child's portrait-
painter of Sicyon, B.C.
370.

rapt attention on a picture [3]Pausias once painted, less in fault than I am when I gaze

[4] Fulvus, Rutuba, and
Pacideianus, were gla-
diators.

with admiration at the battles of our [4]gladiators with their legs thrown well in front, de-

[5] I.e., however roughly
done.

picted in red [5]chalk or even charcoal, when, though they actually fought, the combatants move to and fro their weapons, and give thrusts and parry them? In such a case the slave is called a rascal and a loiterer; but you, a critic shrewd,—a connoisseur of ancient works of art. I'm thought a worthless wretch when I'm attracted by a smoking sacrificial cake; and does *your* wondrous virtue, *your* high soul resist the pleasures a rich banquet gives? Why does this fondness for good living work more harm to me than you? Because I get a beating. And pray how do you deserve less punishment in trying to obtain rich dainties that cannot be gained at little cost? And certainly the banquet's joys, indulged in to excess, pall on the taste; and the unsteady foot will not bear the distempered frame. What?—does the slave do wrong who at nightfall exchanges for a bunch of grapes a ¹scraper from the baths? and does not he act like a slave who sells estates to gratify his gluttony? Then, too, you cannot be consistent for a moment, or arrange your leisure as you should; you shun your thoughts, you're like a runaway and vagabond, now trying to remove your care by wine and now by sleep; but all in vain, for close upon your heels the black companion presses, and pursues you as you flee.

Horace. Whence can I get a stone?

Davus. Where is the need?

Horace. Whence arrows?

Davus. ²Surely he is mad, or he writes poetry.

Horace. If you don't take yourself away at once, you'll join the eight who work now in my Sabine farm.

¹ They used skin-scrapers in bathing, made of horn or metal.

² Davus humorously suggests that there is another fit of poetic phrensy coming upon Horace, and that consequently he will get well abused, and perhaps a beating as before.

Nasidienus, a rich parvenu, gave a banquet, at which Mæcenas, and Fundanius, a celebrated comic poet, were present.

Horace gives a humorous and satirical account of it by the mouth of Fundanius. He describes the ambitious attempts of Nasidienus to impress his guests, and Mæcenas especially, with his great wealth, and also his good taste. The character of Nasidienus throughout is that of a man who shows meanness in his attempt to be lavish, pride in his humility; he is absurd and wearisome in his vain efforts to affect the well-bred gentleman, and utterly devoid of refinement and sensibility.

THE ARRANGEMENT OF THE DINNER-TABLE.

Imus locus, or *Consularis. Medius. Summus.*
Bottom place. Middle place. Top place.

I. MÆCENAS.	II. VIBIDIUS.	III. SERVILIUS BALATRO.

Medius lectus.—Middle couch.

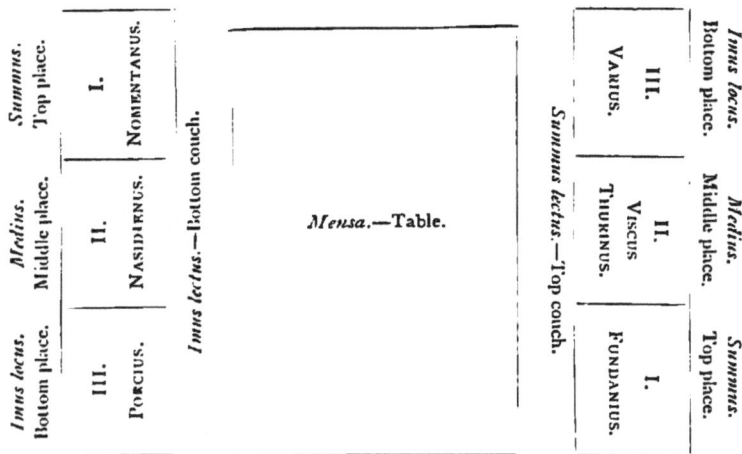

Summus. Top place. — **I.** NOMENTANUS.
Medius. Middle place. — **II.** NASIDIENUS.
Imus locus. Bottom place. — **III.** PORCIUS.

Imus lectus.—Bottom couch.

Mensa.—Table.

Summus lectus.—Top couch.

III. VARIUS. — *Imus locus.* Bottom place.
II. VISCUS THURINUS. — *Medius.* Middle place.
I. FUNDANIUS. — *Summus.* Top place.

The guests did not sit at table, but reclined on the couches.

Horace. How did the wealthy [1] Nasidienus' banquet please you? And I ask, because when I was thinking of inviting you, I was informed that yesterday you had been drinking there since noon.

Fundanius. So well, that I have ne'er enjoyed myself so much in all my life.

Horace. Pray tell [2] me, if you've no objection, what course first appeased your eager appetite?

Fundanius. First, a Lucanian wild boar was served:—[3] 'twas captured, as our host kept telling us, when gentle south winds blew; around the table were placed turnips, lettuces, and radishes, and all that stimulates the failing appetite, as [4] parsnips, fish-brine, lees of Coan wine. When this course had been cleared away, and when one slave in [5] shortest tunic clad had wiped the table, though made but of [6] maple-wood, with purple woollen duster, with the nap still on, and when [7] another had collected all the useless fragments left, and all that might disgust the guests, a [8] swarthy Indian comes slowly forth with Cæcuban wine on a tray, and Alcon with sweet Chian wine [9] not mixed with water from the sea, both slowly walking like the Attic maids with Ceres' sacred baskets on their heads. "Here," says the host, " Mæcenas, if the [10] Alban wine or the Falernian suit your taste better than those on the table, we have both.

Horace. O wretched wealth! But still, Fundanius, I long to know the names of

[1] Nasidienus is pronounced as if Nasidjenus.
He was probably a farmer of the public revenues, and wanted some aid from Mæcenas.
This use of "ut" (line 1) in direct narration belongs more to colloquial Latin.
It was bad taste to begin before three o'clock, as the usual time for the Roman dinner was not at all before that hour.

[2] So Cicero ad Atticum, 13, 42, i., "Si grave non est, velim scire, quid sit causæ?"
No mention is made of the antepast because it was served as it should be. It consisted of eggs, salt fish, and mead.

[3] Such particular description of the food was an instance of bad taste. The boar was really tainted, and was served up with the numerous vegetables and condiments to conceal the fact.

[4] It was bad taste to bring these on so early.

[5] It was bad taste for the slaves to have such unusually short dresses.

[6] Not to have had a table of citron-wood, or one inlaid richly, showed Nasidienus' meanness.

[7] A slave called the "analecta."

[8] There is great humour in the contrast between the haste and over-attention shown by the slave who dusted the table and the absurd gravity and slow movements of the cup-bearers.
It was a token of luxury then to have Ethiopian or Indian slaves.

[9] They used to mix salt water with their wine to excite thirst; and Nasidienus probably omitted this, for fear his guests should drink too much.

[10] Nasidienus shows his meanness by only putting one Italian and one Greek

wine on the table instead of offering his guests Falernian and Lesbian too; and he showed his ostentation by mentioning his possession of what he did not offer.

1 Ironical.

2 Of Thuriæ, a town in Calabria :—he was not the same as either of the "Visci" friends of Horace.
Varius, Sat., I., v., 40.
Pronounced Serv'llyus.
Vibidius was unknown.

3 Porcius was like Nasidienus, a farmer of the public revenues, and very likely toadied him.

4 The fingers were named thus:—
pollex, thumb.
index, 1st finger.
famosus, medius, infamis, 2nd finger.
medicus, 3rd, ring finger.
minimus, 4th finger.

5 *I. e.*, I cannot pretend to his deep knowledge of natural truth.
6 Parody of Æn., ii., 670.
7 Literally, the paleness began to change the face of our state purveyor. There may be some irony in the use of this word "parochus."
8 The real reason, his parsimony, is ironically withheld by Fundanius, who suggests the reasons in the text here given for his paleness and silence.

those who dined with you, when you were treated so 1 delightfully?

Fundanius. Well, I was in the first place on the highest couch, and next to me 2 Thurinus Viscus was, and Varius by him, if I remember right; then on the middle couch, the top seat was filled by Servilius Balatro; Vibidius was in the next, and both of them Mæcenas, who was in the bottom seat, had brought as extra guests. Upon the top seat of the lowest couch was Nomentanus, then the host himself; and on the bottom seat was 3 Porcius, who made himself absurd by gulping down whole cakes at once. But Nomentanus' duty was to point with his 4 first finger to whatever might escape the notice of the guests: for we, I mean the ordinary guests, dined upon fish and game, and shell-fish that contained in them a hidden flavour, far unlike the usual one; indeed, his business was at once quite evident, directly he had handed me the entrails of a plaice and turbot, which I ne'er had tasted until then. He next informed me that the honey-apple was the ruddiest if gathered when the moon was on the wane. 5 What difference it makes, said he, the host himself will better tell you.

Hereupon Vibidius exclaimed to Balatro, If we don't drink so that he feel the cost, "we shall," as Virgil says, "die 6 unavenged;" and so he called for larger glasses. 7 Pale became our entertainer's face, for he feared nothing like hard drinkers, 8 and no doubt because they

slander one too freely, or—[1]because strong
wines quite deaden all nice sense of taste.
Vibidius and Balatro pour into [2]glasses of
the largest size whole bottles at a time, and
so did all the rest except the guests who were
reclining on the lowest couch, [3]for they drank
sparingly enough. Next was brought in a
lamprey sprawling on too small a dish, and
served with prawns that floated in the sauce.
Then said the host, "'Twas caught when full
of spawn, for had it spawned, [4]its flavour
would have been inferior. The sauce is
made of these ingredients : the oil that first
was squeezed from the [5]Venafran press ; then
caviar made from the juices of the Spanish
[6]mackerel ; then wine that's five years old,
while it is boiling, but a wine of Italy ; when
it has boiled, the Chian wine suits better
than all others ; then white pepper and the
vinegar that has fermented [7]Lesbos' grape."

I first showed men the way to cook green
colewort, and the pungent [8]elecampane, but
Curtillus was an Curtillus was the first to teach
unknown gour-
mand.   us how to cook sea-urchins
with the brine upon them, as the [9]liquor that
this shell-fish of the sea itself supplies is
better than the pickle that is [10]sold. Meantime the [11]curtains hung to catch the dirt,
down from the ceiling fell with dreadful crash
upon the [12]dish, and dragged with them more
black dust than the north wind raises in
Campania. We gathered courage when we
found there was no danger, though we had

1 Ironical.

2 Cups made at a pot-
tery in Allifæ, a Samnite
town.

3 Literally, did no harm
to the flagons.
Nomentanus   and
Porcius were parasites,
and   were   afraid   of
offending   Nasidienus,
who was himself afraid
of the expense.

4 Literally, it would
be likely to be worse
after spawning in respect
of its flesh.

5 *I.e.*, from Venafrum,
in Campania. The oil
that ran first from the
press would be the best.
6 From Karthage in
Spain.

7 Methymna was a
town in Lesbos.

8 Elecampane was used
by eastern nations as a
cordial, and rarely in
medicine as a stomachic.

9 The construction is
this: "Ut (id) quod testa
marina remittit (echinus
per se ipse præbet), me-
lius est muriâ (quam mu-
riam) cetarii vendunt.
10 By the fishmonger.
11 The ancients hung
curtains beneath their
ceilings to catch the
dust.
12 Where the precious
lamprey was.

expected that the house itself would fall. Then [1]Rufus, with his head cast down, began to weep, as if a son had come to an untimely death. What would have been the end, had not, with philosophic wisdom, Nomentanus thus restored his friend?—"O Fortune, what divinity so cruel against us as thou? What joy to thee 'tis ever to frustrate the plans of men!" Here Varius could scarce suppress his laughter with a napkin stuffed well in his mouth. But Balatro, with cynical disdain at everything, kept saying, [2]"Such is life," and so you see it is that your repute will never tally with the toil you undergo.—[3]To think that you should be distressed and tortured with all sorts of anxious cares, that I may be magnificently entertained, that no burnt bread, or badly seasoned sauce may be served up; to see that all the slaves are trim and neatly dressed to wait on us!—Include, besides, the possible mischance of hangings falling down, as but just now; the chance, too, that some [4]groom called in to wait should slip and break a dish. But yet misfortune will bring forth to view the talents of a host as of a general, as will success conceal the same. In answer Nasidienus says, "May heaven grant you all the blessings you may ask! You are so kind a man, so courteous a guest!" and then he for his [5]slippers calls and rises to go out. Then on each couch you might observe the whisper buzzing secretly in this, and now in that guest's ear.

[1] Nasidienus was also called Rufus.

[2] Addressed to Nasidienus.

[3] This is the infinitive of indignation, as in Satire ix. of the 1st book, line 72, "Huncine solem tam nigrum surrexe mihi!" Under cover of this pretended consolation, there lurks an ironical enumeration of most of Nasidienus' mistakes.

[4] So in "Mistakes of a Night" a groom waits at table. Nasidienus tried to make a greater show of servants by calling in even the groom, who, awkwardly attempting to clear away the curtains, catches his foot in them, and breaks the dish, making the evil worse.

[5] The guests put on their slippers when they left the "triclinium." Nasidienus meant to go and see if he could not repair his disasters.

Horace. I'd rather see what you describe than any public games ; but tell me, prithee, what you next laughed at.

Fundanius. Well, while Vibidius says to the slaves—" Are the decanters broken too, as wine is not brought when I ask ? "— and whilst we laughed [1] at some pretended joke, with Balatro to help us, [2] thou, great Nasidienus didst return, with brow quite changed, like one who meant to rectify mis-chances by his skill; then followed slaves who bore in a large dish, in which our [3] pulse is mostly served, a [4] crane's dismembered body sprinkled thickly o'er with salt and meal ; the liver of a white [5] goose, not a gander, mind, fed on rich figs ; hares' shoulders too, torn off as though much sweeter so, than if one [6] ate them with the loins ; we then saw black-birds served up with the breast absurdly burnt, and pigeons robbed of the best part ; all nice enough, had [7] but the host not kept on telling us the reason for their being thus prepared, and all their qualities, and him we fled away from, taking vengeance in this way, I mean by tasting nought at all, as though some witch, more venomous than Moorish snakes, had breathed upon the food.

[1] Really at the actual mishaps.

[2] The vocative is used in parody of the epic style.

[3] The Romans' national food was pulse or pottage anciently, and Nasidie-nus had been obliged to use this dish, which was not the usual kind of one, because he had no other.

[4] The stork was prized more than the crane.

[5] Very like "pâté de foie gras." Our word goose does not fix the gender, which was important here.

[6] "Edim" is the old subjunctive.   Confer Epode iii., 3.

[7] Bad taste again.

Vide Sat., i., 8, for Canidia.

I

EPISTLE I.—BOOK I.

Satire brands vices generally; an epistle is addressed specially to one, and peculiarly tinged by the character of the one to whom it is addressed.

This Epistle, addressed to Mæcenas, contains the poet's excuse for having written nothing for three years, that is, since the publication of the Third Book of Odes. It advises calm philosophy, in preference to indiscriminate pursuit of honours, or attention to the great.

DEAR Patron, subject of my first attempts,
fit subject for my last, you're trying to enlist
me in my former training school, though I've
already been before the public quite enough,
and been presented with the wooden sword
that sets me free. My time of life and inclinations are now changed. [1]Veianius, you
know, hung up his sword close by the temple
gate of Hercules, and now lives in the country quite secluded, to prevent his being forced
so oft to beg the public for release, [2]close
by the balcony where nobles view the games.
And I too have a monitor that often rings
into mine ears that hear him well such words
as these :—If wise, in time set free the aged

[1] A celebrated gladiator.

[2] Literally, at the edge of the sand in the amphitheatre.

steed, lest he should stumble at the last and break his wind. So now [1] I give up writing verse, and all my other merry themes, and I am busily engaged in finding out what truth, what virtue is, and think of nothing else :—I'm storing and arranging rules to bring forth, afterwards for action. And to save your possibly inquiring what the sect is, what the school I now attend, I tell you this :—I, bound to hold the dogmas of no one philosopher, go as a guest just where occasion takes me. With the [2] Stoics, I take part in state affairs, and plunge in politics' uncertain sea, true virtue's guardian and stern champion ; sometimes I fall again insensibly into the rules that [3] Aristippus held, and try to pass a philosophic life uninfluenced by circumstance. Just as the night seems long to those whose mistress fails to come, the day to those who work for hire ; and as the year is tedious to minors, whom strict guardianship of mothers keeps in check, so all the time goes slowly and unpleasantly to me, that stays my hopes and plan of strenuously working out some philosophic truths that benefit the poor as well as rich, and will do harm to young and old alike unless attended to. It then remains for me to guide and to console myself with these plain truths. Suppose one cannot vie with others in keen sight, as Lynceus could, yet still, if soreeyed, one would not for that reject the use of salve, nor, if one have no hope of gaining

[1] Mere irony.

[2] The Stoics advocated τὸ πρακτικόν, a busy and energetic life. The Epicureans τὸ λαθεῖν βιώσαντα, a life of retirement and philosophy.

[3] See p. 195, Ep. xvii.

the unconquered [1]Glycon's strength, would
one refuse to guard one's body from the gout
that swells the hands with nodes.   One may
make progress to a small extent, if one may
not make more.

Suppose one's breast be fevered with the
miser's greed of gain, and with a wretched
wish for more ;—well, there are words and
charms by which one may assuage these
perturbations, and may free one's self from
most of the disease of mind. Suppose you be
puffed up with love of praise ; then there's
a well-known remedy that will be able to
restore you, if you thrice read o'er a little
work with guileless heart.   Though jealous,
passionate, or idle, fond of wine or women,
still none are so savage that they can't become more civilized, if they but lend a ready
ear to teaching.   It is virtue to shun vice,
and the first step to wisdom is to give up
folly.   You observe with what great toil of
mind and body you avoid what you think
the worst ills,—I mean small fortune, and want
of success in hunting after place ; just like
an active trader you sail swiftly to remotest
lands, in trying to shun poverty o'er sea, o'er
rock, through flames,—and won't you learn
and listen, and put faith in better men, to
save your caring for that which you foolishly
admire and long to gain? Pray, who that boxes
in our villages and streets would not think
much of being victor at the great Olympic
games, if he had but the hope of gaining

without toil possession of the victor's palm so dear? Yet silver is not worth so much as gold; so, then, gold is not worth so much as virtue. Good citizens, attend; first money must be gained, then virtue after wealth: the whole [1]Exchange from one end to the other rings with words like these; both young and old, with satchel and with slate upon the left arm hung, recite these words by heart. Perchance you've spirit and morality,—nay, eloquence and credit too; yet fifty, or say sixty pounds are wanting to the [2]sum the knights must have; if so, no fourteen ranks for you. And yet the boys say in their sport, "You'll be a king if you shall play the game aright;" and so let moral right be your strong bulwark of defence :—I mean, to be not conscience-stricken, nor grow pale with any crime. Pray tell me which is better, Otho's law or this verse that the boys recite, which gives a kingdom to all those who play the game aright, a verse sung by the [3]Curii and the Camilli e'en when men? Does he advise you better who says, "Wealth, get wealth, by right means if you can, if not get wealth by any means you can," that as a knight, forsooth, you may enjoy a nearer view of [4]Pupius' affecting poetry; or he, who, ever by your side, exhorts and trains you to resist proud fortune's frowns with fearless and undaunted mind? But if the Roman public possibly should ask me why I do not hold the

same ideas as I lounge in the colonnades
they do, or why I do not follow or avoid the
objects of their choice or their aversion, I'll
relate the answer that the wary fox once
made to the sick lion, "'Tis the footprints
turning to your cave, and none away from it,
that frighten me." [1] You people have as many
tastes as heads the hydra had. For what or
whom, pray, shall I imitate? Some men delight
to farm the public revenues, while some hunt
after greedy widows by presenting them with
pastry or with fruit, or try to catch old
men to shut up in preserves, like fish in ponds.
Again, the property of many grows by secret
usury. But granted that men follow different
pursuits ; yet can the same men keep their
fancy for a single moment? No. Suppose
a rich man shall have said, "No bay in all
the world outshines delightful Baiæ :" then
the lake and sea find out the eagerness shown
by the rich proprietor's unfinished plans;
and if his inconsistent whim has prompted
him with omens, as it were, he'll say, "To-
morrow, workmen, [2] take your tools on to
Teanum. Or suppose the marriage couch
be spread within his halls ; he says that nought
excels, that nought is better than a single
life; but if it be not spread, he swears that
married men alone are blest. With what
chains can I hold fast bound this Proteus,
ever changing, as he does, his form? But
how do poor men act? Oh, laugh at them;
they change their garrets, [3] dining-rooms, their

[1] Another form of the proverb, "quot homines, tot sententiæ."

A watering-place in Campania.

[2] The future is often put for the imperative.
Inland town of Campania.
The inconsistency is in the man's suddenly quitting a seaside place for an inland one without reason.

A sea-god who had the power of changing his form.

[3] Triclinia.

baths and barbers, and are just as seasick in
the boat they've hired as is the rich man whom
a larger vessel with three banks of oars conveys.   You laugh at me suppose I meet you
with unevenly cut hair, or if, as possibly may
be, I wear a worn-out jersey'neath a shirt quite
new, or if my coat hang down more upon one
side than the other, still you laugh ; and what,
pray, do you do, when all my thoughts are
inconsistent, when they spurn what once they
tried to gain, then try to get again what just
now they gave up, are tossed about, at
variance with the whole rule of life ; pull
down, build up, change square for round ?
You only think me mad as most men are ;
and do not laugh at me, nor think I need a
doctor or a guardian chosen by the magistrate, although you are protector of my interests,—and feel disgust at the most * trifling
want of taste shown by a friend whose wel-
fare is bound up with yours, who centres all
his hopes in you.   In fine, philosophers are
but one step below the gods, they're rich
and free, raised to high office, fair in mind
(if not in form), [1]supreme as Persia's king,
and gifted with especially good health of
body and mind too, unless, indeed, when
they're afflicted with bad colds.

[1] He was called "The Great King."

The word "sanus" refers not only to bodily health, but to the Stoics' use of it as applied to the philosopher, in contra-distinction to all others who were "insani."

* Literally, on account of a badly pared nail.

EPISTLE II.—BOOK I.

Horace reads Homer again ; writes to Lollius, a friend, and gives him the opinions suggested by the perusal.

———————

WHILE, Lollius, you, eldest of your father's sons, are learning rhetoric at Rome, I've read once more within Præneste's walls [1] the author of the Trojan war, who tells in clearer and in better terms than [2]Crantor or [3]Chrysippus what is virtue, and what vice,—what is expedience, and what its opposite. Now, if you've no engagement, listen to the reason for my thinking thus :—The [4]story in which Greece is said because of Paris' love to have engaged in a protracted strife with Phrygia, contains a history of foolish kings' fierce passions, and their nations' too. [5]Antenor votes that they should rid themselves of the chief [6]cause of war. And what does Paris do? He vows he can't submit to force, although it be to reign in safety, and live happily. Then Nestor hastens anxiously to calm the strife 'twixt Agamemnon and Achilles ; love inflames the first, and anger both alike, and so

A town in Latium, now Palæstrina.
[1] Homer.

[2] A follower of Plato.
[3] The great defender of the Stoic tenets.

[4] Iliad.

[5] One of the most prudent of the Trojans.

[6] *I.e.*, by restoring Helen.

the subjects suffer for the foolish errors of
their kings.   Then deeds of crime were done
outside the walls of Troy, and inside too by
mutiny, by treachery, by guilt, by lust, by
rage.   Next in the Odyssey he shows us in
Ulysses a most excellent example of the
power of virtue and philosophy, who, after
taking Troy, much travelled as he was, exa-
mined many nations' towns and character,
and suffered many hardships in attempts to
gain a safe return both for himself and crew,
and could not be o'erwhelmed by rough misfortune's sea.   You know the story of the
[1] See Odyssey, K. 230. 'Sirens' strains and Circe's magic cups, which
had he, with his crew by folly blinded and
desire, once drunk, he would have been de-
based and brutish 'neath a meretricious mistress' rule, and would have passed his life
changed into filthy dog or sow that wallows
in the mire.   We then, as we do act, are but
mere ciphers, born but to consume earth's
fruits, like suitors of Penelope, true profli-
[2] King of Phæacia, or gates; like subjects of [2]Alcinoüs, who thought
Corcyra, now Corfu.
too much about high living, and who
deemed it a fine thing to sleep till noon each
day that came, and lull their cares to rest by
the melodious lute.   When robbers rise at
night to murder men, pray won't you wake
up from this lethargy to save your life?   And
yet, though you shall care not to take exercise in health, you'll have to take much more
when dropsy has set in ; and should you not
call for a book and light before daybreak,

or fail to give your energies to creditable
business and pursuits, you'll be distressed by
envy or by love. For why, pray, do you
hasten to remove what hurts the eyes, while,
if aught gnaw the mind, you put off treating
that for some long time? The man who has
[1]begun has finished half the work. Then
have the courage to be wise. Begin at once.
Men who defer the time for living a good
life wait like the clown until the river rolls
its floods away. But it rolls gliding on for aye,
and will glide on. Yet possibly wealth is the
object of their search, or else a wife prolific
in childbearing, or wild woods are peace-
fully reclaimed by tillage and the plough.
Let those who have enough wish for nought
more; no house, no farm, no stores of precious metals, draw the fever from the sick
possessor's frame, nor troubles from his heart.
The owner must be well and strong if he
mean to enjoy the wealth he has amassed.
A mansion or estate gives but such pleasure
to the man who longs for more, or dreads to
lose what he has gained, as pictures give to
blear-eyed men, hot fomentations to those
suffering from gout; the strains of lutes to
ears in pain from gathered filth. Unless the
vessel should be clean, whate'er one may
pour into it turns sour. Shun pleasure; pleasure bought by suffering is really pain. The
miser ever is in want; put some fixed limits
to your wish. The envious grow lean with
jealousy as they behold their neighbours'

[1] Well begun is half done.

Phalaris, Agathocles, rich possessions ; nay, Sicilian despots found
and perhaps the Dio-
nysii. no greater torture than this envy. All who
fail to check their rage will wish undone
what sense of wrong and passion urged them
on to do, while they try hurriedly to get
revenge by force for their unsated hate.
Rage is brief madness ; so, then, rule your
mind, for it is or the slave or lord ; restrain
this mind with bridle and with chain. The
trainers teach the horse while tractable with
unformed neck to go the road the rider
guides it on ; and so the hound hunts in the
woods e'er since he barked at the stag's skin
hung in the court. And so do you, while
young, drink in with breast still pure instruction's words : for long, you know, the cask
will keep the flavour that it once, while fresh,
was tainted with. But if you lag behind, or
press on eagerly in front, I tell you this,—" I
do not wait for loiterers, nor try to get before
the rest."

EPISTLE III.—BOOK I.

This Epistle is addressed to Julius Florus, a friend, who had gone with Tiberius to Asia Minor. The poet asks him about Tiberius, about their mutual friends, and about Florus himself, encourages him to study philosophy, and to make friends with Munatius.

DEAR Florus, I should like to know in what tract of the earth Tiberius, Augustus' step-son, serves. Does Thrace or Hebrus' stream, hard bound with icy chain, or does the Hellespont that flows between the towers of Sestos and Abydos, or do Asia's fertile plains and hills detain you? Pray, what composition is that zealous band of youths engaged upon? This, too, I fain would know: who takes upon himself to tell in history the exploits of Augustus? Who is now transmitting to some distant age the story of the wars he waged, and peaces that he made? What's [1] Titius composing, soon to be the theme of Roman tongues?—who boldly drank from the Pindaric spring, and dared to disregard the stores and sources all can use alike. How is he? How does he

It was customary for a retinue of noble youths to accompany state officers on foreign service.

[1] A consul who tried to translate Pindar into Latin.

remember me ? With happy inspiration is
he trying to adapt the measures of the
Theban [1]bard to Latin lyric verse, or does
he storm and rave with turgid style in
tragedy ? And how is Celsus, who has been
advised by me, and still must be advised to
seek resources of his own, and not to pla-
giarize from all those works that once have
passed the Palatine Apollo's temple doors,
lest like a miserable crow he should be
ridiculed, and stripped of all his borrowed
plumes, if possibly the flock of birds should
come to claim their feathers once again?
What style do you yourself attempt ? What
kind of poetry do you now hover busily
about like bees round thyme ? No mean, or
rough, or wildly untrained genius is yours ;
nay, whether you now whet your eloquence
for pleading, or prepare to be a chamber
barrister, or are composing charming songs in
praise of love or wine, you'll gain the first prize
that the victor's ivy crown can give. But
if you could abandon that which checks all
generous thought, and feeds the care you
feel, you then would go where heaven-born
wisdom leads. Let us, both high and low,
extend this work of wisdom in our acts and
thoughts, if we desire to live both valued by
our country, and approved of by ourselves.
You also ought to tell me this in answer,—
whether [2]Plancus' son be loved by you as
he deserves, or, like a wound that's sewn
unskilfully, does your new friendship try in

[1] Pindar.

Celsus Albinovanus, the secretary of Tiberius.

I. e., been received into the public library.

Money and ambition.

[2] Son of Lucius Muna-tius Plancus, consul.

vain to form? and is it being sundered now?
But if hot blood or misconstruction of the
facts sets you at variance like wild steeds
with unbroken necks, I tell you this : wher-
ever in the world you be, unworthy of you as
it is to sunder friendship's closest bond,
a heifer, I have vowed to slay to honour
your return, is feeding now for sacrifice.

EPISTLE IV.—BOOK I.

This Epistle is addressed to Albius Tibullus, the great elegiac poet, who was a dear friend of Horace, and a contemporary of Horace, Ovid, and Propertius.

DEAR Albius, fair critic of my Satires, what shall I suppose you're doing now near Pedum's town? That you're composing something to surpass the epigrams and sonnets Cassius of Parma wrote; or that in meditative mood you roam 'mid healthful groves with thoughts on all that's worthy of the wise and good? Your body ne'er has lacked the spirit's stirring power. For heaven has bestowed on you good looks and wealth, and knowledge how to use that wealth. What greater blessing could a kind nurse wish for her dear charge who, like yourself, thinks what is right, and can express his thoughts, to whom the blessings of [1]repute and influence, and health abundantly belong, together with a tasteful style of living, and no lack of means to keep it up?

'Mid hopes of gain, and care of what you have already gained, 'mid fear of ills to

Pedum, now called Zagarola, was a town in Latium.

[1] Influence and repute, literally.

come, and angry pain at present woe, still think each day that dawns to be your last. For pleasantly will come the time that you shall not expect to live.

When you shall care to laugh at me, a pig from Epicurus' herd of swine, then come and visit me, now fat and sleek with living well.

The Romans used more forcible language in their jests against themselves than we do. For instance, Cicero, in a letter to Atticus, calls himself a "down-right ass," and addresses Piso as "Asine," you donkey.

K

EPISTLE V.—BOOK I.

This Epistle is addressed to Torquatus, a friend and orator, and contains an invitation to celebrate Augustus' approaching birthday, and advises his friend to enjoy life while he may.

TORQUATUS, if you can endure to be my guest and sit down at a homely board, and do not shrink from nothing but plain food, served up on common earthenware, I shall expect you at my house at sunset's hour.

You shall drink wine poured into cask when [1]Taurus was made consul for the second time, the growth of vines between Minturnæ's marsh and Mount [2]Petrinus, in Sinuessa's state. [3]

If you have any better, send your slave with it ; if not, submit to me.

My hearth and household gods have long been bright, my furniture long cleaned to honour you. Away with fruitless hopes, give up the race for gold, and give up 'Moschus' case ; to-morrow is Augustus' birthday and a festival, and is to give us licence and more

Archias was a cabinet-maker at Rome.

Literally, as a guest to recline on couches made by Archias.

The use of the words "olus omne" in the text, entire vegetable diet, to intimate the plainness of the food, is something like our use of the word "mutton." Thus : "Come and take your mutton with me to-morrow."

[1] Titus Statilius Taurus was consul a second time, A.U.C. 728. The wine was six years old, and moderately good.

[2] Now Piedimonte.

[3] In Campania, now Mondragone, and the ruins.

[4] A Mysian rhetori-cian. who was accused of being a wizard.

rest, and we shall be permitted, without fear of loss, to wile away the summer eve with many pleasant anecdotes.

Why should I wish for fortune's gifts if I be not allowed to reap the fruits of them? The man who is too sparing and too hard upon himself in his heir's interest is very nearly mad. I will begin to drink, and ¹tear the garland from my brow, and will not shrink from being thought a rash enthusiast. What does not wine effect? It shows one's truest feelings, makes one's hopes seem realized, inspires the cowardly with ardour for the fray, relieves the anxious mind of all its care, gives fresh accomplishments. And whom does not the flowing bowl make eloquent? Whom does it not set free from care, though pressed by pinching poverty? I'm suited well to see to this, and suitably it's asked of me, and gladly will I see that all the coverlets be clean, and that no dirty dinner-napkin cause disgust, that both the goblet and the dish may be so bright as to reflect your face, that there be none to talk abroad of what true friends have said, to see that spirits quite congenial may meet and may sit side by side; I will ask Butra and Septicius to meet you, and Sabinus, if an earlier engagement or a wish to dine with his own mistress keep him not; and there is room for several extra guests, but overcrowded parties ne'er can be agreeable. Just send a line to say how many you

An interrogative phrase of impatience. "Quo" is the old dative for "cui," in the sense of "quorsum," and there is an ellipsis of "optem."

1 The custom of scattering flowers about during a carousal is not so much alluded to as the habit of tearing the garlands from the brow, and pulling the flowers to pieces that were on the table, a practice which guests would indulge in when merry with wine.

would like to bring, then leave your legal
business, get out by the private door, and so
escape the client as he watches you within
the entrance-room.

EPISTLE VI.—BOOK I.

This Epistle is addressed to a friend, Numicius, to whom the poet recommends a calm philosophy, freedom from superstition, and a proper estimate of riches.

———

NUMICIUS, a calm philosophy's about the one chief thing,—indeed, the only thing that can procure enduring happiness.

Some men can view yon sun and stars, and seasons rolling by in changeless course, with hearts untouched by fear; and what think you of gold and silver, marble, pearls, and purple that enrich the sons of Araby and India :—what of the Circus with its shows, th' applause for the display, the dignities the people's favour brings :—pray, with what limits, with what feelings, looks, and eyes should they be viewed? The man who fears reverse and poverty is quite as much bewildered as the one who longs for gain; 'tis strong emotion that distresses both, directly that the sight of something quite unlooked for terrifies them both. What matters it if he feel joy or grief, desire or

fear; if with dull state he lose his powers
of mind and body too, in stupid wonder at
whatever he has seen that or exceeds or
falls below what he expects to see?

Let, then, the wise man be called mad,
the just unjust, if he pursue e'en virtue to
excess.   Go, then, gaze up at plate, old
marble, and bronze statues, works of art;
admire the purple's hues set off by precious
stones; rejoice that countless eyes gaze on
you as their orator; industrious and early
go to the law courts, and late go home

Nothing was known of
Mutus.

again, for fear some rival should get more
from land his wife in dowry brought, than
you from pleading, and—(what you could
never brook,) sprung as he is from meaner
origin than you—lest he should rather merit
your esteem than you should his.   Whate'er
there be beneath the earth, time will bring
forth to open day, and time will bury and
conceal all that now seems so fair.   Although

The Appian road led
to the villas of the rich
in Campania.
The Roman gentlemen
frequented these resorts
as we do the Burlington
and Rotten Row.
Agrippa's colonnade
was adorned with pic-
tures of the Argonautic
expedition.

Agrippa's colonnade and road of Appius
now know your face so well, you still must
go to that last bourne to which Rome's
noblest kings have gone.   If pleurisy or
Bright's disease assail you, find some remedy
for the complaint.   Of course, you wish to
live a happy life; who don't?   Well, then,
if virtue only can give this, drop luxury, and
see to this with moral bravery.   You think
philosophy a form of words, just as a wood
is made of trees; see, then, that no one
bring his vessel home to port before yourself,

lest you should lose the profits from your
trade with [1] Cibyra or with Bithynia. See

[1] A large city of Phrygia.

that a quarter of a million pounds be gained
completely; add a second quarter, and a
third, and, finally, a fourth to make the
million up. No doubt this money that so
rules the world gives one a dowered wife,

All this is ironical.

gives credit, friends, and noble birth; ay,
handsome person, too; in fine, persuasion and
a winning grace set off the moneyed man.

The Cappadocian king, though rich in
slaves, wants money; don't you be like him.

Ariobarzanes.

Lucullus, as men say, when asked if he could
lend the stage a hundred military cloaks,
said, "How can I supply so many? still,
I'll look and send you all I have." Soon

A general who fought
against Mithridates, and
gained his wealth in the
East.

afterwards he wrote to say he had five thousand cloaks, and that the manager might
take a part or all.

The prætor superin-
tended the appointments
of the public games.

Poor is the house, where there's not more
than is enough, that is not noticed by the
owner's eye, and proves the perquisite of
thievish slaves.

Well, then, if wealth alone can give us

All irony.

lasting happiness, why, be the first to take
this work in hand, the last to give it up. If
influence and splendour make men blest, then
let us buy a slave to tell the names of those we

A slave called the
"nomenclator," who sat

meet and nudge us in the side he guards, and

on the left side, and told

make us shake hands over dirty counters with

his master the names of
those he met.

their weights and scales, and say, "This
man has influence among the Fabian, and
that among the Veline tribe; a third will

1 The consulate.

Gargilius was a freed-
man of Augustus: he
used to agree beforehand
with some one to sell
him a boar outside the
gates, and then bring it
back as though killed in
hunting.

2 The inhabitants of
Cære, in Etruria, gained
the freedom of the city
in return for services
when Rome was sacked
by the Gauls, but they
were afterwards de-
graded for rebellion.
3 They killed some
oxen sacred to the sun.
An elegiac poet of
Colophon.

give the ¹lictor's rods and chair of ivory to
whomsoe'er he will, or will inexorably take
the same away." Call such men "brother,"
or else "father," blandly greet them as relations in the way that suits the age of each.
If he who dines well, lives as men should
live; now day has dawned, why, let us go
where fondness for good living calls; yes,
let us go buy fish and meat, as once Gargilius,
who would give orders that his nets and
hunting spears and slaves should in the
morning be conveyed across the crowded
market-place; so that, forsooth, one mule from
all the pack might bring back home a boar
he—*bought*, the public looking on meanwhile.

Then let us bathe ere we have well
digested food, forgetting what is right, what
wrong, well ²worthy of disfranchisement; a
vicious crew, like that Ulysses, prince of
Ithaca, once had, who thought ³forbidden
pleasure better than their fatherland.

If, as Mimnermus thinks, nought is delightful without love and merriment, why,
spend your life in love and merriment.

Farewell, long life be yours; if you know
aught more true than what you read from
me, sincerely tell me it; if not, join me
in acting on these truths.

EPISTLE VII.—BOOK I.

This Epistle is addressed to Mæcenas, and contains a most candid excuse for his absence.

———

ALTHOUGH I promised to be at my country house but a [1] few days, I broke my word, and you've expected me throughout the whole of August. True. Yet if you wish me to live really well and strong, you will, dear patron, grant me, now that I'm afraid of falling ill, the same indulgence that you grant me when I'm actually ill ; while early figs and the "Sirocco" grace the undertaker with his sable train, while fathers and while loving mothers all are anxious for their children's health, while sedulous attendance on one's patron and the business of the courts bring fevers on, and open dead men's wills. But if midwinter should strew snow upon the Alban hills, your poet will go down then to the [2] sea, and take care of his health ; and well wrapped up, will read with limbs close drawn together ; you, dear friend, he'll visit with [3] spring's harbinger, and spring itself, if you permit him to do so.

[1] "Quinque" is not to be too closely translated.

[2] To Velia or Salernum.

[3] Literally, with the zephyrs and the first swallow.

You've not bestowed your favours upon

The Calabrians were
kind, but rough.
me, as some hosts with rough kindness bid
their guests eat pears. Say they, " I pray
you, eat : " you answer, " I have had
enough." Well, take away all that you will.
No, thank you. Yet you'll take them home
as welcome presents to your little children.

I am quite as much obliged as if I were
sent off well laden with your gift.

Well, as you will; yet you will leave them
here to be consumed to-day by pigs.

The wasteful and the foolish man gives
but what he disdains or loathes. This barren
soil has ever and will ever for all time
produce ungrateful men.

But men who are both good and wise avow
themselves quite ready to assist all who deserve
their aid, and yet they know the difference
between the counters that the actor and the
gambler uses and the sterling coin. I'll show
myself well worthy of your kindness, e'en
commensurately with the high renown of you
who so deserve my gratitude. But if you be
unwilling that I quit yourself and Rome
for any other place, then give me back my

The infinitives in the
text are used as accusa-
tives of substantives, as
in Persius and elsewhere.
once strong chest, my dark hair growing
thickly on my brow ; yes, give me back my
pleasant flow of language ; give me back my
graceful laugh, my fond lament for wanton
Cinara's desertion over wine.

1 Natural history is
often disregarded in
fables.
It happened once that a lean [1] fox had
crept through some small chink into a bin of
corn, and after feeding, when its body was

now full of food, tried vainly to get out again. And to this fox, the weasel, not far off, said this: When lean go to that narrow hole which lean you first went through. If I should be convicted by this simile I give up all, for I don't praise the [1]simple country life when filled with rich and dainty food, nor do I change my independent ease for all the wealth of Araby. You've often praised my modesty; you have been called by me when with you, "king" and "father," and the same although away; test me and see if I can gladly part with all you gave. Telemachus, the son of him who bore so much, said aptly, "Ithaca is not a place that suits the horse, for it lacks spacious champaigns, and does not grow grass abundantly;" so, Menelaus, I will leave your gifts to you, whom they suit better than they suit myself. The humble, humble fortune suits; no longer queenly Rome gives me delight, but Tibur with its quiet streets, or e'en Tarentum's tranquil town.

As [2]Philip once, an energetic and a stout antagonist, and famous too for pleading cases, came back from his business home at two o'clock, and, now in years, complained that [3]the law courts were too far from Carinæ; as they say, he spied some man fresh shaven in a banker's shop, and with a penknife cleaning his nails quietly. Said Philip to his slave—a slave who would with smart despatch do what his master bade,—"Demetrius, away, find out, and bring word from

[1] Literally, the sleep of the people.
Fat birds, such as geese, turkeys, grouse.

Ulysses.

[2] Lucius Marcus Philippus, consul, A.U.C. 698.

[3] As we might say that Hampstead is too far from the courts at Westminster.
Carinæ was a fashionable street where some of the leading men at Rome resided.

what country he is come, what is his character and rank, and parentage and interest."
He goes, comes back and tells his master
that he is an auctioneer, by name Volteius
Mena, of small property but blameless character, known by his class, fond of hard
work in season, and then rest; of gaining
money and then spending it; fond of the
company of a few friends in humble station
like himself; of a fixed home and married
life; the public games and Plain of Mars
when business was all done.

I fain would ask the man himself about
all this you tell me; bid him come to dine
with me. This, Mena really scarcely could
believe, but mused in secret wonderment; in
short, his answer was, "I'm much obliged,
but cannot come."

Is't possible that he refuses *me?* He
both refuses obstinately and or cares nought
for or dreads your company. But in the
morning Philip lights upon Volteius selling
to the [1]coatless common people broken stuff,
and is the first to say, "How do you do?"
He then begins to make his hard work, and
the ties of trade, excuses for not having
called at Philip's house next day, in short,
for failing to perceive and greet him first.

Consider that I pardon you (said Philip), on
condition that you dine with me to-day.

Well, as you will.

Then come at half-past three; now go, and
zealously pursue your trade.

[1] Sans culottes; the poor class wore no toga.

When he had come to dinner, and had talked of anything that chanced to come into his head, he had at last to be informed that it was time to go off home to sleep. When, now a regular attendant on his patron in the morning, and a constant guest, he had been often seen to hurry down to Philip's house as fish will dart at hook concealed by bait ; he then was bid to go with him out to his [1] country seat near Rome, because the Latin holidays had been proclaimed. Once seated in a mule-car, he bestows incessant praise upon the Sabine land and clime. This Philip sees and laughs, and as he tries to find rest and amusement from whatever source he can, and gives Volteius sixty pounds, and promises to lend him sixty more, he strongly urges him to buy a small estate. He buys it, and to cut the story short, instead of a neat townsman turns rough countryman, and talks of nought but furrows and vineyards ; prepares his elms for wedding with the vines, wears out his strength in business, and grows grey with his desire for gain. But when his sheep were lost by theft, his she-goats by the murrain ; when his crops deceived his hopes, his ox grew lean with ploughing the rough soil :—provoked by all this loss, ere morning broke, he seized his horse, and in a rage set off for Philip's house. And when he saw the man all dirty and unshorn, he said, I think, Volteius, you are too laborious, and keep too close at

[1] In the Sabine territory. The "Feriæ Latinæ" were a moveable festival proclaimed at the pleasure of the consul.

work. Said he, I' faith, my patron, you
would call me "wretched" if you cared
to give me the right name. So, then, I pray
you and implore you by your guardian-god,
your friendship, and your hearth and home,
restore me to my former life.

Then let the man who once has seen how
far superior is what he had to what he tried
to gain, come back in time and take again
the lot in life he left. 'Tis right that men
should estimate themselves by standard and
by rule that suits their state.

EPISTLE VIII.—BOOK I.

This Epistle informs a friend, Celsus Albinovanus, one of the retinue o. Tiberius engaged in Armenia, that Horace felt that he was not living as a philosopher should live, and as he had avowed that he would ; inquires after the health and prospects of his friend, and ends with a warning not to forget to bear his new honours without undue pride and elation of mind.

COME now, my pen, invoked by me, compose
a letter of felicitation in reply to Celsus,
aide-de-camp and secretary to the Prince
[1]Tiberius. If Celsus ask what I'm about, say
that although I make fair promises enough,
I live not as I should, and so not as I like ;
yet not because the hail has bruised my
vines, or heat parched up my olives, nor because my herds are struck by murrain in
some distant fields, but all because, less
sound in mind than in whatever portion of
my frame you please, I care to listen to or
learn nought to remove my melancholy
state ; become offended with men who give
me a trusty doctor's aid, grow angry with my
[2]friends for their prompt zeal in saving me
from fatal listlessness ; pursue what does me
harm, shun what I know will do me good,
[3]and, fickle as the wind, at Rome for Tibur

1 The full name was Tiberius Claudius Nero.

I. e., any part of my body is stronger than my mind.

2 He compares his friends' advice to physicians' art.

3 His Sabine villa was near Tibur.

long, at Tibur long for Rome. Then ask
him how he is, how too he does his duty, and
his business, and how he behaves; ask also
how he suits the Prince, and how his train.

If he shall say, "Oh, well enough,"
felicitate him first; then mind you slowly
whisper in his ear these warning words,—"As,
Celsus, you shall bear your honours, so shall
we bear you."

If you bear your accession to fortune with modesty, we shall love you; if with pride, we shall dislike you.

EPISTLE IX.—BOOK I.

A cautious letter of introduction given to Septimius, an acquaintance.

SEPTIMIUS, 'tis clear, Tiberius, more than all other men, perceives your great esteem for me; for when he asks, and by his prayers constrains me, to attempt forsooth to praise and recommend him to yourself, as one well worthy of the high abilities and station of a prince who chooses but the virtuous to know; and when he thinks that I stand in the place of a dear friend to you, he sees and knows what I can do far better than I do myself. I did indeed urge many reasons why I should escape the task, and find excuse; but still I feared lest men should think that I, wrapped up in my own interest alone, pretended to possess less than I do possess, and kept concealed the influence I really have. I then, in trying to avoid reproach for what would merit greater blame, have brought myself to use the licence town-bred confidence can give. So if you think it well to give up modesty in a friend's cause, why, write his name upon your list, and think him brave and true.

Slightly ironical.

L

EPISTLE X.—BOOK I.

This Epistle is written to Fuscus Aristius, an intimate friend and philologist, who preferred living at Rome; and tells him of the advantages of country life, and exhorts him to imitate the Stoics, and live contented with his lot, and not court the rich, which often brings more trouble than advantage.

I, WHO delight in country life, send my regards to Fuscus, who prefers the town,— in which one point, indeed, we are far different; though in all else, almost twin-born, with brothers' feelings, we, like doves that have together lived and loved, each shun whate'er the other shuns, each love whate'er the other loves.

In the words "annuimus pariter" there is an idea of mutual approval, and also the billing of two doves.

You keep [1] the nest; I sing the praises of the pleasant country's streams and rocks edged round with moss and groves. Dost ask the reason? 'Tis because I really live and seem a king the moment that I've left that life that you extol to heaven with shouts of praise; and, like a slave who runs away, "I will not have" the priest's rich food: 'tis bread I want, that now to me is better far than honeyed cakes of meal and cheese. If one

[1] *I.e.*, your home in the city.

Slaves were sometimes fed on the sacrificial cakes left by the priests. So Horace humorously supposes a slave to have run away merely to get plain bread instead of the cloying cake.

should live [1]as nature tells us to, and first a
site on which to build a house must be
looked out, know you a spot that can surpass the happy country fields? Is there a
place where winters are less cold, or where
more pleasant breezes lessen both the dog-
star's rage or Leo's influence, when once
the piercing sun has entered on that mad-
dened sign? Is there a place where carking
care less drives our sleep away? Pray, is
the grass inferior in [2]fragrance or in beauty to
the tesselated floors? Pray, in Rome's streets
does purer water try to burst the leaden
pipes, than that which babbling purls down
winding streams? No doubt, 'mid columns
built of varied marble, trees are reared, and
houses too are praised that look on fields
extended far and near. Though you drive
Nature out by violence, still ever she'll come
back again, and will insensibly o'ercome
and dissipate your ill-conceived disgust. The
man who cannot skilfully compare the fleeces
that absorb Aquinum's dye with Sidon's
purple will not suffer more undoubted or
more heartfelt loss than he will who shall
fail to separate what's false from what is true.
Adversity will sorely try him whom pros-
perity has gladdened overmuch. You will
reluctantly give up whate'er you feel great
admiration for. Shun high estate, for by
one's lowly life one may surpass the noble
and his friends.

The stag once beat the horse in fight, and

[1] This is more in popu-
lar than philosophical
language.

The idea is that the
zodiacal sign Leo is mad-
dened by the rays of the
sun.

[2] The Roman floors
were sometimes strewn
with flowers.
The epithet "Libycis"
implies that the floor was
made of Numidian mar-
ble.
There were plantations
of trees surrounded by
columns at Rome.

Aquinum, a city of the
Volsci in Latium, was ce-
lebrated for its imitation
of the real Tyrian dye.

drove him from the pasturage they shared
alike before, till, worsted in protracted strife,
the horse implored the aid of man, and took
the bit ; but when as a fierce conqueror he
left his foe, he failed to shake the rider from
his back, or bridle from his mouth : so he
who through a fear of poverty gives up his
freedom, which is better far than gold, is
both intemperate and subject to restraint,
and will for ever be a slave because he'll not
know how to live on humble means.   With
him whom his own fortune shall not suit,
the case is like the shoe sometimes, which
will trip up a man, suppose it be too big,
and pinch him if too small.   So, Fuscus,
wisely live contented with your lot, and
don't let me escape reproof when I shall
seem to be amassing more than I can want,

Money should be the and never giving up (the race for gold).
material dispensed, the
mind the dispenser.   And doubtless, money gained is or the lord or

1 Metaphor, from beasts slave of those who gain ; [1]more fit to follow
led with a cord.
others' guidance than to lead the way.

Vacuna was supposed
to be a Sabine goddess,   I read this to my slave to copy down be-
the same as Victoria,
and adored after harvest hind Vacuna's crumbling shrine, contented
as the giver of rest with all else except your absence from myself.
(vaco).

EPISTLE XI.—BOOK I.

This Epistle is addressed to Bullatius, a friend, otherwise not much known. He seems to have been a rich man, the victim of *ennui;* which, in common with many others, he tried to relieve by travelling, instead of engaging energetically in some praiseworthy pursuit. Horace encourages him to live more philosophically, exhorts him to come back, and hints that he himself is happy where'er he be, through a contented mind, not mere change of place.

BULLATIUS, what do you think of [1]Chios and famed Lesbos, what of Samos with neat buildings, what of [2]Sardis, Crœsus' royal home, of Smyrna, and of Colophon? Do they surpass or fall below what rumour says of them, or do they all displease, contrasted with our Plain of Mars and Tiber's stream? Pray, does some one of the Attalic towns suit your desires, or do you now approve of Lebedus, through mere disgust caused by the sea and roads? You know the character of Lebedus, it is a hamlet more untenanted than Gabii, or than Fidenæ; and yet there, forgetful of my friends, and by my friends forgot, I'd gladly watch the raging sea a little distance from the shore. And yet a man who goes from Capua to Rome will not, be-

[1] Islands in the Ægean.

[2] Capital of Lydia.

Ionian cities.

Called so after a king of the Attali. Some of them were Pergamus, Tralles, Thyatira. Lebedus was an Ionian maritime town

Gabii, a town in Latium.
Fidenæ, a small Sabine town.

On the Appian road.

spattered though he be with mud and rain, desire to spend his life in dirty inns ; nor does a man who has caught cold talk loud in praise of bakers' ovens and hot baths, as though they rendered life completely happy ; nor, suppose fierce winds have tossed you on the deep, would you for that cause sell your vessel ere you got back home again.   Fair Rhodes and Mitylene have the same effect on one who is content and thinks aright, as great-coats in the dog days, as thin military training-drawers in storms of snow, as bathing in midwinter in the Tiber's stream, or as a fire in August's heat.   But while you can, and fortune smiles, at Rome praise Samos, Chios, Rhodes, but do not go to them. Take with a grateful hand whatever time the gods have blessed, and don't put off your joy for future days ; so that in what-soever station you have been, you may say that you've gladly lived : for if philosophy and wisdom take away our cares, and not a place that has a wide view of the sea, why, those who haste to other lands but change their clime and not their thoughts.   A busy idleness distresses us ; we go o'er sea and land in search of happiness.

Yet what you seek is here at Rome, or is at (a small town like) Ulubræ, if you but find content.

I.e., he feels no more desire for those beautiful towns than he does for great annoyances.

"Nos" means Romans like Bullatius, among whom Horace lived

Ulubræ was a marshy town in Italy, where Augustus was brought up.

EPISTLE XII.—BOOK I.

This Epistle is addressed to Marcus Iccius, who was at once a soldier and philosopher, and exhorts him to cease his complaints, for which there is no real cause, and to make a friend of Pompeius Grosphus, who was himself the poet's friend.

IF, as you should, dear Iccius, you use the fixed per-centage that you get from your collection of Agrippa's revenues in Sicily, it is impossible for gods to grant you greater affluence. Cease your complaints; for he's not poor who has the power to use whate'er he wants.

Augustus gave Marcus Agrippa the estates.

If you have good digestion, with sound lungs and ¹active feet, the wealth of kings will fail to give you greater boons. If, (as perhaps you do,) surrounded by abundance, you still temperately live on vegetable food and nettles, so you will keep living on, although you suddenly became as rich as Midas was; and this because wealth cannot change a nature like to yours, or else because you philosophically think that virtue is superior to all besides.

¹ *I.e.,* free from gout.

The ordinary nettle, not the sea-nettle. The Italians, even now, in the spring, eat it while young and tender.

Apollo advised Midas to dip his head in Pactolus' stream, and so get golden sand for ever from it.

We are astonished that his neighbours' cattle ate the produce of Democritus's fields,

Democritus was from Abdera, and the originator of the atomic theory.

Argument :—If Democritus, who neglected his property for the study of philosophy, excites our surprise, how much more surprise ought we to feel at your ability to study philosophy, and keep your mind free from sordid ideas amid all your necessary business transactions and dry accounts !

whilst his great mind was deep in abstract speculation : though (we need not feel surprise), for you, 'mid that infectious greed of gain you see, have thoughts for nothing mean, and even now you study natural philosophy ; and learn what agencies restrain the sea, what regulates the seasons ; whether by some forces of their own, or influence of gods, the stars roll in their orbits, or stray from their spheres ; what makes the moon to wane, and then to wax again ; what purpose and what power this union without identity of all the world's great elements possesses ; and whether Empedocles or shrewd Stertinius interpret nature wrong. But whether you be living on the souls, forsooth, of fish, or leek or onion, patronize Pompeius Grosphus, and at once bestow whate'er he ask ; for Grosphus will make no request that is not right and fair. And cheaply gained indeed are friends when good men want some aid. And that you may know how the Roman empire flourishes, I tell you this ; Cantabria is vanquished by the prowess of Agrippa, and Tiberius has by his valour won Armenia ; the king of Parthia on bended knees has owned the prince's sway, and golden Plenty, with her well-stored horn, has spread rich harvests over Italy.

Literally, whilst his active soul was abroad without the body.

Slightly ironical.

Empedocles was from Agrigentum, and a follower of Pythagoras.
Stertinius, called ironically "sapientum octavus," is put to represent the Stoics. He wrote 220 books of Stoic philosophy.

Merely a humorous way of saying, If you live on vegetables, with an ironical allusion to the idea of Empedocles,—that plants had souls.

EPISTLE XIII.—BOOK I.

Horace sends Three Books of Odes just published to Augustus, by Caius Vinius Asella, or Asina, who was probably a neighbour.

———————

As, Vinius, repeatedly and long I told you on your setting out, so give these rolls of parchment with the seal unbroken to the Emperor, [1]if he be well, in spirits, if, in fine, he ask for them ; lest in your zeal for me, as an officious agent and by over-eager efforts, you should err and bring my writings into disrepute.   Suppose, as possibly may be, the bundle of my works seem heavy and distress you, rather throw it quite away than roughly dash it (as an ass might kick its pack away) down in the place to which you're told to carry it and turn your father's surname " Asina " into a jest, and so become the talk of all the town.   Make all the haste you can o'er slope and stream and fen ; and when you've done your purposed work and have arrived at your road's end, then so arrange your burden, and so keep it when arranged, that you don't, as you might, appear to carry your book-parcel as a clown a lamb to market ; or as Pyrrhia, when drunk, the ball of stolen

[1] Augustus was often ill at that time.

A certain Titinius represented Pyrrhia, a maid, as having stolen a ball of wool from her mistress, and being easily detected through her awkward movements when drunk.

wool ; or as a country tribesman holds his slippers and his cap. Don't tell all those you meet what dreadful work you had in carrying those Odes which may attract the eye and ear of great Augustus ; and though often begged to tell your mission, keep straight on your course.   Now go, good-bye ! take care you do not trip in aught, and break the rules I gave.

Rich members of a tribe would sometimes invite poorer country members.

The slippers were worn for entering the triclinium.

The cap to go home in at night.

There were 31 country and 4 city tribes.

EPISTLE XIV.—BOOK I.

This Epistle, addressed nominally to the bailiff or steward of his farm, is really intended by Horace to show his enemies, who envied him the possession of his Sabine estate, that he valued it not so much for its actual worth, as for the opportunity it gave him of escaping their malignity, and pursuing his studies without the annoyance and bustle of a city like Rome: it also explains to his friends why he preferred a country life.

———————

COME, steward of my woodland farm, that makes me my own master once again, which you despise, though dwelt in by five honest families, and wont to send five honest householders to Varia to market :—let us find out whether I more energetically root the vices from my mind, or you the weeds from out my land, and whether Horace or his farm be in a better state. Though the affectionate concern that Lamia shows in mourning for his brother snatched away by death,—ay, grieving inconsolably for him, delays me here, still, heart and soul impel me to that farm, and long to burst the barriers that keep me from the open course to it. *I* say that one who lives a country life is blest; *you*, one who lives at Rome : those

The vilicus was a slave.

Varia was a Sabine town, now called Vicovaro.

L. Ælius Lamia, consul, A.U.C. 756.

whom another's lot so suits, of course dislike their own. Both, foolish as they are, unfairly blame the undeserving place ; it is the mind that is at fault, that never can escape its thoughts. You, when a drudge at everybody's beck and call, begged for the country in your secret prayers ; a steward now, you long for Rome, the plays and baths : you know that I'm consistent, and go with reluctance, when some business that I cannot bear drags me away to town. Our tastes are not alike, and hence we both so disagree ; for he who loves what I do calls delightful what you think a desert and waste wild, and hates what you think beautiful. I see : it is the bagnio and greasy cook-shop that now make you feel this deep regret for Rome, together with the fact that this my little nook will bring forth frankincense and pepper much more readily than grapes ; and that there is no inn close by, nor wanton flute-girl to whose droning notes you may dance clumsily : and that (in spite of these privations) you have still to work the long-neglected fields with hoes ; to give the unyoked ox his food, and satisfy him with the leaves pulled off from trees; and that e'en in your idler moments, if it has rained heavily, [1]Digentia has to be taught by bank and dam to keep its waters from the sunny mead.

Now list, and see what stops us from agreeing on these points. [2]One whom a coat of finest cloth and perfumed hair becomes ;

As clandestinus is derived from clam, so mediastinus is derived from medius ; and meschino, mesquin, from mediastinus.

[1] A stream mentioned again in Epistle xviii., 104.

[2] Himself.

one who, as you well know, won favour from
a greedy mistress by his own unaided charms;
one who has quaffed the clear rich wine from
noon till night, a humble dinner pleases now,
and sleep hard by some stream upon the
grass; nor does it shame one to have once
lived freely, but to fail in giving such life up.
There no one with his jealous eye spoils the
advantages I have, or poisons them with dark
hate's tooth and accusation's power. The
neighbours smile at my unwieldy working of
the field or mill. But you would rather
munch your daily rations with the slaves at
Rome,—you long intensely to be one of them.
And yet my cunning city-overseer begrudges
you the use of fuel, milk, and cheese, and
garden stuff. The ox wants horse's trappings,
and the horse would go to plough. Thus I'll
decide; that both the steward and the over-
seer ply the craft they know.

EPISTLE XV.—BOOK I.

This Epistle is addressed to Caius Numonius Vala, a friend, to inquire about Velia, a town in Lucania, now called Alento; and Salernum, in the Picene district, now called Salerno. The reason for this inquiry was that Augustus had recovered from a dangerous illness by cold bathing, and Antonius Musa, the court physician, had advised Horace to try it.

The construction begins with the words "par est te scribere," in line 25.

DEAR Vala, it is right for you to send me word, and right for me to credit what you say of Velia's weather and Salernum's clime, the character of the inhabitants, and nature of the roads; for the [1]court doctor says that Baiæ's bath is of no use to me; and though 'tis *he* who says it, yet he makes *me* hated when I through the depth of winter take cold baths. And with good reason does the town complain that both its myrtle groves and vapour baths, so famed for drawing from the sinews the rheumatic pains that linger there, are now despised; and with good reason does it bear a grudge against those patients who can bring themselves to bathe their head and stomach in the streams of Clusium or Gabii, and make for colder country haunts. My bathing-place must now be

[1] Antonius Musa made his fortune and reputation by treating Augustus with the cold water cure, after Amilius had greatly reduced him by the opposite treatment.

C'usium, in Etruria, was celebrated through Lars Porsena.

changed, my horse be driven past the well-
known roadside inns. The angry rider,
pulling the left rein, will say this,—" Whither   The left led to Saler-
do you go? My road lies not to Cumæ or   num and Velia ; the right
                                                   to Baiæ and Cumæ.
Baiæ,"—although, indeed, a horse obeys the
bit, not words. 'Tis right too that you say
which people are supported by the greater
stores of corn, and if they drink from cisterns, or pure water brought from ever-flowing
wells,—for I care nought for wines that district can produce ; when at my country home
I can digest and bear all sorts of food and
drink, but when I've come down to the sea
I want some rich and mellow wine to drive
my cares away, to bring high hopes, and
course both through my veins and soul, to
give me words to recommend me to the
girl I love in ¹Velia's town, with all the charm   ₁ Velia was a town in
of youth. 'Tis right too that you say which   Lower Italy, or Lucania.
district can supply more boars ; beneath the
waters of which sea are found more fish and
more sea-urchins; so that I may go home from
the place, fat, and a real " bon vivant " too.   The Phæacians were
    A certain Mænius, when, after spending   noted for their luxury.
                                                   Mænius Pantolabus,
with great spirit all his mother and his father   often quoted before as
left him, he began to be thought quite a wit,   a notorious profligate.
                                                   Horace compares him-
a merry jester, with no settled home ; who   self to him.
now would dine with this man, now with that ;
who could not tell the difference between
a friend or foe when hungry, and relentlessly
got up all sorts of charges against any one
you please, the shambles' plague and storm
and all-devouring gulf, would swallow greed-

ily whate'er he had obtained. When he
had wrung some trifling gift from those who
patronized rascality, or were afraid of it, he'd
dine upon a dish of tripe or else bad lamb,
and eat enough to feed three bears; so that
forsooth, like old fault-finder Bestius, he
might well say that spendthrifts should be
branded on the belly with a red-hot metal
plate. Besides, when he had quite consumed
whatever richer plunder he had gained, he'd
say, " I' faith, I'm not surprised at all who
waste their goods in gluttony, for there's
nought better than a well-fed thrush, nought
finer than a large sow's paunch."

Well, really, I'm like him; for I commend
a safe and humble state when I lack means
for better things, and readily put up with what
you please 'mid common fare; but when it is
my luck to gain some better and some richer
food, I then declare that ye alone are wise,
alone know how to live, whose landed property is seen in your trim country seats.

Bestius was a bad-tempered old miser, who loudly reviled the profligate and luxurious.

EPISTLE XVI.—BOOK I.

This Epistle is addressed to Titus Quintius Crispinus, Consul, A. U. C. 745. The argument runs briefly thus:—I am happy, dear friend, and one of the chief outward causes of this happiness is my Sabine home : take care that you may be as happy as you deserve, and as you are said to be, by acting on the philosophic maxim, "Know thyself," and by keeping your mind free from undue passion and emotion.

DEAR Quintius, I'll write you a complete description of the shape and situation of the land, to save your asking if my farm support its owner by its crops of corn or olive-berries, mead and orchard, or by elms encircled with the vine.   There is a chain of hills unbroken, save where they are parted by a shady vale : yet still so that the rising sun beams on the right side, and that, as he quits the sky with setting car, he warms the left.   You would approve the mildness of the clime.   What would you think, suppose I told you that the [1]brambles bore the cherry and the plum abundantly ?—that both the esculent and scarlet oak rejoiced the cattle with a rich supply of mast, their owner with their spreading shade ? You would vow that Tarentum, closer brought

[1] Poetical traces of the golden age.

M

to Rome, was putting forth its leafy beauty here.

¹There is a spring too (of such size) as well to give its name e'en to the brook that flows from it, since nor with purer nor with clearer stream does Hebrus wind round Thrace. Its waters can cure headache, and have other virtues too.   And this retreat is dear to me ;

² *I. e.*, can please by its own merits alone. nay, if you but believe me, e'en ²delightful in itself, and keeps me well and strong through autumn's sickly time.

You live as you should live, if you do not belie your high repute ; we all of us at Rome have long been proudly talking of your happiness, yet still I fear lest you should rather trust what others say of you than what you think yourself. I fear, too, lest you should suppose that any but the wise and good enjoy real happiness ; and lest, if but the people should declare that you are strong and well, you should conceal the hidden fever at meal-times, until your hands are palsied, and get greased with sauce and fat.   A fool's false shame hides sores instead of curing them. If any one should talk of wars by you conducted both on land and sea, and were to gratify your ear with words like these,— "May Jove, who has your interest and that of Rome at heart, long keep us ignorant whether the nation prize your safety more, or you the nation's ;" you could see in that the praise an emperor should gain : and when you let yourself be called both wise

and virtuous, pray, do you answer, "So
I am"?

"Yes, for I surely feel delight as much
as you in being called both good and wise."

And yet the people who bestowed this
honour on you but to-day, will, if they please,
to-morrow take it back; just as, in case
they have conferred the consulship on some
unworthy man, they will deprive him of the
same :—say they, "Come, give it up, 'tis mine."
Dejectedly I give it up, and then withdraw.
And if the people were to cry out that I was
a thief, vow that I was not chaste, urge that
I killed my father with the strangling-rope,
should I be angry at such false reproach, and
change from pale to red, and red to pale? *The plural shows that
Whom but the vicious man, and one who *there were several alter-
nations of colour.*
needs correction, does or undeserved renown
or false detraction terrify?

But who is the good man? The ¹man who ¹ *According to the peo-*
keeps the senators' decrees, the written law *ple's idea.*
and principles of equity; by whose decision
many an important suit is settled, by whose
legal promise money's safe, and by whose
evidence a cause is won.   And yet the man's
whole family and all his neighbours see that
he is base at heart and specious with a fair
outside.   Suppose a slave should say to me, *Argument : — a s'ave
"I have not stolen aught, or run away;" I *should not be thought
good and careful who is*
answer, "You're rewarded, and escape the *only free from gross
faults.*
galling lash." Then if he say, "I've done no
murder;" I reply, "Then you shall not be *Horace probably means
himself in the epithet*
food for crows upon the cross."   But if he *"Sabellus," taken from
his Sabine farm.*

say, " Then I am good and honest ;" any fair
and truthful man like me would shake his
head and say, " No, no :"—the wolf once
caught fears pitfalls, hawks, the hated snare,
and gurnet dread the hook concealed by bait ;
but really good men hate to do what's wrong
through love of virtue, while you will abstain
from crime through nought but dread of
punishment. Let there be hope that you will
not be caught, you'll work all crimes, e'en
sacrilege ; and when out of a thousand

¹ One peck, of course. pecks of beans you steal but ¹one, my
loss, but not your crime, is less to me on
that account. Whene'er your good man,
whom each law court and each bench of
magistrates regards, propitiates his gods with
offered pig or ox, and has cried out in loud
voice, " Father Janus, hear ! Apollo, hear ! "
he mutters, fearful lest he should be heard,

² Laverna was the god-
dess of stealthy theft. " O fair ²Laverna, grant that I escape detec-
tion : grant that I may seem both just and
pure, and throw a veil of night o'er all my
crimes and knavery!" I don't see how the
miser who stoops down in crossings of the
streets to pick a penny up stuck in the
ground is better than a slave, or aught more
free ; for he who covets will feel fear as well ;
and so the man who lives in fear will never,
as I think, be free. The man who ever

Argument :—the miser
is like a cowardly soldier,
who has fled, been taken
prisoner, and become a
slave ; whose work is
useful to others, but dis-
honourable to himself. hurries on, and is so trammelled in his quest
of gain, will throw away his shield of truth,
and leave his post in virtue's ranks ; when
you can sell your captive, spare his life ; for

he will be a slave to some one's good; let
him, so hardy as he is, feed cattle and work
at the plough; let him go with his master out
to sea, and as a trader winter on the waves;
let him make cheap the price of grain; help
to import both corn and stores. But he
who's really good and wise will dare to say,
"O Pentheus, king of Thebes, pray what   Like Bacchus in the
indignity will you compel me to submit to   Bacchæ of Euripides.
and endure?" "I'll take away your wealth."
"You mean my cattle, land and fortune, furniture and plate : yes, you may take them all."
"I'll bind you fast with manacles and fetters,
ay, and keep you in some cruel jailer's
power." "The god himself will set me free
directly that I will." Methinks this is his
meaning,—I shall die ; death is the bourne
of all this earthly state.

EPISTLE XVII.—BOOK I.

This is an Epistle addressed to Scæva, a Roman knight, in which the poet endeavours to show that business is preferable to inaction, and that it is desirable to gain the friendship of the great, although caution is needed in its cultivation, and, above all, an absence of servility and importunate begging.

———————

ALTHOUGH, dear Scæva, you want no advice, besides your own, and know the means by which one possibly may, as one should, behave in the society of those in higher rank ; yet learn what thinks your dear old friend who still himself needs teaching, (at his age of forty,)—though 'tis just as if a blind man would fain show the way,—yet list and see if I say aught that you would care to use for your own good.   If pleasant rest and sleep till seven o'clock delight you, if the dust and din of carriage wheels, or public-house close by annoy you, I will bid you go to ¹Ferentinum.   For not to the rich man's lot alone falls happiness, nor has he lived so badly who from birth to death has passed unnoticed through the world.   If

¹ A very quiet town in New Latium.

you shall care to further your friends' interests and live yourself with luxury, poor as
you are, go to the wealthy noble. Said the
[1]Cynic, "Aristippus would not care to dwell
with nobles, could he dine on herbs and be
content." Said [2]Aristippus, "If the man
who censures me knew how to live with
nobles, he would be disgusted with his
herbs." Now tell me which of these men's
words and actions you approve of, or since
you are younger, listen to the reason why the
view that Aristippus held is better; for, as
story tells, he used to trick the Cynic's biting
gibes like this :—"I play the jester, but 'tis
for myself, while you are but the people's
fool; my plan is more correct and brilliant
too; I court a noble with attention, so that
I may have a horse to ride and patron to
support me, while you beg for worthless stuff,
inferior to him who gives, however much you
style yourself quite independent." Yet all
kinds of life, position, or possessions suited
Aristippus well, who ever tried to rise, but
still was mostly satisfied with what he had.
Yet, on the other hand, I shall be much
amazed if any change of life will suit the man
whom hard endurance clothes with ragged
cloak with its two folds. The one will not
wait till he get a purple dress, but clad in
aught you please will walk through most
frequented spots and with good taste support
both characters. The other will avoid as
worse than dog or snake a cloak of rich

1 Diogenes.

2 A philosopher of Cy-
rene, pupil of Socrates,
and founder of the Cy-
renaic school.

Milesian wool; nay, he will die of cold if you don't give him back his rags. Pray give them back, and let the poor fool live. To do great deeds in war, and show one's countrymen the captive foe in chains, are tasks wellnigh divine, and aim at immortality. So 'tis no trifling merit to please nobles' taste. You know it is not every man who has the luck to [1]visit Corinth's town. The man who feels no hopes of some success is wont to give up his pursuit; and what of him who has already reached the goal? Has he done what a man should do? (You cannot tell.) Yet here or nowhere is the pith of this our argument. One shirks the burden as too great for his small mind and puny frame. The other takes the load and bears it to the goal. Or virtue is an empty term, or he who makes the trial fairly claims the honour and reward. Those men who in their patron's presence do not tell how poor they are, will gain more than the one who begs; it matters something whether one should modestly accept or rudely seize, and yet this was and is the source and origin of all your [2]aims. The man who says, " My sister has no dowry, my dear mother's very poor, my farm cannot be sold, and is not sure enough in yield to keep me," really cries out, " Give me bread." Another says in whining tones, " For me too [3]shall be cut a slice from this your gift which can be shared." And yet, (as in the fable,) if the [4]raven could but feed and stay

[1] Because of the expensive mistresses, cheating priests, and slaves.

[2] Viz., to gain a better position, more influence, and wealth.

[3] The future shows the impudence of the mendicant.
[4] As the raven that found a bit of food, croaked loud and attracted others, so one who loudly begs, attracts others and spoils his own enjoyment.

its croaking, it would have more food, and
much less bickering and jealousy.   The man
who finds fault with the rugged road—the
bitter cold and heavy rain,—laments the
breaking of a box or stealing of his travelling
money when he's taken as companion to his
patron to Brundusium or to Surrentum's   Brundusium, now
pleasant town—does only reproduce the   Brindisi.
                                           Surrentum, now
shrewd tricks of the courtesan, who oft   Sorrento.
bewails the loss of some small chain, or often
of an anklet, torn from her, so that henceforth real losses and real grief are not believed
at all ; nor does one, if once mocked, care
to lift up the beggar in the streets, though
he may really have a broken leg, and though
abundant tears flow down his cheeks, and
though he swear by the ¹impostor's sacred   Osiris was an Egyp-
god, and say, "Believe me, I'm not jesting,   tian god.
cruel people, raise the poor lame man."   "Find
one who knows you not," the neighbours
with hoarse shouts rejoin.

EPISTLE XVIII.—BOOK I.

An Epistle addressed to the same Lollius to which the Second Epistle is addressed. It contains rules for a suitable demeanour to those above one in rank, and advocates the philosophy of moderation.

FREE-SPOKEN Lollius, if I mistake you not, you'll take care not to look the parasite when you avow yourself the friend; for as staid married women will be different in ways and life to courtesans, so will the friend be far removed from treacherous toadies' ways. There is a fault quite opposite to this, and almost worse, and that is clownish roughness coupled with disgusting want of taste, that tries to recommend itself by hair cropped close, e'en to the skin, by unclean teeth, in vain endeavour to be styled mere freedom from conventional restrictions, and called sterling worth. But virtue is the golden mean, and quite removed from great defect or great excess. One sort of men, too prone to fulsome flattery, like the buffoons who sit by hosts at table, so shrink at the noble's nod, so echo his expressions, so take up the

words that fall haphazard from his lips, that
one would think a boy were saying a heart-
lesson to some harsh [1] Orbilius, or that an
actor played the parasite in comedy. Another
quarrels ofttimes for the [2] merest trifle, and
equipped with absurd arguments as arms,
defends what is absurd, and says, " Forsooth, how can it be that I should not be
credited above the rest, and fearlessly blurt
out whate'er I really think ?—a second life's
not worth enough to make me hold my
peace." But pray what is the difference
about ? Is it to see which gladiator is more
skilled, or is't to see if the Minucian or
Appian road lead one better to Brundisium ?
Those whom expensive lust or gambling's
reckless hazard brings to beggary, whom
boastful pride makes dress beyond their
means, whom restless thirst and hunger after
gold holds fast, whom shame at poverty
and dread of it entirely sways, a rich friend
often much more vicious, hates and shuns, or
if he do not hate them, orders all their life ;
and as fond mothers wish their children
to excel them, so he fain would that the
friend should be more wise and virtuous than
he is, and says what is nearly true,—" Don't
vie with me, *my* wealth admits this folly,
while *you* have but humble means ; a coat
with no spare cloth becomes the prudent
comrade, don't you ape my rank." Eutra-
pelus would give all those he wished to harm
rich clothes to wear, for in such case, men

[1] Orbilius plagosus was the schoolmaster of the day.

[2] Literally, for a goat's hair.

Castor and Dolichos were two gladiators.

dreaming that they're blest, will form fresh
plans and hopes, when they put on the finer
dress ; will sleep until broad day, put off for
some low courtesan polite attention that a
patron needs, will borrow money at high interest, at last—will turn out gladiator, or for hire
will drive a market gardener's horse to town.
See that you never strive to pry into your
patron's hidden thoughts, keep fast a secret
trust, though plied by wine and cause for rage,
don't praise your own pursuits, or blame
another man's, and don't write poetry when he
shall care to hunt. 'Twas through such difference that erst the friendship the twin brothers,
Zethus and Amphion felt, was sundered, till
the lute was hushed, so hated by the harsher
brother.   For Amphion is supposed to have
conceded to his brother's character, and so
do you yield to the gentle sway of some
loved noble friend, and always, when he shall
lead out into the fields his mules all laden

¹ Meleager was one of
the combatants at the
Calydonian boar hunt
(Ovid, Met., 8, 299), and
the son of King Œneus.

with such toils as ¹ Meleager used to catch the
wild boars with, together with his hounds—
rise and throw off the roughness of your
Muse so impolite, that you may dine with
him off what is very pleasant food, gained
as it was by toil, toil such as the old Romans
used to take, so beneficial to repute and
health and strength, especially when you are
strong and well, and can outrun the hound,
or master the wild boar. Besides, there is
not one who wields more gracefully the arms
of manly exercise ; you know with what

'acclaim from the surrounding throng you
manage the sham fighting in the plain
of Mars;—in fine, when quite a boy, you
bore hard service and a campaign in Canta-
bria, led by a [1] general who took down from   [1] Augustus.
the fanes of Parthia once captured ensigns,
and who now reduces to the power of Rome
whatever distant region is not yet subdued.
And lest you should withdraw, and be away
without just grounds, (when asked to see
your patron, think of this,) although you are
engaged on nought that does not suit the
rule of life and harmonize with it, you some-
times take light recreation on your own   Therefore you can have
estate; mock forces portion out the boats;   no just excuse.
the fight at Actium is shown by means of
slaves with you as admiral, as though real
foes engaged; your brother takes the other
side; a lake does for the Adriatic Sea; and
this, until swift victory crown one or other
of you with her bays.   All those who
think that you agree with their pursuits [2] will   [2] In gladiatorial exhi-
countenance your sport with fullest meed   bitions the people expressed their favour by
of praise.   Then next, to give advice to you.   turning their thumbs
downwards, and showed
if aught you need adviser's aid, examine well   their aversion by turning
them upwards.
what you say of each man, and whom you
say it to.   Shun the inquisitive, for they are
babblers too; and those whose ears are
curious to learn, don't keep a secret faithfully; and words once uttered fly away beyond recall.   And let no handsome slave
inflame your heart with love within the
splendid marble threshold of your august

friend ; lest he who owns the handsome, precious girl, should gratify you by some trifling
gift, or should annoy you by tenaciously with-
holding it. Repeatedly regard the character of
him you recommend, lest afterwards another's
faults bring shame upon your head. Sometimes we are deceived, and offer to a noble's
notice one unworthy of it, so, if you should
be misled, give up the company of him whom
his own errors shall keep down, so that you
may preserve the one whose worth you really
know, and guard the one who trusts to your
protection if false charges should assail him ;
and when he's carped at by all with envy's
tooth, pray, do you see that danger will
soon come to you ? For when your neighbour's house wall is in flames, *your* fortunes
are at stake, and fires will gather strength if
left alone. To court a noble friend delights
all those who have not tried, but those who
have are diffident. So while your bark is on
the open sea, take care the wind don't
change and bear you back to port. The sad
the cheerful hate, the merry hate the sad, the
quick the sober, and the careless hate the
energetic and the active ; nay, all those who
drink rich wine from midnight hate the man
who shirks his wine, although he swear he is
afraid of being feverish by night. Remove
that haughty gravity that clouds your brow.
Full oft the really modest man looks like
a double-dealing character, and the reserved
like the morose. What'er your state, read

well the writings of philosophers, and talk
with them, and find out by what means one
may pass calmly through this life, and
whether an insatiate desire for more distress and harass men, or dread of losing
life's bare necessaries ; whether virtue can
be taught or comes instinctively ; what les-
sens cares, what makes one satisfied in heart,
what gives us thorough peace of mind ; distinction, or delightful gain, or a secluded path,
and course of life unnoticed by the world.
And what, pray, think you, are my thoughts,
dear friend, what, think you, are my prayers
whene'er ¹Digentia's cool stream refreshes
me, a stream ²Mandela's citizens drink from,
a village that contracts one's skin with cold ?
My thoughts and prayers are these :—" Let
me retain what I now have, or even less, and
so live the remainder of my life, if heaven
grant me any further time to live ; let me
have a good store of books, and food to last
each year ; and let me not be tossed in
doubts and fears about th' uncertain time to
come ; but I need only pray to heaven as to
blessings that it gives or takes away ; let it
give life and health with means, and I myself
will find content.

¹ See page 52.

² Now called Bardela.

EPISTLE XIX.—BOOK I.

The poet shows the folly of some who would imitate, and the envy of others who would censure him.

DEAR Patron, so well read in Greek and Latin, if you list to old [1]Cratinus' rules, no verses can be long in vogue or last, which water-drinkers write. E'er since the time that Bacchus [2]ranked enthusiastic bards among his regiments of Fauns and Satyrs, the sweet Muses mostly smelt of wine at morn. [3]'Tis proved that Homer loved good wine, because he praised it so. E'en Ennius, that founder of all poetry, ne'er started forth to sing of martial deeds, unless inspired by wine. To those who drink no wine I'll give the law courts and the prætor's bench, and take away the gift of song from the morose. [4]When prætor-like I this declared, the bards ne'er ceased to vie in drinking hard by night, and reeking of the wine by day. And pray, suppose a man should ape old Cato's ways by looking wildly fierce, and walking

[1] Cratinus was one of the old comic writers.

[2] " Adscripsit " is a military term.

[3] Vide Iliad, 15, line 264.

[4] " Edico " was the official word the prætor used.

with bare feet, and wearing coats some sorry
weaver made ; would he show Cato's virtue
to the life, and [1]Cato's character ? A tongue
that tried to emulate the rhetoric [2]Timagenes
displayed made Codrus, from [3]Iarbas sprung,
once burst the vessels of his lungs through
wishing to be thought a man of taste, and
striving to gain fame for eloquence.   A model
one may copy in its faults misleads us ; why,
if I grew pale by accident, these would-be
bards would drink the cumin that makes thin
the blood. O plagiarists, ye abject creatures !
oh, how often have your laboured efforts
stirred my rage and ridicule ! I was the first
to tread with steps original on ground ne'er
trod before, I followed no one else.   Those
who rely upon themselves, like queen bees
lead the swarm.   I was the first to introduce
to Latium th' iambic of [4]Archilochus, the
first to follow both his measures and his
spirit, not the subject that once made
[5]Lycambes hang himself.   But that you give
me not less meed of praise, through this my
fear of altering his metre or the composition
of his lines, I tell you this,—that Sappho
regulates her poetry so full of force, by metre
that Archilochus composed, as does Alcæus ;
but he differs in the subject-matter and
arrangement too, nor does he pick out some
[6]Lycambes to lampoon in biting verse, nor
plait a noose for [7]Neobule's neck in his
defaming lines.   Such strains as those
Alcæus once or Sappho sang, untold before

[1] Cato Uticensis.

[2] Timagenes, a rhetorician from Alexandria, was brought captive to Rome.

[3] Iarbita, or descendant of Iarbas, was the same as Codrus, an African.

[4] Native of Paros.

[5] Lycambes was a Theban who promised his daughter to Archilochus, and afterwards refused her, for which he was assailed by the poet in such biting lines that he and his daughter both hanged themselves.

[6] As Archilochus did ; literally, father-in-law.
[7] Literally, for a bride.

N

by any tongue, I, as the Roman lyric bard,
made known, and sweet it is to show the
nobly born a style unsung before, and to be
read by noble eyes and held in noble hands.
Pray, would you care to know why the ungrateful reader praises my small works at home
and likes them well, yet still unfairly cries them
down abroad ? (Well, here's the cause :) I do
not try to curry favour with the fickle crowd
by some expensive feast, or by a gift of
worn-out clothes ; nor do I deign, wont as I
am to listen to or be the champion of famous
bards, to canvass cliques of petty critics
in their lecture chairs,—and hence their rage
at me. Suppose I've said,—" I feel ashamed
to read my works, which are not fit for a
large audience to hear,"—and so to give to
trifles undue weight ; the critic then replies,
—" You're mocking us, and keeping for
Augustus' ear alone those works of yours.
You trust that you alone distil poetic honey
from your lips, delighted with yourself."
Now I'm afraid to treat all this with cynical
disdain, and that I be not wounded by
the bitter malice of my foe, I cry aloud,
" The place you choose don't suit, I beg
a few days' grace ;" for even jest engenders
hot dispute and rage, and rage fierce enmity
and deadly feuds.

EPISTLE XX.—BOOK I.

This is a sort of epilogue to the First Book of the Epistles, in which the poet describes his volume as desirous of appearing in print, and foretells an early repentance of the desire.

My book, you seem to gaze with wistful eyes
at Janus' and Vertumnus' fanes, so that, no
doubt, you may be laid on shelves for sale in
our best shops for books, made smooth by
pumice stone ;—you hate to be locked up or
sealed, so pleasant to a modest work ;—nay,
you complain because you're shown to few,
and praise the general haunts of men, and
yet you were not trained to this.   Well, go
down quickly to the place to which you long
to go, but there'll be no return for you once
issued to the world.   You'll say, " Unhappy
book, what have I done ? what did I want ? "
when any one has injured you, and when you
see yourself packed in some narrow space,
and when the reader dozes and is wearied
out ; but if the prophet err not, through a
hatred of your folly, you'll be dear to Rome

The Sosii were like our Mudie.

The parchment was rough outside until smoothed by pumice stone.

The Forum was on lower ground ; as was the Sosii's shop.

but till the novel charm is past, and when
you have begun to be well thumbed by
vulgar hands, in cold neglect you'll be food
for the lazy moths, or suffer banishment
to Utica in Africa, or in a parcel you'll be
sent to Lerida in Spain.   Then he who gave
advice unheeded thus, will laugh, like him
who in a rage thrust on a rock his miserable
ass when obstinate; for who would care
to save another 'gainst his will? Besides,
this lot awaits you, that a childish dotage
shall steal over you, while teaching boys
their A B C in outskirts of the town.   But
when warm summer days have gained a
larger audience, you'll say that I, from freed-
man-father sprung, possessed of small estate,
tried hard to rise beyond my humble lot ;—
and tell them this to give me merit that may
compensate for want of birth.   You'll also
tell that I in peace and war have suited well
the leading men at Rome, am small in frame,
grey ere my time, fond of the sun, soon
angry, but in such a way, that I am also soon
appeased.   Suppose, as possibly may be,
some one should ask my age, then let him
know that I had lived full four-and-forty
years when Lollius took Lepidus to share
his [1] office in the state.

Modern name for Ilerda.

[1] The consulate.

EPISTLE I.—BOOK II.

An Epistle to Augustus, who complained that the poet (laureate) had not addressed him. In this epistle Horace defends the poets of modern times against the absurd taste of the public, shared in, to some extent, by Augustus himself, for antique poems simply from their antiquity. It also contains a sketch of the progress of Latin poetry.

SINCE you, great prince, by your unaided strength, have to conduct affairs so numerous and of such moment, guard the Roman empire by your martial skill, adorn it by your character, improve it by your laws, I should retard the national advantage were I to take up your time with more than a few words. Once Romulus and father Bacchus, Castor and his brother too, who, after doing deeds of high renown, were deified, while they reclaimed waste lands, and civilized the human race, allayed fierce war, built towns, and settled landed property, complained that the return of gratitude they hoped to gain was not commensurate with their deserts. That[1] hero who once crushed the hydra's dreaded might, and killed those monsters famed in story, in per-

[1] Hercules.

forming toils imposed by fate, found out that
envy was subdued but when the objects of its
hate were dead.   For those men who depress
pursuits inferior to theirs, but dazzle by their
splendour when alive, although when dead
they will be loved.   To you we now pay

Clever flattery to Au- timely honour while you're with us, and build
gustus.
shrines for men to grasp as they swear by your
'name, confessing thus that nought like you
will e'er arise, or has arisen yet.   But this
your people, wise and just in this one point,
I mean in their preferring you to Roman and
Greek generals, yet estimate all else by plans
and methods very different, and or disdain or
hate all that they see but what is past and
gone, and has outlived its proper age : and
are such champions of all that's old, as to avow
that erst upon the Alban Mount the Muses
read out those twelve tables that forbid all
crime, which the Decemviri proclaimed as
law ; read out the treaties made by Tarquin,
struck at Gabii, or framed by Romulus with
the stern Sabines' moral race; the yearly

Especially of the bro- chronicles of the chief priests, and ancient
thers Marcii and Attius
Navius. volumes of the soothsayers.   If, just because

1 Homer and Archilo- all the most ancient ¹works Greek poets wrote
chus.
are also better than the rest, the Roman

2 Literally, weighed in writers too are therefore ²rated thus, it is no
the same scale.
use to waste our words.

An absurd argument
advanced by logicians.   'Tis as absurd as the logicians' argument,
1. Olives and nuts both " There is nought hard inside an olive, so
produce oil.
2. There is nothing there's nothing hard outside a nut."
hard inside a nut. There-
fore there is nothing hard Ironical.   And so, no doubt, we're highly blest
inside an olive.

by fortune, so we paint, and sing, and wrestle
with more skill than Greeks, who know so
well what wrestling oil implies.　If age make
poems better, just like wine, I'd gladly know
how many years would stamp the poet's works
with value.　Ought a bard who died a hundred
years ago to be ranked with those perfect ones
of old, or numbered with the worthless modern
ones?　Let some fixed limit stay dispute.

Well, then, one who has lived a hundred
years is ancient and approved.

But what of him who was a month or a year
younger when he died, among which class
will it be right for him to rank,—among
the ancient bards, or those whom modern
times, and times to come, would never own?

Oh yes, that one you named, who's younger
by a mere brief month, or even a whole year,
shall fairly rank with older bards.

I take, then, this concession, and by slow
degrees remove one year and then another, as
I'd pluck away the hairs from horses' tails,
till he who has recourse to calendars, and
estimates the poet's merit by his age, and
thinks nought worth attention but what death
has consecrated, shall fall vanquished by the
process of the falling heap.　Then Ennius,*

Marginal notes:

3. There is nothing hard outside an olive. Therefore there is not outside a nut. Reductio ad absurdum. Horace does not give it in full as it would be well understood by Augustus and his readers.

A supposed dialogist says this.

An example of the logical argument "sorites"—metaphor from a gradually diminishing heap, like Cicero's "argumentatio acervalis," Cic. Div. 2, 4, 11. It consisted of an accumulation of propositions differing slightly, the first of which could not well be opposed. and the rest followed almost insensibly from the first.

* Ennius professed that Homer's soul and genius had entered into him, and promised his countrymen that he would write verses as good as Homer wrote; and as our critics think so highly of him, he is not at all nervous about the result of his boasting.

" Pythagorea somnia" means the process of transmigration believed in by Pythagoras.

both wise and grand, indeed a second Homer (as our critics say), seems to feel safe about the issue of his boasting, and his dreamy theories of transmigration.

Nay, more; is not [1]Nævius still often read, and still fresh in our memories? He is, so sacred are all poems of antiquity. Whene'er our critics hold debates about the merits of each bard, [2]Pacuvius bears off the reputation of a skilled, and [3]Accius of a sublime old man. [4]Afranius's Roman comedies are said to be just like the Greek ones of Menander, while we're told that Plautus hurries on to the *dénouement* just as Epicharmus did of Sicily, that [5]Statius excels in dignity, and Terence more in skill. The works of these men, queenly Rome now learns by heart, and sits in crowded theatre to view; these men, esteems and thinks real poets from the age of tragic [6]Livius to our own times. The common people sometimes judge aright, but sometimes they go wrong. If they admire and praise the bards of old so much that they prefer nought else to them, compare nought with them, they are wrong; if they believe that they composed much in too rough, admit they wrote much in too slovenly a style, they have good taste, and side with me, and judge with [7]heaven's countenance. I don't indeed assail the lines of Livius, or think that they should be erased, which I remember once [8]Orbilius, who birched so much, read out for me, a little boy, to learn;

[1] Nævius was a much older and worse poet, though still read by every one. He wrote tragedies and comedies.

[2] Pacuvius, son of Ennius's sister, wrote twelve tragedies, and was eighty years old when he published his ninth tragedy.

[3] Accius was an old orator and tragedian.

[4] Comœdiæ togatæ were comedies founded on Roman custom, and had Roman dress. Comœdiæ palliatæ were founded on Grecian customs, and had Greek dress. Afranius flourished about A.U.C. 660.

[5] Caius Cæcilius Statius was a Gaul by birth, originally a slave, and afterwards a friend of Ennius, and a comic poet.

[6] Livius Andronicus was an old tragic poet.

[7] When Jove is angry men go wrong; when he is propitious they go right.

[8] Orbilius Pupillus, a native of Beneventum, an ancient city of Samnium, now Benevento,—came to teach at Rome in his fiftieth year.

but I am much surprised that they think such
lines excellent, quite free from faults and
nearly perfect, when in all their works, if but
a few fortuitous expressions, if a line or two
a little neater than the rest have ta'en the eye,
this gains reception for and recommends the
whole work to the public praise.   I cannot
bear that aught should meet with blame, not
since men think it coarsely or ungracefully
composed, but merely from its modern style.
Nor can I bear that great applause and rich
rewards be claimed for ancient bards instead
of sufferance.   Were I to doubt if [1]Atta's
comedy be a success or no, the older men
would all cry out that shame was nowhere
to be found, since I attempted to find fault
with pieces such as dignified [2]Æsopus, such
as polished Roscius are wont to act, and
this because they think nought right but what
suits their own taste, or else because they
think it quite beneath them to adopt the
taste of younger men, and to admit when old
that what they learnt as beardless boys is
now but worthy of neglect.   But he who
praises [3]Numa's Salian strain, and fain would
seem alone to know what he, like me, knows
nothing of, is not a champion loud in his
praise of genius long buried in oblivion, but
he assails the modern works; us moderns
and our works he hates maliciously.   And
yet had Greeks disliked, as much as we,
all novelty, what work would now be old? or
what would national enjoyment have for all

Emico means to shoot forth so as to attract attention.
Ducit means conducts to, or gains admittance for a poem to theatres, &c: where it could scarcely go without such beauties, slight as they be.

1 Atta means a lame man, from αἴσσω, to limp or start, a sobriquet given to Titus Quinctius Atta, who was lame. A play was said to be successful (stare), or to be hissed off the stage (cadere); literally, move across the saffron and flowers with which the stage was strewn. 2 Two celebrated tragic actors of the age just passed, Roscius was defended by Cicero, and Æsopus was his friend.

3 Sung by the priests of Mars in solemn procession, and very imperfectly understood. Numa introduced the sacerdotal order of the Salii for preserving the ancilia, or sacred shields.

alike to read and wear by constant use? As
soon as Greece (the Persian war now done)
began to cultivate the arts, and by degrees
fall into luxury through fortune's smiles, she
was devoted now to training in gymnastic
schools, now to the race, bestowed her
patronage on men who carved in marble,
ivory, or bronze, gazed with rapt look and
thought upon some masterpiece of painting,
found delight in flute-girls' piping now, and
now in tragic actors' plays. Just as a baby-
girl would play while under nurse's care, so
Greece, soon cloyed, gave up the eager object
of her search. And pray what takes our
fancy, or excites dislike, that you'd suppose
would never change? This love for art both
fav'ring peace and fortune's smiles produced.
'Twas long our joy and custom too to rise
betimes and open doors, explain the law to
clients, to invest our wealth made safe by
definite receipts, to learn from old men, and
instruct the young in means by which their
fortunes could increase, and the expense of
luxury grow less.

But now our fickle public have quite
changed their inclinations, and are fired by
nought but strong desire for scribbling verse.
Young men, grave fathers, all with locks engirt
by bay, now as they dine read o'er their lines
for writing down. Nay, I myself, who vow that
I don't write a line, am found to be more false
than ¹Parthians, for, waking ere sunrise, I
call for pen and parchment and bookchest.

Literally, to invest
money secured by cor-
rect names. The lender
had the borrower's name
written in his ledger.

Proverbially false.

Though one who knows not seamanship shuns
steering, though but those who know their
use dare give sick men a remedy,—for as
the proverb is, "Physicians but their art pro-
fess, the artisan his craft alone attempts,"—
yet all alike, skilled or unskilled, write verses
now. Still learn from these remarks what great
advantages this trifling error and delusion
has. The poet's mind is not addicted much
to greed of gain ; 'tis poetry he loves ; he is
wrapped up in that ; he smiles at loss, the
flight of slaves, and fire ; he purposes no fraud
against a partner or a youthful ward ; he lives
on farinaceous food and household bread,
although unsuited to hard service and a
coward, still he's a good citizen. And if you
grant that matters of grave import can be
furthered by more trifling ones, the poet
shapes the unformed lisping speech of children ; turns their ears in tender youth from
filthy conversation ; afterwards he trains the
heart as well by kind instruction ; he corrects rough manners, envy, rage ; records all
noble deeds ; he furnishes the time to come
with ample precedent, consoles the destitute
and sick at heart. Whence could unmarried
maidens and chaste boys learn how to beg
for heaven's aid, had not the poet shown
them how ? The band of youths and girls
pray for assistance, and soon feel the gods'
propitious help ; they pray for rain in winning accents taught them by the bard, avert
disease, drive off the dangers of portentous

Southernwood, much
used for various ailments.

dread, gain peace and bounteous harvests for
the year. The gods above and gods below
are all alike appeased by song. The swains
of old, so stout to toil, so happy in their
humble means, at the glad season after harvest home, as they refreshed their bodies,—
ay, and e'en their minds, that bore hard
toil through hopes of ending it :—amid the
partners of their toil, their children and their
faithful wives, used to obtain good-will of
Ceres by an offered pig, and of Silvanus by

Fescennia was a town new milk, and of the guardian-god who ever
of Etruria, where nuptial
songs were invented. tells us how short-lived we are, by flowers
and wine ; and by this custom was found out
the freedom of all rural song, which in alternate strains poured forth the raillery of
clowns. And this free custom, gladly owned,
each harvest-time would crack the harmless
joke, until the jest, now biting, 'gan to
change to rage, and with its unrestrained
assaults t'attack the noblest families. Men
felt the smart, when now assailed by malice'
tooth that drew blood with its bite : when
even those as yet unharmed were anxious for
the general good. Besides, a law was passed,
and penalty inflicted, to protect all men from
being satirized ; so poets changed their style,
compelled to praise, and thus to please,
through fear of being beaten with a club to

1 When Corinth was death. Then captive [1]Greece took captive
destroyed by the Ro-
mans, A.U.C. 608. her rude conqueror, and introduced the fine
arts into rustic Latium ; so the rough mea-
sures of old times then passed away, and

elegance of style drove out the coarser taste,
though still for many years, and even yet,
some trace remains of the rough style. For
long it was before the Roman writer turned
his shrewd mind to the pages of Greek works,
and when the second Punic war was done, at
peace, then for a time began to see what worthy
model Sophocles, or [1]Thespis, or old Æschylus could give. He next essayed his powers in
fit translation of their works, and naturally of
a lofty mind and full of fire, was satisfied with
the result. For well the tragic spirit breathes
in him, and he is happy in new turns of
phrase or word, and yet he ignorantly thinks
correction is disgrace, and fears its use.
[2]'Tis thought that comedy is very easy to
compose, because it gets its subjects out of
general life ; yet in proportion to the less
excuse it has, so much the harder is the task.
Just see how poorly [3]Plautus represents the
rôle of youthful lover, niggard father, or of
treacherous pimp. How grand, forsooth,
[4]Dossennus is in showing up voracious para-
sites ! with what a careless air he treads the
comic stage ! for he delights in filling out his
coffers well, quite careless after that whether
his play be hissed or have a run. Yet those
whom a desire for fame drives in her fickle
car to write dramatic works, a listless audience
dispirits, an attentive one puffs up with pride.
So slight, so small the cause, that does depress
or raise the mind that's eager for applause.
But to destruction with the drama, if or praise

[1] Thespis was called the "father of tragedy."

[2] The mere fact of people supposing it so easy prevents their excusing what they otherwise might excuse.

[3] Compared with Menander, Diphilus, and Philemo. He shows the difficulty of comedy by quoting some poor delineations.

[4] A comic writer, otherwise unknown.

withheld so wear me out, or praise bestowed
conduct me home so blest. [1]This often scares
and stops from writing e'en th' intrepid
bard; I mean that the more numerous mob,
inferior in merit and in rank, unskilled, ob-
tuse, prepared to come to blows suppose
the knights object, call for a bear-bait or a
boxing-match e'en in the middle of the play;
for this is what the populace applauds.
Yet e'en the pleasure which our *knights* now
feel is now no longer that of ear but eye,
that gazes now on this, and now on that
vain show. But now-a-days 'tis four whole
hours or more before the curtain falls, while
troops of horse, and regiments of foot, are
put to flight: then kings made captives by
reverse, with hands tied fast behind them,
are dragged on the stage, while Gallic cars,
sedans, and carriages, and men of war, all
hurry on, while iv'ry statues, and all Corinth's
riches, are borne past. Were but Democritus
alive, he'd laugh, suppose a creature, blending
in its form the panther and the camel, differing in kind, or rare white elephant, should
draw the crowd's attention, nay, he'd watch
the people much more narrowly e'en than
the games, because he'd think they offered
him a finer sight than any actor could: in fine,
he would imagine that composers [2]wasted all
their toil in writing for the stupid mob. For
pray, what power of voice can drown the noise
with which our theatres now ring? Why,
one would think [3]Garganus' groves or Tuscan

[1] Excuse for not writing at all, or writing so as to suit the vitiated taste of the age.

Literally, is raised: for the Romans had their curtain drawn down upon the stage until the play began.

A giraffe.

[2] Literally, he'd think that writers were relating their plays to a deaf ass.

[3] A woody mountain in Apulia.

sea was groaning to the blast, so great the
din with which our plays and works of art
and wealth from foreign lands are viewed;
and when the actor, decked with these, has
stood upon the stage, the people loudly clap
their hands. Well, has he said aught yet?
Not he, indeed. What takes their fancy then?
O 'tis his cloak that rivals violets with its
Tarentine dye; and lest, as possibly you may,
you think that I "damn with faint praise" a
style I care not for myself, though others
treat it well, I tell you this;—that bard seems
able to [1]achieve the greatest feats in poetry
who works upon my heart by all his fictions,
stirs my rage and then allays it, fills my breast
with terrors feigned as by magician's wand,
and places me in fancy now at [2]Athens, now
at Thebes. Yet come and give some countenance to those as well who rather trust a
reader's taste than brook the proud disdain
a public audience will show, suppose you
care to fill [3]that library so worthy of Apollo,
and to stimulate the poets' zeal, that with
more ardour they may go unto the Muses'
verdant hill. Then, as the proverb runs, [4]that
I may cut *my* vines down too, we poets ofttimes do ourselves much harm by giving
you our books to read when full of care
and wearied out; when we feel deeply hurt
suppose some friend has dared to criticise a
single line; or when unasked we read again
a passage read before; when we complain
that no advantage comes from all our toil, or

[1] "To walk on the tight rope" was a proverb for any difficult task.

[2] The plots of most dramatic works were laid in these places.

[3] The Palatine library established by Augustus.

[4] *I.e.*, to be severe against others as well as myself.

This all refers to Augustus.

Literally, spun out with nice or delicate thread.

² *I. e.*, the emperor.

³ The merit of Augustus is likened to a goddess. And those who panegyrize him are guardians of that goddess's temple.

⁴ Chœrilus was a poet of Iasus, a Carian town.

⁵ It is said that Chœrilus received a piece of gold for every good line he made in Alexander's praise.

⁶ He showed more sense in doing that.

⁷ Bœotian dulness was proverbial.

The argument is, that Augustus, on the other hand, only favoured the best poets.

£8,000 to each was perhaps given.

from those poems ¹so exquisitely composed :
—and when we hope that matters will result
in this, that on the instant ²you have learnt
that we are writing verses, you will kindly,
though unasked, send for us, and enrich us
with your gifts, and bind us by our gratitude
to write. Yet still, it is worth while to learn
what sort of ³guardians of its temple the
imperial excellence may have, so tested both
in cabinet and field, and not to be entrusted
to unworthy poets' pens. That ⁴Chœrilus we
read of, who for his rough, ill-formed lines,
set down in his receipts so many coins with
⁵Philip's royal head upon them, was thought
highly of by Alexander, the great king. But
just as ink, when touched, will leave a mark
and stain upon the hands, so, oft composers
sully noble deeds by their imperfect lines.
Yet that same king who lavishly bought
poetry so weak at such a price, ⁶by procla-
mation ordered that no man should paint his
portrait but Apelles, no one but Lysippus
mould in bronze a statue to express brave
Alexander's lineaments. But were you to
invite that keen discrimination in inspecting
arts, to judge of books and these our Muses'
gifts, you'd vow that he was born in thick
⁷Bœotian air. But bards whom you esteem,
like Virgil and like Varius, do not disgrace
your estimate of them ; nor yet the gifts which
they've received, and which reflect great
praise upon the ⁸giver ; nor with greater life-
like clearness are the features shown when

cast in bronze than are the characters and
feelings of distinguished men by poets' works;
nor would I sooner write my prosy satires in
their humble style than sing in epic verse of
your exploits, or tell the situation of the
lands you have subdued, their streams, the
castles ta'en by you though placed on hills,
the foreign realms, wars ended by your skilful
conduct through the whole world's space, and
Rome, the dread of Parthians while you are
Emperor, were my abilities but equal to
my will. But neither does your majesty
allow a feeble lay to pass, nor am I bold
enough to try a task beyond my strength; for
over-acted zeal does foolishly disgust the
man it loves, especially whene'er it tries to
recommend itself by the poetic art, for men
learn quicker, and remember with more will-
ingness what any one laughs at, than what
he may approve of and respect. I care nought
for a service that may possibly annoy me, nor
do I desire to have my portrait painted with
distorted features, nor be caricatured in
some weak verse, lest I should have to blush
when I received so coarse a gift, and lest,
stretched out in 'open box, with him who   ¹ To show the worth-
penned my praise, I should be carried down   lessness of the contents.
to streets where men sell frankincense and
unguent, grocery, and all that is wrapped up
in worthless manuscripts.

O

EPISTLE II.—BOOK II.

The poet makes various excuses to Julius Florus, a friend of his, and aide-de-camp to Tiberius, for not sending him any composition, according to a sort of promise made when Tiberius left Rome.

DEAR Florus, trusty friend of prince Tiberius

¹ the good and famed, suppose a man, as possibly he might, should wish to sell a slave born, say at Tibur or at Gabii, and were to thus negotiate with you :—This slave is fair and bright, and handsome too, from head to foot, and shall become and ²be your property for four-and-sixty pounds ;—a home-born slave, well fitted to perform his owner's slightest wish, one too who knows a little Greek, and is adapted for whatever duty you may please ; you'll mould him to whate'er you like, as does the potter the moist clay. Nay, more, he'll sing a strain that's pleasant as one drinks one's wine, though it lack art and skill ;—why, all these great professions make one doubt the facts, when men bestow excessive praise on wares they would palm off on us. Suppose he further said, I'm not at all

¹ Tiberius acted like a good man, and was a great general while Augustus lived.

² I. e., continue to be.

The argument is that Florus is no more right in blaming Horace's idleness than one who, after purchasing a slave with defects mentioned by the dealer, brings a lawsuit against the vendor.

obliged to sell; though poor, I do not owe a
penny piece; besides, no other dealer would
do this for you, nor is it any one you like
who'd get the same advantage easily from
me;—he once failed in some trifling duty,
and as will occur, he hid behind the stairs
through terror of the whip that hung upon
the wall;—give me my price, unless his
shirking work, that sole exception to his
merit, cause offence: methinks in such a
case the man would bear the price away,
and dread no legal penalty; and say, You
bought a slave, and knew of his defects, [1]the
verdict is as good as given for defendant; do
you still assail him and annoy him by an unjust suit? So *I* told *you* when leaving Rome
that I was idle, had no energies for such a
task, to save your fiercely finding fault with
me, because no answer to your letter came.
What good did I then gain, if still you now
impugn the points that make for me? Besides this, you complain that I don't keep
my word, nor send the verses you look for.
When once a soldier of Lucullus, wearied out,
while snoring fast asleep at night, had lost
completely the small store he had amassed by
unremitting toil, he, angry with himself and
with the enemy, like some fierce wolf made
keener by the tooth of hunger, as they say,
hurled down king Mithridates' soldiers from
a garrison, though strongly fortified, and rich
in treasure-stores. Grown famous for that
deed, he was adorned with medals of dis-

[1] There is no chance
of your succeeding in a
suit.

Argument, — A poet
in easy circumstances
should make poetry but
an amusement.

1 £160.

tinction, and received a 'sum of money too.
It happened nearly at that time the general
who wished to overthrow some fort, began
with words that might have well inspired
a coward with some spirit for the fray, to
urge him on like this,—"Brave soldier, go
with lucky steps where your own valour calls,
for you will reap rich guerdon for your
services.   Ha! pray why stand you there?"
Then shrewdly, though a thorough clown, he
said,— "he who has lost his purse will go,
yes, *he* will go where you would have him
go."   So first 'twas my good fortune to be
reared at Rome, and taught how much
Achilles' rage once harmed the Greeks.
Then Athens kindly gave me tastes a little
more refined; so that I longed to draw
distinctions between right and wrong, and
study truth in Academus' grove.   But
troublous times withdrew me from this
pleasant place, and then the tide of civil
strife bore me, though knowing nought of
war, to fight against a foe, who was to prove
no match for great Augustus' strength;
and me, the moment that Philippi's field
dismissed me humbled, with my hopes thus
nipped, and reft of house and farm my
father left, dread poverty that makes one
bold, impelled to write; while now that I've
enough, pray, what strong remedy shall ever
rid me of my folly, if I don't conceive it better
far to rest than keep on scribbling lines?
Besides, years, as they roll along, deprive

us of each gift we have ; they've stripped
[1]me of my merriment, the joys of love, of
feasting, and of sport; they're trying now
to wrest my art of writing from me too.
What would you have me do ?   In fine, we
do not all admire and like the same pursuits ; you take delight in lyric verse,
another loves iambic lines, a third likes
satires such as [2]Bion wrote, and caustic
wit.   I almost think that even three men
differ as they dine together, calling as they
do, with varied taste, for food quite opposite
in kind.   What should I give you, what
take care that I don't give ?   You there
reject that dish the other bids me bring;
while what you ask for is beyond a doubt
annoying and distasteful to the other two.
Then, what is more than all I've said, do
you suppose that I can write at Rome 'mid
all these toils and cares ?   One calls me to
be bail, another bids me give up all my
duties, and go hear him read his poetry,
a third lies ill in the [3]north end of Rome,
a fourth in the [4]extremest south,—yet both
must be called on ; a tolerable distance that,
you see, to walk.   [5]Yet still you say the streets
are clear, so that there is no hindrance to
deep thought.   Not so; some builder with his
mules and porters hurries by in eager haste ;
the huge crane raises now a block of stone,
and now a beam of wood; the gloomy
trains of mourners jostle with unwieldy
wains ; a mad dog swiftly runs in this direc-

[1] He was fifty years old.

[2] A philosopher and poet, pupil of Theo-phrastus.

[3] Literally, on the Quirinal hill
[4] On the Aventine.

[5] Horace says this only to refute it.

tion, while in that a sow besmeared with mud goes rushing past.   Go, then, and with poetic thought compose the tuneful lines. All those who write, love groves and flee from towns, and, as they ought to be, are votaries of Bacchus, who delights in sleep and shade.   And do you wish me, 'mid this bustle both by night and day, to sing and follow in the bard's unhackneyed tread? Why, e'en a genius who has picked out calm Athens to dwell in, and has devoted [1]seven years to study, and grown old in reading books and careful thought, comes forth at Rome more silent than a statue, and full often makes the public shake their sides with laughter,—and amid this sea of business, and this stormy bustle of the town, should I think *myself* able to build rhymes to wake the lute's full tones?   There were at Rome two brothers once, an orator and barrister, so dear that when one spoke the other heard what was but praise, so much so, that the former called the latter Gracchus, and the latter called the former Mucius. And how does that mad wish for praise less influence our tuneful bards?   I write the ode, another elegiac verse, and (as we read) we say,—" O wondrous sight, [2]and work elaborate ! "   Just notice first with what proud looks, with what a stately mien we gaze up at Apollo's temple open to the Roman bard.   Then, after, if, as possibly may be, you've time, go in with us and stand a little

Marginal notes:

" I nunc " are ironical words.

[1] Only to express a longer time than usual.

Gracchus was a celebrated orator ; Mucius Scævola, a distinguished civil lawyer mentioned by Cicero, Or. i. 3.

[2] Literally, finished by the nine Muses. These bad poet's compliments are compared to gladiators using foils.

distance off, and hear the works read we
both bring, and why each for himself so
weaves the poet's crown.   Like gladiators
in their Samnite dress, with slow contention,
we ourselves sustain wounds or inflict them
on our foe e'en till the lights are lit.

I go off home in his idea, Alcæus, and
pray who is he in mine? Who but [1]Calli-
machus? Or, if he seem to wish for more,
he then becomes [2]Mimnermus, and believes
himself more famed because he now has
gained the name he longed to gain.

I bear with much to soothe the fretful
race of bards when I compose, and, [3]cringing,
try to gain the public praise. But since
this zeal for poetry is gone, and I am now
myself again, [4]let me refuse to listen, as
they read their works quite free from fear of
rivalry from me. Composers of bad lines
are ridiculed, 'tis true, yet they exult in
writing, think themselves divine, and if one
praise them not, they praise themselves unasked whate'er in happy vanity they have
composed. But he who shall desire to write
a poem really made as it should be, will
take th' impartial critic's judgment when he
takes his tablets in his hands; he'll bring
himself to blot out from his works all words
that shall be mean in style, shall not be
serious enough, and shall roll on unworthy
of esteem, although they may reluctantly
withdraw, and linger still within the poet's
sacred shrine; he'll kindly rescue from their

Gladiators used to represent the Samnites conquered by Romans, a show which the Romans were fond of, and which usually lasted till night.

[1] A poet of Cyrene.

[2] A poet of Colophon.

[3] Ironical.

[4] *I.e.*, don't force me to write again, and be subject to the same annoyances.

Metaphor from a muddy stream. The poet's study is compared to Vesta's shrine, which none but the Pontifex Maximus could enter.

long oblivion, and for the people's good
bring into vogue expressive terms which,
though once used by men like Cato and
Cethegus in the plain old times, unsightly
mould and long neglect keeps hid from
view; he will adopt new words which custom,
the great source of language, has produced ;
impassioned, clear, and very like a limpid
stream, he'll pour out all his stores, and will
enrich his country's tongue by fruitful flow
of eloquence ; he'll prune too flowery a
style, make smooth with his judicious taste
what's rough ; he will erase lines that are
spiritless ; he will look like the actor in the
pantomime, and shift from one part to
another as the man who dances like a
nimble satyr now, now like the clumsy
Cyclops moves. I'd rather seem a silly and
unskilful writer, if my faults but give me joy,
or pass at least unnoticed by, than know my
art and be distressed by secret rage. There
was a man at Argos once, and well known
too, who thought that he was listening to
some [1]splendid tragedies,—one who would sit
and clap his hands delighted in the empty
theatre ; yet he was one who could observe
life's duties as he ought, a neighbour really
kind, a courteous host, and gentle to his
wife ; nay, one who could forgive his slaves,
and not get in a rage about a flask of wine
they might have tampered with, one too who
kept himself [2]from open danger safe ;—and
when he was restored by his relation's aid

Cato the Censor.

Marcus Cethegus, consul, A.U.C. 548.

"Ringi" is used of dogs who are angry, and just going to bite.

[1] *I. e.*, when no plays were being represented.

[2] Literally, who could avoid a rock and open well.

and care, and had expelled his mental
malady by [1]strongest remedies, and was himself again, he said, " I' faith, dear friends,
you've killed, not saved, a man, from whom
his pleasure and delusion so delightful has
been wrested thus ! "

Well, then, it surely is expedient for me to
give up trifling and be wise, and leave for
children play so fit for them, and cease to
hunt for words to set to Latin lyric strains ;
and rather learn completely both the harmony and measures of real life.

[2]And hence it is, I meditate and call to mind
in silent thought reflections such as these :—
Suppose no ample draughts of water were
to quench your thirst, you'd tell the doctor
of your state ; and can't you bring yourself to
tell some one that your desires increase as
fast as do your gains ? Suppose your wound
would not heal up when treated by a root or
herb shown for your use, you would indig-
nantly reject the treatment by the root or herb
that did no good. You had already heard
the common people say, " Misguided folly
quits the mind of him to whom the gods give
wealth," and though you have become no
wiser since you gained more gold, will you
still cling to their false teaching ? Yet if
wealth could give you wisdom, free you from
your wish for more, or fear of loss, you well
might blush for shame if there should be, in
all the world, one man more covetous than
you. If what one buys in [3]all due form

1 Hellebore was the
usual cure for madness.

2 Soliloquy from here
to the end.

3 Previous to the reign
of Servius Tullius every-
thing was sold by weight,
and even as late as
Horace's time the old
custom was retained of
the purchaser striking
the balance with a brass
coin, and giving the
coin to the vendor as
price.

become one's own, still, if you credit what
the lawyers say, prescriptive right gives
ownership sometimes; the land that gives
you food is virtually yours, [1]and the rich
owner's bailiff feels that you are really the
possessor. when he harrows fields that are to
yield their corn for you; you pay a price,
and get for it grapes, kids, sheep, casks of
wine; and surely by that means you purchase
by degrees a piece of land that once perchance
was purchased for [2]two thousand pounds or
more; what matters it whether your income
be derived from money paid just lately, or in
years gone by? A man, who long ago
bought land [3]in Latium, or in Etruria, has
still to dine off herbs he buys, though he
don't think he has; nay, more, he has to
boil hot water at the fall of chilly night with
fuel he has bought, and yet he calls all that
his own as far as where the poplar planted
close by stays all quarrels among neighbours,
by appointing unchanged boundaries;—as
though, forsooth, there's aught that does
belong to one for aye, when in brief fleeting
space by favour, or by purchase, or by force,
or, last of all, by death, it takes fresh owners
and falls into other hands. So, then, since
lasting ownership belongs to none, and heir
comes after heir as wave comes after wave,
what is the good of owning streets and
barns?—What use to own Lucanian downs
that join Calabrian, if death, that cannot be
begged off by bribes, mow down the high

[1] Orbius was a rich landed proprietor, who sold the produce of his fields.

[2] Really £2,400.

[3] Aricia, now La Riccia, was in Latium.
Veii, now Isola Farnese, was in Etruria.

and low alike? Some have no precious
stones, no statues formed of marble or of
ivory, no Tuscan statuettes, no pictures,
plate, no vestments stained with Moorish
purple dye,—and [1]there is one who does not
care to have all this. Why, of two brothers,
one prefers ease, pleasure, and perfumes,
to Herod's rich palm groves,—the other,
wealthy, restless, keeps reclaiming wild
woodland with fire and axe from light
till dark, that guardian deity alone can tell
who regulates our horoscope, and always
is with us; that god whose nature is like
man's, who dies with each of us, whose looks
will change from joy to grief. So, then,
I will enjoy my modest competence, and
take from it whate'er occasion shall require,
and will not fear what thoughts my heir may
form of me, because he find no more than I
have left him in my will. And yet I never
shall forget how much the open-hearted and
the cheerful differ from the spendthrift, or how
much the thrifty differ from the niggardly.
For there's a difference between a reckless
squandering of means, and an avoidance
of a miserly unwillingness to spend or care
to get more than's enough; and one would
better choose, like boys sometimes, their
[2]Easter holidays, to hastily enjoy a short and
pleasant time. Let all disgusting meanness
in one's house be far removed. On large or
humble means I still shall live with uniform
consistency; suppose I be not borne along

[1] He uses "est," not "sit," to show that he means definitely the philosopher.

[2] Five days' holiday, from March 19th to the 23rd.

with well-filled sails by fav'ring winds, yet
still I don't drag on my life amid adversity's
rough storms; in strength, in genius, appearance, merit, rank, and means, I'm ever running midway in the race of life. Suppose you
be no miser, then I say, well done; but,
pray, has every vice besides fled from you
with that one ? Pray is your heart quite
free from all insatiate desire for place ?—
quite free from dread of death ? quite free
from rage ?—Can you deride the vulgar view
of dreams, of incantations' mystery, strange
natural phenomena, the sorceress, the ghost
by night, and magic's awful power ?—And
do you gratefully compute the years you've
lived?—excuse your friends' mistakes?—grow
both a gentler and a better man as age

I. e., the mere fact of comes on ? If not, pray, how much better
your not being a miser
is very far from making are you for the riddance of one moral
you a philosopher.
weed out of so large a crop? If you can't
live aright, give place to those who can ;
you've had enough of love, and banqueting,
and wine ; 'tis time for you to leave, lest
younger men, whom gaiety and pleasure
better suit, should laugh at you for having
drunk too deep a draught, and drive you off
the stage of life.

ARS POETICA.

The Art of Poetry was written in a letter to Lucius Piso, who was after-wards Prefect of the City at Rome, and to his two sons. The absence of continuity in the ideas expressed and the general character of the work, give rise to the belief that it was more a sketch by letter of what he intended afterwards to amplify and systematize.

———————

SUPPOSE a painter should elect to join a horse's neck unto a human head, and then to spread the plumage of all sorts of birds upon his canvas. While the limbs were chosen from such motley sources, that the picture of a lovely woman at the top should end in the portrayal of some monster of the deep of hideous blackness, would you then, my friends, when once let in to see this work, refrain from ridicule ?

Consider, then, ye Pisos, (father and sons too), that every book where empty fiction shall be formed like the chimæras of distem-pered brains, in such a way that neither head nor foot be given to a model that is uniform,[2] will be extremely like that wretched daub.

[3]Yet surely both the painter and the poet ever have enjoyed fair licence to attempt the strangest works.

[1] From line 1 to 23 he describes the simplicity and uniformity of all works of art.

[2] The word "uni" by poetic prolepsis is put for "ita ut una sit."

[3] An objector says this.

Of course, and we [1]demand and grant in turn such privilege, yet not so far that fierceness should be classed with gentleness, the snake dwell with the bird in peace, the tiger with the lamb.

Oft one or two descriptions of the senator's broad purple stripe are foisted into tragic and heroic works of great pretensions, for effect, though Dian's grove and altar, winding streams as they purl swiftly through delightful fields, the river Rhine, or rainbow, is the subject of the poet's pen. Yet here was not the place for such digression.

And I dare say you can [2]paint a cypress well enough: though what's the good of that, if sitters pay their price, and then are represented swimming from a wreck bereft of all their goods?

Again: suppose a noble jar is being fashioned by the potter, how, pray, as the wheel turns round, is but a paltry pitcher the result?

In fine, be works of any style you please, if they observe consistency and uniformity.

[3]Ye Pisos, father and sons worthy of your father, most of us bards are misled by a mere semblance of what's right. For instance, I try to be terse, and I turn out obscure; then those who aim at a smooth, easy flow, lack fire and force; those who pretend to the sublime are but bombastic; those who are too cautious and too fearful of a storm are grovelling in style; while others, in their eager wish to represent a single subject in

astonishingly varied lights, make the proverbial mistake of painting dolphins in a
wood, and wild boars in the sea.   Unskilled
attempts to shun mistakes but lead us on to
fresh defects.   Why, near Æmilius' gladiatorial school there dwells a brazier, who will
better than all others mould in bronze e'en
[1]nails and waving hair, though he will prove
unlucky in his work's completion, for he'll
not know how to suitably arrange the whole.
If I were thinking of composing aught, I'd
no more care to be like him than to live
with a nose awry, admired though I were for
my black eyes and hair.

Choose, then, ye authors, subjects suited
to your powers, and find out long before
what load your shoulders can, and what they
cannot, bear.   Nor fluency nor clear arrangement will be lacked by him who has selected
themes adapted to his wit.

The merit and the grace, if I mistake not,
of arrangement, will consist in authors of
projected poems saying, in their work's first
lines, what then must needs be said, in putting off and for the moment keeping in
reserve most of their thoughts and plot,—in
choosing this, rejecting that.

Then, with a critic's care and judgment in
disposing words, one will express one's self
with admirable skill, suppose a clever combination shall have made an old word seem
quite new.   And if, as possibly may be, one
be obliged to illustrate an abstruse matter by

[1] They required very delicate casting.

some modern terms, it will then be one's lot to frame words never heard by Romans [1] of old times; and this same licence, if but moderately used, will be allowed, [2] and new and recently coined words will be in vogue, suppose their origin be Greek, and only a small number thence derived. But why, pray, shall our public grant to Statius and Plautus licence not allowed to Virgil and to Varius? Why am I looked upon with jealousy, if I can add a few new words and phrases, when the language Ennius and [3] Cato used has found fresh stores for their own country's tongue, and brought new terms in vogue? It aye has been, and aye will be allowed, one to bring into daily use a term stamped with the current mark. As by their leaves the woods are changed each autumn that comes round, and as the earliest fall off, so words once used die out, and, like the young words newly coined, will grow and thrive.

Death claims us and our works alike, ay, though the 'harbour by Augustus made protects our fleets from north winds' rage (a work well worthy of a king), or though that marsh,[5] long barren, fit for boats alone, now finds food for the towns around, and feels the plough sunk deep in earth; or Tiber,[6] shown a better course, has changed its channel erst destructive to our crops, still, all that

---

[1] Cethegus was a celebrated orator, called "Suadæ medulla,"—the essence of persuasion.
"Cinctutus" means wearing a girdle as the ancients did, while the more feminate moderns wore the tunic ungirded.

[2] As, for instance, centimanus, tauriformis, beluosus, intermundia, qualitas, æqualibritas, veriloquium, essentia, indoloria.
C. Cæcilius Statius, of Gallic origin: a slave by birth, and comic poet.

[3] Cato the Censor is meant.

[4] The Portus Julius, formed by a junction of the waters of the Avernian and Lucrine lakes.
[5] The draining of the Pontine marshes.

[6] Augustus prevented the inundations caused by the Tiber, by building moles and making dams, and repairing the banks.

man can do will come to nought : far less,
then, can the favour and the influence that
language has remain unchanged. Oft terms
that now are obsolete will be brought
in again, and those in vogue will fall into
disuse, if custom, that controls the choice
and right and rule of speech, shall will it
so. Great Homer showed us in what metre
the exploits of kings and generals and all
war's horrors could be told. At first the
sad lament, and afterwards pleased feelings,
too, were shown in elegiac verse. Yet still
philologists contend, and their contention's
undecided, as to who first introduced the
humbler elegy. The rage he felt stirred up
[1]Archilochus with the iambic he himself composed. This metre the low shoe of comedy,
and this the stately tragic buskin, chose as fit
for dialogue, both since it drowned the noise
the people made when in the theatre, and
since 'twas naturally formed for action. But
the Muses gave to lyric poetry the art of
representing gods and demigods ; the boxer's
victory ; the steed first in the race ; the
young man's loves, and the free speech that
wine begets. And why am I called " bard "
by all, if I have not the power or the skill
t'observe distinctions made, and the com-
plexion of each several work ? Why with
false modesty do I prefer to keep so ignorant
than to find out the truth ?

A comic subject is unsuited for description
in the tragic metre, while a tragic theme

[1] Not even ten lines his works are extant.

P

will not bear treating in familiar verse
that's nearly fit for comedy. Let each style
fitly keep the place it has assigned to it.
[1]Yet sometimes even comedy is spoken in a
grander tone, [2]or else an angry father rails
against his son with cheeks that swell with
rage, and [3]Telephus and [4]Peleus, tragic
though their lot, ofttimes express their grief
in simple style : when both in poverty and
exile they give up inflated terms and words
of wondrous length if they intend to move
the listener's feelings by their plaint. 'Tis
not enough that poetry be written with regard
to art ; let it be tender too, and draw the
hearer's heart whithersoe'er it will. Just as
the human face smiles upon those who smile,
so it shows sympathy with those who weep ;
and so, if you want me to weep, you must
first grieve yourself, and then, you actor of
the lot of Telephus or Peleus, your misfor-
tunes will touch me. But if you utter words
unsuited to the part, I shall or fall asleep
or laugh. A mournful tone the sorrow-
stricken face becomes, a threatening the
enraged ; but merry words become the gay,
and grave the stern : and surely nature trains
in early years the feelings of our hearts to
suit each phase of fate ; makes us feel joy,
excites to rage, or bows us to the earth and
tortures with deep woe, then gives those
feelings vent by speech's explanation. Yet
suppose the speaker's words be not adapted
to his state, the Roman knights and common

[1] *Vide* Terence, "Adel-phi," 5, 3, 3. Demea speaks.
[2] Terence, "The Self-Tormentor," 5, 4.
[3] Telephus was a son of Hercules, and King of Mysia.
[4] Peleus was the father of Achilles and son of Æacus. He killed his brother and went mad.

people too will raise a loud derisive laugh. 'Twill make great difference whether the actor play the part of god or demigod ; of one of ripe old age, or one impetuous, and in the bloom of youth ; of matron ruling her own house, or of attentive nurse ; of roving trader, or of tiller of green fields ; of some fierce Colchian or effeminate Assyrian ; of one brought up at Thebes, or at the rival town ; or follow what tradition tells, or be consistent in invention. If, as possibly may be, you put * upon the stage once more the great Achilles' part, let him be ever active, passionate, implacable, and fierce ; let him swear laws were never made for him ; with him let might be right. But let [1] Medea be untamable and resolute, but [2] Ino quickly moved to tears ; [3] Ixion treacherous ; [4] Io in exile wandering ; [5] Orestes sternly mad. Suppose you represent upon the stage some plot untried before, and dare t'invent new characters : let the same model that you started with be kept quite to the end, and see that it be uniform. 'Tis hard to portray characters that many have, as if distinctively your own ; and one does better to spin out Homeric themes to several acts, than if one were the first to publish subjects both unknown and undescribed before. A subject from the general store will be distinctively one's own, if one spend little time on hackneyed views of it that all alike can claim, and if one do not set one's self to

* The prefix "re" is the word "reponis" implies "after so many others."

[1] Medea was a sorceress of Colchis who helped her lover Jason to obtain the golden fleece, and prevented the father Æetes from pursuing by strewing the sea with her brother's limbs. When Jason repudiated her to marry Creusa. she killed her own children by Jason and burned Creusa to death.

[2] Ino was the wife of Athamas. King of Thebes, who went raving mad, and pursued her until she threw herself into the sea, and, together with her sister Melicerta, was changed into a sea-goddess.

[3] Ixion was king of the Lapithæ in Thessaly, and murdered his father-in-law to avoid paying the nuptial present. Jupiter took him into heaven to purify him, and he there made an unsuccessful attack on Juno's chastity, for which he was bound to a revolving wheel in Tartarus.

[4] Io was daughter of Inachus, King of Argos, beloved by Jupiter, and turned into a cow through fear of Juno. Juno drove her mad ; but ultimately she married Osiris, King of Egypt.

[5] Orestes killed his mother, Clytemnestra, for her murder of his father and her husband Agamemnon. He was driven mad by the Furies, was tried at Argos, but acquitted by Minerva's casting vote and Apollo's aid,

translate closely word for word, or through a servile imitation get involved in limits so confined that shame or the work's plan prevent one's extrication.

Don't begin like this, as Homer's imitators erst: "I'll sing of Priam's lot, and of the celebrated war." For what will such a boasting author give us worthy of his high-flown strain? Why, as the proverb goes, the mountains are in labour, but an absurd mouse will come to birth. And how much better writes this poet, who shows taste in all his works!—

[1] "Describe, I pray, my Muse, the hero who, when Troy was ta'en, saw characters of many men, and saw their states." His purpose is to give a brilliant narrative after a modest opening, not a spiritless account after commencing with quite dazzling arrogance; and this he does so that he may in order bring to notice all his wonderful conceptions like the truth: such as [2] Antiphates or Scylla, Polyphemus or Charybdis; he does not begin his tale of Diomede's return from Troy with Meleager's [3] death, or his relation of the Trojan war with [4] Helen's wondrous birth; he ever hastens to his poem's issue,—hurries on his readers to his plot's main action, just as though they knew it well; omits all that he knows will gain no lustre in the handling; and so frames his fiction, so well blends the false with true, that the chief plot agrees well

[1] The first lines of the Odyssey.

[2] Antiphates, a king of the Læstrygones, who sunk the Greek fleet returning with Ulysses from Troy, and devoured one of his crew: *vide* Odyssey, 10, 100. Scylla and Charybdis: *vide* Odyssey, "ii," 12, line 85; and Polyphemus, Odyssey, "i," 9, line 187.

[3] A description by Antimachus, a cyclic poet.

[4] Referring to Jupiter's amour with Leda in the form of a swan.

with the opening, and the end with the
chief plot.

Just listen, Piso, to what I and all the
public with me look for from you: if you
want an audience t'applaud until the [1] curtain's drop, and one that means to sit until
the actor cries, "Now clap your hands;"
you must then strongly mark the character
that suits each time of life, and draw a
graceful disposition of men's characters aye
changing as the years roll on. The child
that can now clearly speak and firmly walk,
plays gladly with its mates; gets in a
rage with thoughtless haste, and easily
calms down again, and changes every hour
that goes.

Again, the stripling freed at last from the
attendant's rule, delights in keeping dogs
and horses, or in training on the sunny
[2] Campus' grass; seduced to vice with all the
pliancy of wax; rough to all those who give
him good advice; slow to advance his
interest, but reckless in expenditure; elated,
eager in desires, and swift to give up what
he just now loved.

But manhood's age, with feelings and pursuits all changed, seeks influence and friendship's aid; tries hard to gain distinction;
takes care not to do what it would afterwards
be very glad to change. But many draw-
backs oft beset the old, because, perhaps,
they try to gain still more, and wretchedly
avoid to touch, and dare not use what they've

[1] The curtain of the Roman stage was not dropped at the end of the play, but raised.

[2] I.e., the Campus Martius.

amassed; or else because they do whate'er
they do with chilling caution and procrasti-
nate, are slow to hope, lethargic, ever looking
for some future time, morose and peevish,
praising time they spent when they were
boys; reprovers, too, and censurers of
younger men. Life up to forty years of age
brings much advantage in its train, and
afterwards takes much away. Then, to
prevent the chance of characters that suit
the old being assigned to those in manhood's
prime, or those that suit a man to a mere
boy, we should keep our attention fixed on
those that properly belong to, and so suit
the several times of life. A thing is either
done upon the stage or done [1] elsewhere,
and tidings of it brought. What falls upon
the ear stirs not men's feelings as does what
is witnessed by the trusty eye, to tell them
which the audience require no messenger. Yet
still don't bring upon the stage what should
be done more privately, and keep much from
men's sight which some eye-witness' eloquence
may afterwards make known. Let no Medea
slay her sons before the public gaze, and let
no wicked [2] Atreus openly cook entrails for
that horrid feast, nor [3] Procue turn into a
bird, or [4] Cadmus into snake. I don't believe, and loathe whate'er you show me like
to this.

Again, don't let the play that means to be
called for and have a run, be shorter or e'en
longer than five acts, and let no god take

[1] Such as suicides and deaths.

[2] Atreus, the father of Menelaus and Agamemnon, was King of Argos and Mycenæ, and served up his brother Thyestes' sons at a banquet to the father.

[3] Procue was daughter of Pandion, King of Athens, sister to Philomela and wife of Tereus. She killed her son Itys, and served him up to his father: she was changed into a swallow, Philomela into a nightingale, and Tereus into a hoopoe.

[4] Cadmus was the founder of Thebes, and the inventor of alphabetic writing.

part in it, unless some case of difficult
distress arise to need such champion ; and
let not a fourth character try to intrude his
speech. See that the chorus take part in the
play, and do its duty thoroughly, and let it
not sing aught between the acts that does
not aid and fitly suit the plot. Then let it
side with honesty and virtue, and give kind
advice, restrain the passionate, and ever
quell the threats of pride. Let it praise
meals that humble boards can give, praise
justice' benefits, the written law, and peace
with gates not leaguered by the foe. Let it
keep secrets safe, pray to the gods, and beg
that fortune may once more upon the
wretched smile, and leave the proud in
misery. The flute was not, as now, brass-
bound, and rivalling the trumpet's notes, but
thin in tone and plain in form, with but few
stops ; was fitted to accompany and aid the
chorus, and fill with its sound the rows of
seats not yet too closely packed ; for thither
certainly a public flocked that one could
count, since few and moderate, and pure
and modest, were the people there. But
when the Romans widened out their empire's
bounds by conquest, and when ampler walls
girt in the towns, and when on holidays
men's guardian gods were made propitious
fearlessly by wine drunk in the day, then
greater freedom was conferred on measures
and on rhythm. And, pray, what taste could
the unlettered clown, when freed from toil,

show in incongruous society with educated
men,—the base born with the nobleman?
And so the player on the flute gave gestures
and more scenic splendour to his art, and
now to right, and now to left, trailed tragic
trains across the stage ; so, too, shrill tones
were added to the lute's deep notes, and
bolder fancy-flights found vent in words
unheard before, and what the chorus said,
with quick perception of true interest and
keen foresight, were very like unerring oracles
from Delphi sent.

[1] The bard who strove in tragic verse to
gain the prize of tragedy, the goat so value-
less, soon after brought nude on the stage,
wild satyrs (a new style), and roughly, though
not losing the [2] grave character of god or
demigod, tried raillery, because the audience, when now the sacrifice was done, were
drunk and riotous, and had to be kept in
their seats by some enticement and by
pleasing novelty.

But 'twill be suitable so to commend to
public taste the bantering, the witty satyrs—
so to temper tragic gravity with comic jest—
that neither god nor demigod who shall be
brought upon the stage, and who just now
was seen, in royal gold and purple dressed,
go from a palace to an humble hut and utter
vulgar words, or in attempts to shun a style
that's tame, affect a meaningless obscurity.
Real Tragedy, that does not deign to babble
trifling lines, will, [3] like staid matron bade to

[1] Description of the satyric drama.

[2] These characters were brought on the stage as well.

[3] There were some sacred rites at which married women danced, such as those of Cybele.

dance on holidays, mix with the wanton
satyrs, and still keep a show of modesty.

[1] I never shall, ye Pisos, as a writer of
satyric drama, be content with simple ordinary terms alone, nor shall I try so hard to
differ from the usual character of tragedy
that it should make no difference if some
slave and bold woman who obtained more
than [2] two hundred pounds by cheating her
old master, or if a Silenus, guardian and
attendant to the [3] god he reared, should speak.
I will so aim at a satyric drama, formed
artistically from an ordinary theme, that any
one you like should hope to do the same,
but when he tried his skill should labour
very hard and spend much toil in vain ; so
much do continuity and combination tell :
such grace is sometimes given to a common
theme.   If I be critic, let the satyrs, brought
from woods upon the stage, take care that
never, like street-boys in towns or idlers in
the market-place, they act or play the wanton
rake in lines effeminately soft, or chatter
noisily in filthy and defaming speech.   Indeed, at this the Roman [4] gentlemen, the free-
born and the rich, are much annoyed ; nor
do they willingly acknowledge or present the
crown of bay to what the people's lowest
dregs approve.[5]

Short syllables when followed by long ones
are called iambics ; a quick measure this,
which quickness gave the name of " trimeter
iambics " to the verse, though made of pure

[1] He mentions the kind of writing that suits the satyric drama.

[2] The talent was about £250 in value.

[3] I.e., Bacchus.

[4] Slaves and freedmen were those who had no recognised fathers, so those who had a father would be "ingenui."

[5] Literally, "if the purchaser of parched peas and nuts approve anything."

iambics from the first foot to the last, it had
six beats. And not so long ago, the measure
with obliging readiness admitted steady
spondees to its early heritage of laws, but
not so far as to give up iambics in the second
and fourth feet as readily as comrades yield.
Yet this iambus in the second and fourth feet
is seldom seen in those [1] fine trimeters of
Accius men like so now, and (by its absence)
stigmatises Ennius's lines hurled on the stage
with spondees' mighty weight, by charging
them with far too hasty and too careless composition, or with want of skill. It is not any .
critic in the world who sees a rhythmical
defect, and so a licence that he don't deserve
is granted to the Roman bard. And just for
that should I transgress due limits, and write
by no rule, and think that none will see—
or should I rather think that every man will
see the errors I may make, and so pursue a
plan that's safe, and cautiously attempt but
what may find some tolerance? In fine, I
have avoided blame, but earned no praise.
Ye Pisos, turn the pages of the best Greek
writers over, both by day and night.

But yet your ancestors praised Plautus'
measures and his wit, though they admired
both his measures and his wit too freely, not
to say absurdly, if but you and I know how
to separate a pointless joke from really witty
repartee, and can but mark the pauses off,
and have good ear to time and tune.

'Twas said that Thespis was the author of

a kind of tragedy not known before, and
that he rode about the streets in wains
together with his poetry for men to sing and
act, whose faces were smeared o'er with lees
of wine.

Then after him came Æschylus, who first
used tragic characters and tragic trains well
worthy of the name ; who covered o'er the
stage with ordinary planks, and taught the
actors how to speak in grander tones and
use the stately buskin's aid. [1] Next ancient
Comedy came in, and was in vogue with
most. But speech's freedom here became a
fault, and showed excess that merited some
legal check, and so a law [2] was passed, and
then the chorus to its shame was dumb, for
it had lost its licence to abuse. More
modern bards left nought untried, and those
perhaps gained most renown who dared to
quit the path the Greeks had trod, and celebrate our nation's deeds, though it were
[3] tragedy or [4] comedy they put upon the
stage. And Latium would not be now more
powerful in valour and in martial glory than
she is in speech if but correction's labour
and delay did not disgust each bard she has.
[5] Ye scions of Pompilius, find fault with
dramas that both course of time and much
erasure have not well corrected ; ay, un-
numbered times emended to the greatest
nicety. Yet just because Democritus thinks
genius more blest than miserable art, and
shuts the uninspired bard off from the

[1] *I. e*, after Thespis, Æschylus, Cratinus, Eupolis, Aristophanes.

[2] Decrees were passed by Antimachus and Syracosius perhaps B.C. 410.

[3] Fabulæ prætextatæ, or rarely, prætextæ, were Latin tragedies with a Roman plot, and so called because illustrious men clad in the toga prætexta, or nobleman's dress, acted in them. They were opposite to the " fabulæ crepidatæ," or Latin tragedies with a Greek plot.
[4] Fabulæ togatæ were Latin comedies with a Roman plot, opposed to fabulæ palliatæ, or those with a Greek plot. They were so called from the toga, or national dress.
[5] The nominative is used, as in Sat. 2, 2, 107, as a declaration more than an appeal.
Calpus was a son of Numa Pompilius, and the Pisos were called Calpurnii from him.

Of course this is irony
against the would-be
poets of the day, who
were quite ignorant, and
devoid of genius or art.

Muses' hill, most writers give up paring
nails and shaving beard, haunt secret spots,
and shun the bath.

And doubtless they will gain the longed-
for name of " bard," if they have ne'er let

[1] Licinus was made a
senator for his hatred of
Pompey. Such an ele-
vation for a barber gave
rise to the epitaph,—
" Marmoreo tumulo Li-
cinus jacet, at Cato
nullo,
Pompeius parvo, quis
putet esse deos?"
which might be rendered
thus :—
" The barber lies in
  splendid marble tomb;
  no stone
Points out great Cato's
  place of rest :
Where Pompey sleeps
  an humble slab de-
  clares alone:
That gods exist, who
  could have guessed?
For Anticyra, see Sat.
2, 3, 83.
[2] There is no good rea-
son why I should care to
be a poet according to
their standard.

[1] Licinus our barber cut the hair from heads
that hellebore from three Anticyras could
never cure.

O stupid that I am to rid myself of bile
when spring-time comes ! for did I not, no
other would write poetry in better style.

[2] But there's nought in it worth all this.
So, then, I'll do the whetstone's work, which
can make sharp the steel, although itself it
cannot cut : and so, though I write nought
myself, I will explain the author's work and
duty too ; the stores from which he draws
material ; what makes and trains the bard ;
what suits him, what does not ; what the
result of merit in the art, and what of
ignorance. The sense of the philosopher is
the real source of writing well. The works
of men who followed Socrates will show you
subjects to write on ; and words will readily
attend a subject carefully thought out.

He who has learnt his duty to his country
and his friends ; who knows what love to
show a parent, brother, or a guest ; the
duties of a senator or judge ; the office of a
general on service sent,—beyond a doubt
knows how to give each character its proper
traits. I'll bid the man who draws a picture
of " *the real*" with skill, regard the copy life

and morals give, and get expressions thence
instinct with life. Sometimes a drama
showily set off with ordinary truths, in which
the characters are duly marked, although
devoid of grace and dignity and art, delights
the public more, more forcibly attracts, than
lines devoid of fact, and light melodious
verse.

The Muse gave to the Greeks both genius
and power to speak in neat and fluent tones;
to Greeks who cared for nothing but renown.
But Roman boys learn how to subdivide
the pound by lengthy sums into minutest
parts. Now let the money-lender's son
tell this : Suppose a twelfth from five-
twelfths be subtracted, what remains? You
might have said, " The third part of a
pound." Well done ! you'll want no aid to
guard your property. Suppose a twelfth be
added, what does that come to? It comes
to half a pound. And yet when once cor-
rupting avarice and care for gain like this
has tinged our thoughts, do we expect that
poems worthy of [1] immortal fame can be
composed?

The Romans paid much more attention to arithmetic than poetry. A side blow is aimed here at their avarice and eager pursuit of wealth.

The poet's aim is to instruct or please, or
tell what is at once instructive and an aid
to life. In all didactic poetry be brief. so
that the minds you teach may swiftly learn.
and faithfully retain your words. All that is
needless touches not the mind already full
of thought on what is said. Let fiction
made to please be very like the truth, and.

1 Literally, worthy to be rubbed with cedar oil and stored up in smooth cypress chest. The cedar gave an oil that protected things from decay, and the cypress wood was used for the same purpose.

let no drama claim an indiscriminate belief,
nor represent some monstrous incident.

[1] Our companies of older men deride what
lacks instructive truth, while younger knights
with arrogance despise grave poetry. But he
[2] gains full applause who with instruction
blends what is attractive by delighting and
informing equally all those who read.

Such books pay our best publishers, are
sent abroad for sale, and win undying fame
for the now celebrated bard.

But there are faults one well may overlook, for neither does the string sound as
the hand and inclination wills, but often
answers sharp when one would have a flat;
nor will the arrow from the bow aye hit the
mark. But when a poem's greater part is
beautiful, I shall not be disgusted with a few
mistakes that carelessness has caused, or
human weakness failed to guard against.
Well, what then is the rule?

Just as a copyist is not excused, if, though
forewarned, he ever make the same mistake;
just as the harpist is laughed at who always
strikes the same wrong note: so, in my
judgment, he who's very carelesss is as bad
as that notorious bard [3] Chœrilus; for him I
wonder at and laugh when he shows two or
three good lines, and also am annoyed when-
e'er a poet really good grows careless in his
work. Although one well may be allowed
to show less vigilance in such long works as
Homer wrote. As painting is, so poetry:

[1] More than 45 years of age.

[2] Literally, is wont to gain every vote. "Punc-
ta" were dots on waxen tablets as signs of votes
before the introduction of separate ballots.

[3] Chœrilus only made seven good lines in de-
scribing all the exploits of Alexander.
Compare Ep. 2, 1, 232.

there will be pictures to attract you more on
nearer view, and some you'll like when seen
more distantly.　One loves the gloom;
another will prefer to be viewed in broad
day, if it dread not the critic's nice perception : one has pleased but once, another will
please though viewed many times.　And do
you, elder of the Pisos, though you're trained
to right by what your father says, and have
good taste yourself, still take this rule to
heart and well remember it, that moderate
and passable proficiency can in some cases
be allowed.　To put a case : the barrister
and pleader of but ordinary power does not
come near the excellence of our best members of the bar, and still is valued ; but nor
gods nor men, nor even pillars where the
books are hung for sale, have granted aught
but failure or complete success to bards.
As at a pleasant feast discordant music, and
coarse unguent, and the poppy-seed mixed
with bad honey, cause disgust, because the
meal might be prolonged without such needless aid ; so poetry, both made and introduced for giving pleasure to the soul, sinks
to the lowest depths if it but fall a little
short of highest excellence.　The man who
cannot take part in the games ne'er tries to
wield the weapons on the plain of Mars ; and
he who is unskilled at tennis, quoits, or
hoop, tries not to gain distinction so, lest
the dense throng that crowds around
should safely raise a laugh ; but he who

The Corsican and Sar-dinian honey had the worst flavour ; that of Mount Hymettus and Hybla the best.

knows not aught of poetry still dares to write.

1 One of the bad poets says this.

[1]Well, pray, why not? says one : I'm free-born ; nay, more—nobly born ! Besides, I'm

2 Really £3,200.

rated as possessing [2]the three thousand pounds or more the knights require ; in fine, my life is irreproachable.

But, Piso, you'll not say or do aught that don't suit your genius, so excellent is both your judgment and your intellect. Yet still, if e'er you shall have written aught,

3 Spurius Mæcius Tar-pa, *vide* Sat., 1, 10, page 60.

submit it [3]to our shrewdest critic's ears; your father's too and mine : and put the manu-script by privately till more than eight years have gone by, for you'll be able to emend what you've not published ; but words oi ce sent forth can ne'er return. Once Orpheus, heaven's priest and gods' interpreter, made savage men who lived in woods give up their

4 He means acorns and raw flesh, such as beasts only ought to eat.

murders and disgusting [4]food ; and he, through this, was said to have soothed savage tigers', ay, and lions' rage. Amphion, too, that founder of the Theban town, was said to have moved rocks at his lute's sound, and led them wheresoe'er he would by mild persuasion's power. Their wisdom in old times was this,—to separate the national from private rights, things sacred from pro-fane ; to stay the sexes from a lawless inter-course ; frame rules for man and wife ; build

5 Before the use of brass or bronze.

towns ; [5]carve laws on oak. By means like this, respect and fame accrued to the immor-tal bard and to his poetry. Then, after them, great Homer and [1]Tyrtæus roused the manly mind to martial deeds in fight; the oracle's response was told in song, the path of life marked out; kings' favour sought in Muses' strains, and relaxation and cessation from long toil found out: and this I tell you, lest perchance the Muse of lyric poetry, and Phœbus, god of song, should make you feel ashamed of them. It has been questioned whether poetry that's really good is made from nature's gift or skill: but I can't see what study could effect without rich vein of genius, nor genius untrained; so much the one requires the other's aid, and with such harmony conspires to work the end in view.

The man who purposes to reach the wished-for goal will bear much and do much when young, endure both heat and cold, refrain from women and from wine; and so the minstrel who sings Pythian strains will [2]learn before and [2]fear the critic's blame. 'Tis not enough to say, I am composing poetry of wondrous excellence; "a murrain seize the last," as boys say [3]in their game: it is disgraceful to be left behind, and really to confess that I don't know what I have never learned. Just as a crier who collects a crowd to buy his wares, the poet who is rich in land and money placed at interest, bids those who flatter him come for rewards. But should he be a man who can give a good dinner with nice taste, be

[1] Tyrtæus was an Athenian, who, in the second Messenian war, was sent out by the Athenians to help Sparta as a general. His harangue to his soldiers was in verse.

[2] The perfects are used aoristically. He compares the intending poet to one going to run in the Olympic games.

[3] The umpire in a boy's race used to say, The first shall be a conqueror, and him I will acknowledge gladly; but the last I will reject as though tainted by some foul disease.

surety for a poor man of small credit, and
relive a man entangled in a gloomy lawsuit, I shall feel amazed if he, so rich, shall
know [1] how to distinguish false friends from
the true.   So whether you have given aught,
or whether you shall mean to give to any one,
don't bring him [2] full of joy to hear the
verses you have made, for he'll cry out,
" How charmingly, how well, how suitably
composed ! "   Pale with [3] emotion he will
grow at the more tragic parts : he'll even
drop a tear from sympathetic eyes ; leap
from his seat ; and, lastly, dance with joy.

Just as hired mutes, who weep at funerals,
almost exceed in words and acts of grief
real mourners, so these false admirers are
apparently affected more than those who are
sincere.

'Tis said that wealthy nobles ply with oft-
repeated bumpers and test well with wine
all those whose inmost feelings they would
know, to see if they be worthy of their
patronage ; so, if you shall be writing poetry,
ne'er let the crafty mind, that lies concealed
as though in fox's skin, deceive.   If to
[4] Quintilius you read your lines, he'd say,
" Pray alter this and that."   And if, when
you had tried in vain two or three times,
you vowed you could not do aught better,
then he'd bid you rub them out, and place
again upon thought's anvil such rough lines.
But if you rather would defend your fault
than alter it, he would not waste another

[1] Horace means that the flatterers and para-sites will prevent him.

[2] Because of the gift.

[3] That is, feigned, or induced merely through gratitude.

[4] Quintilius Varus of Cremona.   See the 24th Ode of Book I., where Horace mourns his death.

word or spend more fruitless toil to stay
your admiration of yourself and works without a single rival in the field. A man of
honesty and sense will censure careless lines,
blame rough ones, draw his pen crosswise,
and will fix a black mark to those that are
devoid of taste ; will cut out bold redundant
ornament, oblige the writer to throw light
on what's obscure. He will arraign a phrase
that is ambiguous ; will mark what should
be changed : in fine, will be a critic such as
[1]Aristarchus was, and will not say, " Pray
why should I offend my friend in trifles such
as these ?" For trifles such as these will
bring to grave [2]mischance a poet once
laughed at and heard unfavourably on the
stage. The prudent fear to touch mad
bards, and shun them as they would a man
whom plaguing itch or jaundice, frenzy or
sad lunacy distressed ; boys heap abuse upon
their heads, and all who are regardless
of their safety follow them.

If, while he spouts his lines with head
aloft, and wanders carelessly about, like
fowler bent on catching birds, he fall into a
well or pit, although he loudly cry, " Bring
aid, my countrymen !" there would not be a
man who'd care to help him out. And
should one care to render aid and throw a
rope to him, how do you know that he did
not on purpose jump into the hole, and does
not wish to be preserved ?

I will describe and tell the end of the

[1] He was proverbially the greatest critic.

[2] Such a repute as Chœrilus, Bavius, and Mævius had.

Fovea Gorea = a pitfall.

1 Empedocles, a famous natural philosopher of Agr.gentum.
Sicilian bard. ¹ Empedocles, with eager wish to be thought an immortal god, deliberately leapt into Mount Ætna's blazing jaws.

Let poets have the right and privilege to choose their death; for those who save a man against his will but seem as if they
² I. e., tried to commit suicide.
killed. And this is not the first ² time he had acted thus, nor if he be dragged back will he act like a man, and lay aside his wish for death so infamous. Nor is it clear why he writes poetry at all: whether because he may have desecrated his own father's grave, or sacrilegiously removed a sad memorial of lightning's force. But still beyond a doubt he's mad, and like a bear, if he has but been able to break through the bars that close his den, this troublesome rehearser chases those who care for poetry and those who don't alike: and if he has once caught a man, he keeps him, and by reading wearies him to death, just like a leech that does not mean to leave the skin till sated with the blood it draws.

J. AND W. RIDER, PRINTERS, LONDON.

† Wept long: ye streams,‡ ye hazel-trees, knew
    well

The Nymphs' deep grief; what time the mother
    fell

Beside, and clasping to her heart her son,

Alas! a piteous corpse, cried out, as none

But mothers § can, on cruel fate and heaven.

No, Daphnis, in those days no steers were driven

To drink, when fed, from cooling streams; no
    draught

Of grateful water from the river quaff'd

  * 19—44. *Mo.* We've reached the cave; I thus begin: "When
Daphnis died the Nymphs shed tears; his mother clasped her son's
cold corpse and called upon the gods reproachfully: the flocks and
herds were all unfed, the very lions roared aloud in grief: for
Daphnis tamed the tiger, founded Bacchus' rural worship, was the
glory of his friends: and now he's dead, a curse lies on the land, and
where good seed was sown, there springs the noisome weed. Let us
then raise his tomb and write his epitaph."

  † Line 21. *Flebant*, as Conington says, with a pause after it at the
beginning of the verse, is meant to add to the melancholy effect.
The two monosyllables in the translation are an attempt to preserve
the same effect.

  ‡ Compare Scott :—
           "Call it not vain: they do not err:
           Who say that when the poet dies,
           Mute Nature mourns her worshipper
           And celebrates his obsequies:
           Who say tall cliff and cavern lone
           For the departed bard make moan." . . .

  § The position of *mater* shows that it is meant to be emphatic.

THE BUCOLICS, or ECLOGUES OF VIRGIL, with Notes based
    on those in Conington's Edition, a Life of Virgil, more than 100 Woodcuts
from Rich's "Antiquities," and an Illustrated Article on the Ancient Musical
Instruments, translated into English Heroic Verse. Fcap. 8vo, cloth boards,
illuminated, gilt edges, 5s. London : LONGMANS & Co., Paternoster Row.

(1) Square and circular altars, with cavity at the top for the fire, and orifice at the side or bottom for libations to flow through.

(4) Altar in a street at Pompeii, in front of a picture of the Lares Viales, or overseers of streets and roads.

(2) Altar in a sacred grove, before a statue of Diana, taken from the Arch of Trajan.

(5) *Opilio*, a shepherd watching his sheep.

(3) Altar on the steps in front of the Temple of Fortune at Pompeii.

(6) Pandean pipe (*arundo*) or (*avena*), made of several stalks of reed, cane, or wild oat.

This omen, thus at once began :* "There is

In the Carpathian† ocean's vast abyss,

By Neptune lov'd, a prophet who rides o'er

The sea, drawn by strange creatures, horse‡ before

And fish behind : his name is Proteus, and

Sea-green his hue : he to his fatherland,

Equus bipes. A mythic creature called a sea-horse, poetically attached to the marine chariot of Neptune and Proteus.

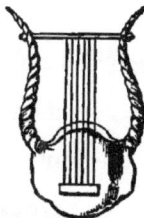

Testudo. A variety of the lyre, with a sounding bottom, over which the chords were drawn to increase the fullness of the sound.

Pallene,§ now returns, and to the ports

Of Thessaly : we Nymphs him in our thoughts,

* ARGUMENT.—She bids him go to Pallene in Macedonia with her, and there find Proteus, the prophetic old man of the sea, who would tell him the cause and cure of the evil, but only under the stress of persevering violence, as he would endeavour to elude the pressure by his power of transforming himself into all kinds of shapes.

† The geography is, as usual, vague, the Carpathian Sea being strictly between Rhodes and Crete.

‡ See illustration to *Equus bipes.*

§ This points to a legend to which other writers refer, though it was not known by Homer ; one version being that Proteus originally

From thee she fled. Her mates, the Dryad band,

With cries fill'd e'en the mountain-tops, the land

Of Thrace so brave, where Rhesus* reign'd in years

Gone by,—each height of Rhodope† shed tears,

The Getans,‡ Attic Orithyia,§ rills

Of Hebrus, wept with tall Pangæan‖ hills.

He oft, his love-sick bosom solacing,

Upon the hollow lute¶ of thee would sing,

His own dear wife,—of thee, when morn arose,

On the lone shore,—of thee at evening's close.

He e'en through Tænarus'** dread entrance pass'd

Pluto's deep portals, that grove overcast

---

* Rhesus was supposed to be a son of one of the Muses, and a king of Thrace, who was robbed of his horse and killed by Diomedes and Ulysses before Troy.

† Rhodope was a mountain range in Thrace, a part of the Hæmus.

‡ The Getans were classed by the ancients among the Thracians. They resided on the banks of the Danube, and bordered on the Dacians.

§ Orithyia was supposed to be the nymph of the country of Attica. Acte was the old name for Attica: so that Actias is appropriate as an epithet intimating that she was the daughter of Erechtheus.—Con.

‖ The Pangæan mountain was in Thrace, on the borders of Macedonia, near Philippi.

¶ See illustration on page 43 to Testudo.

** Tænarus was a promontory and town in Laconia; on the promontory was a temple of Neptune, and near it a cavern, the fabled entrance to the infernal regions: it was also famous for its black marble.

THE FOURTH GEORGIC OF VIRGIL, with Notes, a Life, Illustrations, and an Illustrated Article on the Gladiators, translated into Heroic Verse. New Edition, in an elegant binding, 4s. 6d. London: LONGMANS & Co., Paternoster Row.

XLVIII.

It is curious to observe[1] the different estimations two men make of one another's[2] happiness. [3][Each of them surveys the external appearance of the other's situation, and thinks him happier, when comparing it with the secret disquieting circumstances of his own ;][3] and so it is that, all the world over, be we favoured as we may,[4] there is ever something[5] which others have, and we have not, necessary to the completion of our felicity. I think, therefore,[6] upon the whole, there is no such thing as positive happiness in this world, and a man can only be deemed felicitous as he is in comparison less affected with positive evil.[7]

XLIX.

1. Compare the metrical system of Virgil with that of Lucretius.

2. Derive *excuso, ambitio, secretus, egregius, sestertius, profecto, erudio, securis, ancile, Salii,* and *Luperci.*

---

[1] *Operae pretium est* with infinitive. Distinguish *observare* and *animadvertere.*

[2] The Latins were fond of bringing parts of words like *alius* and *alter* together, *e.g., alii alia fecére,* " some did one thing, one another ; " or, again, *alter alterum interfecit,* "one killed the other."

[3] Turn this sentence as if the English ran thus : " For as often as (*quoties*) whether of the two you please compares the external appearance (*speciem*) of the other's condition with those things which inwardly vex himself, he thinks him happier."

[4] Turn as if " However much the gods favour us." Remember the construction of *quamvis* and *quanquam,* and their different use and meaning.

[5] Render by *aliquid boni,* and you will so escape the difficulty of a substantive for " happiness." Avoid *felicitas, beatitas, beatitudo,* although the last two were coined by Cicero. It is not the peculiarities of a language we should imitate, but the usual forms and words.

[6] You may obviate the difficulty here by a direct quotation from Horace, introduced thus : " Wherefore I think that expression (*illud*) of Flaccus is true," " *Nihil est ab omni parte beatum.* "

[7] Avoid the unsupported ablative after the oblique case of the comparative.

SELECTIONS FOR LATIN PROSE, specially arranged for the Army and Middle-Class Student, and to discourage *cram.* By R. M. MILLINGTON, M.A. Crown 8vo, 3s. 6d. KEY, 5s. London : LONGMANS & Co., Paternoster Row.

dam, quo et, qualis vera gloria, et quid sit honestum ergà rem-publicam studium faciliùs intelligas. Triplex igitur, ut opinor, est hujus quaestionis deliberatio. Primùm, utrum gloriae cupido rei-publicae necne prosit, quaerendum est. Deinde, quùm duo sint gloriae genera, utrum horum ab optimo quoque anteferendum. Tertium disputandi genus est de gloriâ et honesti ergà rem-publicam studii comparatione. Nimirùm ex amore famae permulta civitati bona sunt, et semper erunt orta, et ab egregiis viris facta : sed haud scio an, rei-publicae utilitate omissâ, suo privato commodo, ut servitent, illa fecerint.

XXVI.

1 *a*. A fresh loan was being entered into for building a wall, which was let by the censors on contract, to be constructed of hewn stone.

   b. Philippus stumbles on Vulteius in the morning, as he sells his cheap brokery to the coatless rabble, and bids him good morning first.

2. *Manipulus :* a name given to a company of soldiers, because Romulus tied a bundle (*manipulus*) of hay to the standards.

Aedepol : a lengthened vocative of *Pollux,* and more correctly written *Edepol.*

Ecastor : the vocative of *Castor,* with a demonstrative prefix *e.*

Mediastinus : as *clandestinus* is formed from *clam,* so *mediastinus* is formed from *medius.*

Medius-fidius (= as true as heaven !) is *Deus,* with the demonstrative prefix *me* and the adjective *fidius,* πίστιος.

Mehercule : the vocative of *Hercules,* with a demonstrative prefix.

Nudius-tertius: nudius = *nunc dies,* with a numeral to suit the number of days since : as, *nudiusquartus,* it is four days since.

THE LATIN RENDERINGS AND SOLUTIONS TO THE CRITICAL QUESTIONS. Price 5s. London: LONGMANS & Co. Paternoster Row.

By a glance you can measure her form, and discover
If a misshapen leg or splay foot be veil'd over.
For you surely don't wish that a trick should be play'd
On you, and that my price I should get ere I've laid
Out my wares for inspection.   Thus, taken to task,
The offender to these lines attention may ask :
Says ¹Callimachus, " Often the hunter* the hare

* *Venatio* (hunting of wild beasts).

Will course through the deep snow, and yet never will care
E'en to touch it when kill'd, or with arrow pierc'd through.
And, as apposite, add, " It is this that we do :
For what all can obtain with such ease we pass by,
And to reach what eludes the pursuer we try."
Do you dream that the tide of fierce passion—that grief,
Or life's cares from such paltry lines e'er find relief ?
Is it not better far nature's bounds to search out,
To the passions—to learn what we can do without,

¹ A distinguished Greek poet and grammarian of Cyrene.

THE FIRST BOOK OF THE SATIRES OF HORACE, in ENGLISH VERSE, with
Illustrations from Rich's " Antiquities," Notes (based on those in Orelli), a Life of Horace, and
Illustrated Articles on the Roman House, Amphitheatre, Theatre, and Circus.   Price 4s.   By
R. M. MILLINGTON, M.A. LONGMANS & Co., 39, Paternoster Row. To be followed by the SECOND
BOOK OF THE SATIRES AND THE EPISTLES.

shall from the yoke his steers set free: nor shall
wool learn to falsely imitate all kinds of hues, but in
the mead, without the dyer's aid, the ram shall
change the colour of his fleece for sweetly-blushing
purple now, anon for yellow saffron's dye: lambs
[1]as they graze shall be clothed with the scarlet's
hues. "[2]Blest ages, speed ye onward," to their spindles
sang the Parcae, who in concert tell th' unaltered
will of fate.

[3]Assume, dear offspring of the gods, great son of
Jove, successive highest offices of state; soon will the
time be here. See how the whole world nods with
all its weight of vaulted arch: the earth, the ocean-
tracts, and azure deep of air! See how all nature
joys in the approaching age! Oh, [4]may a few years
at the close of life be left me—time enough and
breath inspired enough to sing thy deeds! Nor
Thracian Orpheus, no, nor Linus, though the one
his mother, and his sire the other aid—Calliopea,
Orpheus, Linus, beautiful Apollo's self—shall then
surpass myself in song. [5]If Pan himself should vie
with me in song, e'en with Arcadia for judge, Pan
would confess himself surpassed, e'en with Arcadia as
judge. [6]Begin, then, infant, with thy smile to re-

[1] 45. *Pascentis = pascentes.*

[2] 46. Compare the use of the Greek οὗτος with this vocative of
Talia.

[3] 48—59. Let him now take his seat upon his throne: the
whole world with expectant longing waits for him, and shakes at
his approach as temples at the coming of their gods. May I live
long enough to tell of his glory! the theme would raise me of
itself above all bards, both human and divine.

[4] 53. *Quantum* refers to *tam longae,* but is connected in sense
with *maneat.* The confusion is from the number of predicates.

[5] 58. The Arcadians would be excellent critics, and would
favour their own god Pan.

[6] 60—63. Let him smile on his mother, she has earned his
smiles; without her smile he ne'er can come to honour.

VIRGIL'S ECLOGUES FOR THE STUDENT, with Notes.
   translated into Rhythmic Prose. Price 2s. 6d. London: LONG-
MANS & Co., Paternoster Row.